SIX CHARACTERS IN SEARCH OF AN AUTHOR AND OTHER PLAYS

Luigi Pirandello was born of rich, middle-class parents in Girgenti (Agrigento), Sicily, on 28 June 1867. As a young man he studied at the Universities of Palermo, Rome and Bonn, where he gained his doctorate in 1891. His first published work, *Mal giocondo* (1889), was a collection of poems. It was followed by other volumes of poems, critical essays, novels, short stories and over forty plays. In 1894 he married Antoinetta Portulano, the daughter of his father's business associate. Financial disaster and a severe illness brought on by the birth of their third child drove his wife to a hysterical form of insanity. Only in 1918, when her presence in the family constituted a real threat to their daughter's safety, did Pirandello agree to have his wife committed to an asylum. The enormous emotional strain he felt at this time is reflected in the intense pessimism found in his work. Pirandello's first real success in the theatre came about in 1921 when *Six Characters in Search of an Author* was performed. *Henry IV* followed the next year and confirmed his position as a playwright. In the following years Pirandello travelled abroad extensively. He embarked on a career as a producer and in 1925 founded his Art Theatre in Rome. He was awarded the Nobel Prize for Literature in 1934 and died in Rome on 10 December 1936.

Mark Musa holds the title of Distinguished Professor of Italian Studies at Indiana University. He is a graduate of Rutgers University, the University of Florence and the Johns Hopkins University. He is also a former Guggenheim Fellow. Best known for his translations of the Italian classics (Dante, Petrarch, Boccaccio, Machiavelli and the poetry of the Middle Ages and twentieth century) and for his Dante criticism, he has also published in Penguin his widely acclaimed translation of Dante's *Divine Comedy: Volume 1: Inferno*; *Volume II: Purgatory*; *and Volume III: Paradise*; as well as *The Portable Dante* and *The Portable Machiavelli*.

SIX CHARACTERS IN SEARCH OF AN AUTHOR AND OTHER PLAYS

LUIGI PIRANDELLO

PENGUIN BOOKS

PENGUIN BOOKS

Published by the Penguin Group
Penguin Books Ltd, 80 Strand, London WC2R 0RL, England
Penguin Putnam Inc., 375 Hudson Street, New York, New York 10014, USA
Penguin Books Australia Ltd, 250 Camberwell Road, Camberwell, Victoria 3124, Australia
Penguin Books Canada Ltd, 10 Alcorn Avenue, Toronto, Ontario, Canada M4V 3B2
Penguin Books India (P) Ltd, 11 Community Centre, Panchsheel Park, New Delhi – 110 017, India
Penguin Books (NZ) Ltd, Cnr Rosedale and Airborne Roads, Albany, Auckland, New Zealand
Penguin Books (South Africa) (Pty) Ltd, 24 Sturdee Avenue, Rosebank 2196, South Africa

Penguin Books Ltd, Registered Offices: 80 Strand, London WC2R 0RL, England

www.penguin.com

Published in Penguin Books 1995

16

Translation and introduction copyright © Mark Musa, 1995
All rights reserved

The moral right of the translator has been asserted

Set in 10/12 Bembo Monophoto
Filmset by Datix International Limited, Bungay, Suffolk
Printed in England by Clays Ltd, St Ives plc

For Gene and Francesca Raskin
with Love

CONTENTS

INTRODUCTION

In 1924, Pirandello added to his comedy, *Six Characters in Search of an Author*, written three years before, a Preface. It was conceived in a polemical spirit, in part directed to his critics as self-defence and counter-argument and in part to his audience, who had refused to understand his art. But even now it assumes for the critic a capital importance: it is the key to penetrating the not-easy Pirandellian world and is a sure aid to interpeting not only the play that the Preface discusses but also *So It Is (If You Think So)* and *Henry IV*.

In the first part of the Preface Pirandello discusses his theory of art; in the second he presents a critical interpretation of his *Six Characters*. It is the first part that I find most interesting. Pirandello, servant of 'fantasia' – the inventive force – needs to interpret that which his imagination creates from a universal point of view. The imagination has an absolute value, autonomous and present in each author *as nature spontaneously revealed*.

'The mystery of artistic creation', Pirandello writes in the Preface, 'is the same mystery as natural birth.' Nature is a creative force, and an author is nothing other than a means through which nature proceeds and works and produces. An author has only two choices: either accept that nature works through him as medium, so that the creation of art takes place, or refuse to provide a medium for nature, so that creation is renounced.

In the second part of the Preface Pirandello discusses a problem which is fundamental to *Six Characters* as well as the other plays in this collection: the conflict between 'having form' and 'being form'. All that which 'has form' is condemned to continual change, which ends by destroying that form. All that which 'is form' is immutable and eternal both in time and in space. Every work of art, every character born alive in the mind of an author and fixed in life by means of the word, is form. A character is static in form and cannot ever undergo change. A human being who 'has form' because of his very nature will be constrained to act entirely differently, changing from day to day.

The problem is at the centre of the Pirandellian thematic, one he will address again in *Vestire gli ignudi* (*To Dress the Naked,* 1922). But here he limits it to the human condition without touching on the life of art. The protagonist Ersilia wants to fix herself in a form that would make her appear better than she is, and then to attempt suicide. In *Six Characters* the attempt is double: the Father, like every other character, is form, but as human symbol he rebels against the fixity of the form in which he feels himself bound. The Father suffers from having been caught in a particular moment of his life and to have been judged solely for this. It is a position opposite to that of Ersilia. For any human, both positions are false. In human affairs there cannot be fixity of form. Nevertheless, all of Pirandello's characters are possessed of this dual force: as characters in themselves they *are form* – immutable and eternal – as symbols of human beings they *have form*, often fighting against the mutability of that form. When a man wishes to stop his life in order to assume an unchangeable form, as is the case of Henry IV, he no longer lives; or he tries to change his life into a form created by his imagination, or tries to become his own character in an illusory comedy as in *Il Giuoco delle parti* (*The Play of Parts,* 1913), which is the play the Director in *Six Characters* happens to be rehearsing when the six characters walk into the theatre.

Pirandello observes often in the Preface that in *Six Characters* an orderly and sequential dramatic development, in the traditional sense of the term, is lacking. But this is not accidental. The drama of the six characters is not one that could be organized in the mind of the author, whatever the outcome of telling their story might be. Dramatic construction must instead bend itself to present a drama refused by that author. The six characters are caught in an effort to represent themselves seeking a life. And so the comedy is built around 'situations', lacking logical development, which are continually interrupted and contradicted. So that the universal sense that Pirandello is seeking may be clear, it is necessary to pay attention to the value he gives to the words 'spirit' and 'nature'. Again it is the Preface that helps us. The Father, Daughter and Son are realized as 'spirit', while the Mother is realized as 'nature'.

'Spirit' for Pirandello is equivalent, in our view, to the pure intellective force, to the possibility, that is, of understanding oneself fully, one's own capacities, and even more important, the limits of one's intelligence and knowledge. At an inferior level, precisely because she is unconscious of herself and her limits, is 'nature'. The Mother of *Six Characters* is not even conscious of being a character. She arrives on stage with the other characters but does not know why. She knows only that she is Mother, and as Mother she knows only that she must follow her family. Pirandello addresses this problem only in *Six Characters* and in the Preface; however, precedents do exist. In *So It Is (If You Think So)*, for example, a clear contrapositioning of 'spirit' and 'nature' occurs: Laudisi, who appears as 'spirit' in the comedy, laughs at all the other characters, who exhaust themselves seeking the truth. Laudisi knows himself and the limits of his understanding; he knows the past and has already discounted for himself that the truth can ever be discovered. In a certain sense Laudisi is beyond any truth, and throughout the play he remains as if outside it. 'Spirit' laughs at 'nature'; 'nature' itself can only weep, because it does not understand.

Examining *Six Characters* we see how Pirandello weaves together three levels of drama: the drama of the six characters refused by their author, who must struggle to realize themselves and fix their action in a play written by another; the human drama of suffering that each of the six characters lives; and the drama that Pirandello himself attempts to represent for the first time: his fantasy in the act of creation.

It is a completely new undertaking that requires new solutions. And Pirandello seeks and experiments with a technical solution, creating the new perspective of descending values, with character-spirit, character-nature, and character-presence; and a philosophical solution, counterposing that which is form and that which has form. The greater or lesser understanding of the various characters in the face of the problem creates the completely new perspective in which Pirandello fixes them: spirit, nature and pure presence. As created characters they are stable, immutable and eternal truth; as human figures they are unstable, changeable and ephemeral reality, like the Director and the actors. At the end of the play, when the characters have completed the action they are compelled to complete, the Young Boy commits suicide. A great confusion arises on stage. One actor shouts, 'Reality!' – the Young Boy is truly dead. Others cannot believe it and shout, 'Make-believe!' – the Young Boy cannot be dead. Among the contrasting voices rebounds that of the Father: 'But what make-believe! Reality, reality, sir! Reality!' Having intuited a new dimension, Pirandello must construct his play in a new way. That which may appear as illogical construction or disordered dramatic development is instead the resolution of the true drama of the creating author, who necessarily constructs 'illogically', by means of scenes and 'situations' oddly juxtaposed.

The original idea for the events Pirandello exploits in *Six Characters* first came to his mind as material for a novel. But he refused to write that novel. Even though there was plenty of interesting material, to Pirandello it seemed to lack that universality for which, and only for which, he chose to write. He could not narrate, as some others did, only for the pleasure of narrating. He wanted something more from his art, and that something was absent.

In 1910, Pirandello saw *Six Characters* as a tragic plot and nothing more. So he abandoned the idea. Only eleven years later, in 1921, did he finally find a way to use the tragic plot and add to it that which was lacking. In sending the six characters in search of another author he found a universal sense: to translate into images his fantasy in the act of creating. Even in 1917, the story tormented him, and Pirandello was still seeking a solution, as he reveals in the following light-hearted comment:

And a strangeness so sad, so sad: Six Characters in Search of an Author; a novel to be written. Perhaps you understand. Six characters, taken up in a terrible drama, who come up close to me, to be composed in a novel, an obsession, and I don't want to know about it, and I say to them that it is useless and they don't matter to me, and that nothing any longer matters to me; and they who show me all of their wounds, I chase them away – and so at the end the novel to be written will come out to be written. And many, many other ideas I still have in mind.

(Rome, 23 July 1917)

In the short story *La tragedia di un personaggio* (*The Tragedy of a Character*, 1911), Pirandello presents himself in conversation with a character, Doctor Fileno, who had come forth for the first time the night before from the pages of a novel someone had given Pirandello to read. The character laments about an author unable to understand him and begs Pirandello to write about him again, in order to give him the life to which he rightly aspires. Pirandello agrees that his author has not made good use of him; however, he refuses his request. The following is the argument the Doctor uses to plead his cause before his new author. It is clear that here is the germ of Pirandello's play. Doctor Fileno speaks the same words and phrases which Pirandello will put into the mouth of the Father ten years later:

> No one can know better than yourself that we are living beings, more alive than those who breathe and dress; perhaps we are less real, but we are certainly more true. One is born into the world in many different ways and you know that nature serves as the instrument of the human fantasy to continue her work of creation. And he who is fortunate enough to be born of the creative activity of the spirit of man is given by nature a longer and more superior life than he who is born of the womb. He who is born a character, who is so lucky to be born alive, does not have to worry about dying. He never dies. Man dies, the writer, the natural instrument of nature dies, but the created character never dies. And in order to live eternally he need not be of exceptional calibre. Tell me, who was Sancho Panza? Tell me, who was Don Abbondio? And yet they live eternally. As living germs they had the good fortune to find a very fertile fantasy, a fantasy that knew how to raise them and nourish them for eternity.

The stages of this play can be summarized in this way: 1910, the incident; 1911, one character who seeks an author; 1917, the possibility of applying Doctor Fileno's drama to the incident of the six characters; 1921, the play; 1924, the Preface to the comedy. The cycle begun in 1910 is finally concluded.

To what we might call this external story, may be added an

internal story: one that leads up to the new positions of thought Pirandello reached in 1921. Let us refer back to *Pensaci Giacomino* (*Think About It, Giacomino*) and *Liolà*, both of 1916. Here there is nothing to be found to anticipate what comes. The conflict between having form and being form has not even been suggested. These are only human dramas of characters who fight each other and within themselves. Then, in 1917, Pirandello directly confronts the problem of truth in *So It Is* (*If You Think So*). The central poetic of the work (just as for the novel that preceded the play) is the human impossibility of reaching truth or even determining if truth exists. Truth must exist, Pirandello seems to say, but finding it is beyond human capability. Truth appears behind a thick black veil and reveals itself as that which each one of us desires it to be. Truth, then, is relative. That which is true for one person may not be true for another. Each person sees, through an impenetrable veil, a vague phantasm which he or she gives the name of truth, but it is only his or her truth.

So It Is (*If You Think So*) is considered to be Pirandello's major contribution to the so-called 'theatre of the grotesque' – a name given to an innovative type of tragicomic drama which appeared in Italy as a reaction to naturalism and in which characters are treated like puppets, controlled by blind, mysterious forces. There is no development of character in the play. The fact that Pirandello added to the title of the play 'A Parable' indicates that the recreation of reality is not his main concern and the action of the play has little to do with the external circumstances of the unreal realness of the story-plot.

The play is about the futile attempt on the part of a group of townspeople to establish whether it is Signor Ponza or Signora Frola, his mother-in-law, who is crazy concerning the identity of Signor Ponza's wife. According to Frola she is her daughter; for Ponza she is not the daughter of Frola but rather his new second wife. Ponza, the newly arrived secretary of the town's prefect, becomes the centre of interest for the unmerciful curiosity of middle-class superiority. The 'truth' for which the play searches is not so much in the heavily veiled figure whose voice is heard but once at the end of the play as it is in the play's very structure and symmetrical design itself: in the first act Ponza and Frola make their case and produce evidence to support it; in act two Ponza and Frola confront one another; act three is the conclusion where the supposed revelation of the 'truth' takes place. In the meantime the character of Laudisi seems to be floating above this formal structure, as each act ends in silence followed by his burst of laughter.

The issue is not whether the Agazzi family and friends can find out the truth about the Ponza-Frola family but whether they should be doing so at all. This Laudisi makes quite clear in the course of the play. While the audience may be asking itself, as is the chorus of townspeople on stage, 'Who is lying?' the fact remains that it is the insensitivity of the Agazzi clan and the pain resulting from it that holds the play together and moves it along. And the message of the play may well be that whether or not that veiled lady be Frola's daughter or Ponza's second wife, she does not exist in or for herself; she exists only in so far as Ponza and Frola exist – she is there for them and for each of them in his or her own way. Truth then is Love and Compassion.

The plea for compassion and disinterested love that underlies *So It Is*, and which is the structure supporting the actions of Ponza, his wife and his mother-in-law, is not present in *Six Characters* and *Henry IV*. What these three plays do have in common, however, is the confrontation of form and life. I believe the themes that preoccupied Pirandello the most are all to be found in one way or another in *Henry IV*: the relativity of language, perception and freedom, the game of life with people assigned to various roles, madness, 'being form' and 'having form', reality and illusion are some of them.

Pirandello began writing *Henry IV* immediately after the opening fiasco of *Six Characters* in Rome. He wrote it in four months. He will never deal with the theme of madness in any of the twenty plays he writes after that. The play opened in Milan on 24 February 1922. The critics had their reservations about it, but compared to *Six Characters* it was well received. Only one critic, Silvio d'Amico, claimed it was a masterpiece. It was not until *Six Characters* had its enormous success in Paris the following year that the critics unanimously agreed on masterpiece status for *Henry IV*.

The play, which is subtitled 'A Tragedy', is traditional in its structure. It respects the Aristotelian unities and has a climax and denouement, all of which are not easily found in *Six Characters*. The elements are logically and clearly presented in spite of the fact that the protagonist is both sane and insane. Henry lives in the world of art; his world is one he, a mad man, has created himself, having left the world of the living for the ideal work of art. He is a part of history in which nothing changes, since events have been lived out and fixed in immutable form. With history every effect follows its cause. This is the cry of the Father in *Six Characters* and it is what Henry announces to his Secret Counsellors who are so important to an understanding of Henry's psyche early in the play. Henry appears rather late in the first act and only after a long and lively scene during which the Counsellors step in and out of their roles – moving from history ('being form') to their present-day selves ('having form') as they train a new member of their group who has just joined them and who has for months been preparing himself for the wrong part in their play within a play.

Henry IV, the man with no name of his own (his name is followed by dots in the list of characters), is both an actor in Pirandello's play and the star of his own play which he also happens to be directing in a stage setting of his own choosing. Henry, like his mentor Pirandello, becomes the creative artist himself as he creates his own play within a play. He also directs it and is his own make-up artist and wardrobe man, and at times in the play we even catch him watching himself perform – as would an audience. The play, like *Six Characters* then, is a play within a play and like *So It Is* deals with relativism: how crazy is crazy? And even the plea for compassion and love mentioned earlier in connection with *So It Is* is answered in a brief scene between Henry and his old servant John. But *Henry IV* is much more: like no other character in Pirandello's large corpus of plays Henry seems to have it all! He is theatre in all its many facets! And with the words 'per sempre' ('forever') he brings the curtain down on his tregedy as he who 'has form' 'becomes form': illusion virtually becomes reality.

SELECTED FURTHER READING

Barbina, Alfredo, *Bibliografia della critica pirandelliana (1889–1961)*, Florence, 1967.

Bentley, Eric, *In Search of Truth,* New York, 1953.

Büdel, Oscar, *Pirandello*, New York and London, 1966.

Cambon, Glauco (ed.), *Pirandello: A collection of Critical Essays*, Eaglewood Cliffs, New Jersey, 1967.

Donati, Corrado, *Bibliografia della critica pirandelliana (1962–1981)*, Florence, 1986.

Fergusson, Francis, *The Idea of a Theater*, Princeton, 1949.

Giudice, Gaspare, *Luigi Pirandello*, Turin, 1963.

Giudice, Gaspare, *Pirandello: A Bibliography* (trans. Alastair Hamilton), New York, London and Toronto, 1975.

Illiano, Antonio, *Metapsichica e letteratura in Pirandello*, Florence, 1982.

MacClintock, Lander, *The Age of Pirandello*, Bloomington, 1951.

Oliver, Roger W., *Dreams of Passion: The Theater of Luigi Pirandello*, New York, 1979.

Ragusa, Olga, *Luigi Pirandello, An Approach to his Theatre*, Edinburgh, 1980.

Starkie, Walter, *Luigi Pirandello*, Berkeley, 1965.

Valency, Maurice, *The End of the World: An Introduction to Contemporary Drama*, New York and Oxford, 1980.

*SIX CHARACTERS IN SEARCH OF
AN AUTHOR*

LIST OF CHARACTERS

Characters in the play to be played:

THE FATHER
THE MOTHER
THE STEPDAUGHTER
THE SON
THE YOUNG BOY
THE CHILD
MADAME PACE

Actors in the play being played:

THE DIRECTOR
THE LEADING LADY
THE LEADING MAN
A YOUNG ACTOR
A YOUNG ACTRESS
A THIRD ACTOR
A FOURTH ACTOR
A FIFTH ACTOR
OTHER ACTORS AND ACTRESSES
THE PROMPTER
THE STAGE MANAGER
THE PROPERTY MAN
THE TECHNICIAN
THE DIRECTOR'S SECRETARY
USHER
STAGE HANDS

ACT ONE

Upon entering the theatre, the audience finds the curtain already raised and the stage the way it is during the day without the wings or scenery in view, semi-dark and empty, so that from the beginning the audience will have the impression of an impromptu performance.

Two sets of stairs, one at the right, the other at the left, that serve to connect the stage with the theatre hall. On the stage the cover for the prompter's box has been removed and is to one side of the opening.

On the other side, towards the front, a small table and a chair with its back to the audience for the DIRECTOR. Two more tables, one bigger, one smaller, with several chairs around, set up in front ready to be used in case they should be needed for the rehearsals. More chairs here and there to the right and left for the ACTORS. And in the background to one side, a piano half hidden.

Once the theatre lights are dimmed, from the door on stage the TECHNICIAN *appears dressed in dark-blue overalls with a bag hanging from his belt; from a corner backstage he picks up a few rigging boards, puts them down up front and kneels down to nail them. While the hammering is going on there enters from the direction of the dressing-rooms the* STAGE MANAGER.

STAGE MANAGER: Hey, what are you doing?

TECHNICIAN: What am I doing? I'm nailing.

STAGE MANAGER: At this hour? [*He looks at his watch.*] It's already ten-thirty. Before you know it the director will be here for the rehearsal.

TECHNICIAN: Hey, I've gotta have time for my work too!

STAGE MANAGER: And you will, but not now.

TECHNICIAN: Then when?

STAGE MANAGER: When rehearsals are over. Come on, let's get everything out of here, and let me prepare the stage for the second act of *Il Giuoco delle parti.*★

★ 'The Play of Parts'

The [TECHNICIAN, *huffing and muttering, picks up the wooden boards and goes off. In the meantime, the* ACTORS *in the company begin to come through the stage door — men and women, first one, then another, then two together, in no particular order: nine or ten, as many as are supposed to take part in the rehearsals of Pirandello's play* Il Giuoco delle parti *according to the assignment of the day. They enter and greet the* STAGE MANAGER *and exchange cordialities and good mornings among themselves. Some head for their dressing-rooms; others, among whom is the* PROMPTER, *who has the script of the play rolled up under his arm, stop on the stage and wait for the* STAGE MANAGER *to begin the rehearsal, and in the meantime, sitting or standing in a group, they talk to each other; some will light up a cigarette, others complain about their part in the play, another will be reading some news to a companion from a theatrical magazine. It would be a good idea for the* ACTRESSES *as well as* ACTORS *to be dressed in clothes that are rather light and cheerful-looking, and that this first improvised scene be very vivacious in its naturalness. At a certain point one of the cast might sit at the piano and begin playing some dance music and some of the younger* ACTORS *and* ACTRESSES *begin to dance.*]

STAGE MANAGER [*clapping his hands to bring things to order*]: OK, come on, cut it out! Here comes the Director.

[*All of a sudden the music and dancing stop. The* ACTORS *turn and look into the audience and from the lobby door enters the* DIRECTOR *who, with hat planted firmly on his head and walking-stick under his arm and a hefty cigar in his mouth, comes down the aisle between the seats, and, greeted by the cast, he climbs one of the two small staircases leading to the stage. The* SECRETARY *hands him the mail: some newspapers and a bound script.*]

DIRECTOR: Letters?

SECRETARY: Not one. This is all the mail.

DIRECTOR [*handing him the bound script*]: Take it to my office. [*Then, looking around and addressing the* STAGE MANAGER:] You can't see a thing here. Would you please give us a little light?

STAGE MANAGER: Right away.

[*He gives the order. And a short time later the right side of the*

6

stage where the ACTORS *are is all lit up by a bright white light. In the meantime the* PROMPTER *will have taken his place in the box, put on the light and set the script out before him.*]

DIRECTOR [*clapping his hands*]: OK, let's go, time to begin. [*To the* STAGE MANAGER:] Anyone missing?

STAGE MANAGER: The leading lady's missing.

DIRECTOR: As usual! [*He looks at his watch.*] We're already ten minutes late. Do me a favour and make a note of it. That way she'll learn to be on time for rehearsals.

[*No sooner has he finished his reprimand than from the back of the theatre can be heard the voice of the* LEADING LADY.]

LEADING LADY: No, no, for God's sake. Here I am. I'm here. [*She is all dressed in white with a big, bold hat on her head and a cute little dog in her arms; she runs down the aisle between the rows of seats and quickly climbs up one of the staircases.*]

DIRECTOR: So you've made up your mind to keep us waiting for ever.

LEADING LADY: Forgive me. I tried so hard to find a car to arrive on time! But I see you haven't begun yet. And it's not time for me to make my entrance yet. [*Then, calling the* STAGE MANAGER *by name and handing the little dog to him:*] Please, would you put him in my dressing-room for me?

DIRECTOR [*muttering*]: Now the little dog too! As if there weren't enough dogs here already. [*He claps his hands again and turns to the* PROMPTER.] OK, let's go with Act Two of *Il Giuoco delle parti*. [*Sitting in the armchair:*] Your attention, ladies and gentlemen. Who's on stage?

[*The* ACTORS *and* ACTRESSES *clear the front of the stage and sit to one side except for the three who are to begin the rehearsal and the* LEADING LADY *who, paying no attention to the* DIRECTOR's *question, goes and sits in front of one of the two little tables.*]

DIRECTOR [*to the* LEADING LADY]: So then you *are* in this scene?

LEADING LADY: Who, me? No sir.

DIRECTOR [*fed up*]: Well, then, please remove yourself, for Christ's sake!

[*The* LEADING LADY *gets up and sits next to the other* ACTORS *who have already retreated to one side.*]

DIRECTOR [*to the* PROMPTER]: Begin, begin.

PROMPTER [*reading the script*]: 'In the house of Leone Gala. A strange set that serves as a dining-room and a study.'

DIRECTOR [*turning to the* STAGE MANAGER]: We'll use the red room set.

STAGE MANAGER [*writing it down on a piece of paper*]: The red one. That's fine.

PROMPTER [*continuing to read the script*]: 'Table already set and desk with books and papers. Bookshelves and china cabinets with elegant table furnishings. Exit rear to Leone's bedroom. Exit left to the kitchen. Main exit to the right.'

DIRECTOR [*getting up and pointing*]: So now, pay close attention: over there, the main exit; over here, the kitchen. [*Turning to the* ACTOR *who will play the part of Socrates:*] You enter and exit from here. [*To the* STAGE MANAGER:] We'll need a screen to the rear and put up the curtains. [*He returns to his seat.*]

STAGE MANAGER [*taking note*]: Right you are.

PROMPTER [*reading as before*]: 'Scene One. Leone Gala, Guido Venanzi, Filippo, alias Socrates.' [*To the* DIRECTOR:] Should I read the stage directions too?

DIRECTOR: Certainly, of course. I must have told you that a hundred times.

PROMPTER [*reading as before*]: 'When the curtain goes up, Leone Gala wearing a chef's hat and apron, is intent on beating an egg in a bowl with a wooden spoon. Filippo, also in the trappings of a cook, is beating another. Guido Venanzi is seated and listening.'

LEADING MAN [*to the* DIRECTOR]: Excuse me, do I really have to wear this chef's hat?

DIRECTOR [*annoyed by the comment*]: I would think so [*pointing to the script*], since it's written there.

LEADING MAN: Forgive me, but it's silly.

DIRECTOR [*jumping up in a rage*]: Silly? Silly? What can I do if France can't produce any good theatre and we are reduced to putting on Pirandello plays which you have to be lucky to understand and which are written in a way never to please either critics or actors or public.

[*The* ACTORS *laugh. At this point the* DIRECTOR, *getting up and going to the* LEADING MAN, *shouts:*]

The chef's hat. Yes sir, put it on and beat the eggs. Do you think that this egg-beating business is simply that? If so, you're in trouble. You have to represent the shell of those eggs you are beating!

[*The* ACTORS *start to laugh again and to make ironic comments to each other.*]

Quiet now, and listen to my explanations. [*Turning again to the* LEADING MAN:] Yes sir, the shell: that is to say, the empty form of reason without the insides of instinct, which is blind! You stand for reason, and your wife is instinct in a game of assigned roles, according to which you, who play your own role, purposely become the puppet of yourself. Do you understand?

LEADING MAN [*dropping his arms*]: Not at all.

DIRECTOR [*returning to his place*]: Neither do I. Let's get on with it. In any case you'll like the way it turns out! [*In a more intimate tone:*] Do me a favour and face three-quarters, otherwise between the abstruseness of the dialogue and the fact that you can't make yourself heard by the audience, the whole thing will flop. [*Clapping his hands again:*] Attention please. Let's get going.

PROMPTER: Excuse me, sir, would you mind if I get into my box? There's a bit of a draught out here.

DIRECTOR: Sure. Go right ahead.

[*In the meantime, the theatre* USHER, *wearing his gold and silver braided cap, has entered the hall and gone down the aisle between the rows of seats. He is approaching the stage to announce to the* STAGE MANAGER *the arrival of the* SIX CHARACTERS *who, also having entered the theatre, are following him at a certain distance. They appear to be somewhat puzzled and lost as they look around the hall.*

To stage this play one must take every possible precaution to achieve the effect that these SIX CHARACTERS *are not be confused with the company of* ACTORS. *The arrangement of the* ACTORS *and the* CHARACTERS (*indicated in the stage directions*) *when they go on stage will undoubtedly be helpful: for example, using different kinds of coloured lighting by means of special reflectors. But the most suitable and efficacious means suggested here is the*

9

use of special masks for the CHARACTERS: *masks made specifically with a kind of material that perspiration will not cause to lose its form and at the same time light enough for the actors to be able to wear; they must be cut and made in such a way as to allow freedom to the eyes, the nose and mouth. This will also be a way of representing the profound meaning of the play. The* CHARACTERS, *in fact, should not appear to be unreal figures but rather created reality, the creations of immutable fantasy; therefore, more real and substantial than the changeable naturalness of the* ACTORS. *The masks will help to give the impression of the figure created by means of art and fixed immutably in the expression of its own fundamental sentiment, which, in the case of the* FATHER, *would be remorse; revenge for the* STEPDAUGHTER; *disdain for the* SON; *grief for the* MOTHER (*who will have permanent tears of wax fixed in the discolouring under her eyes, and along the cheeks, as seen in the paintings and statues of the grieving Virgin Mother in churches; also, her clothing should be of a special material and style, not extravagant, but with severe pleats and a kind of sculptural voluminousness; in other words, in such a way that it does not give the impression that it was made of a material easy to find in any city store and that could be put together by any dressmaker*).*

The FATHER *is about 50 years old, with reddish hair, thin at the temples but not bald, however; thick moustaches curving around his still youthful mouth, which often opens in an uncertain and futile smile. He is pale, especially his large forehead; blue oval-shaped eyes that are very bright and piercing; he wears light-coloured trousers and a dark jacket; at times he is smooth and sweet, at times harsh and rough.*

The MOTHER *seems frightened and crushed as if by an intolerable weight of shame and humiliation. Wearing a thick widow's veil of crêpe, she is dressed in a meek black, and when she lifts her veil, she reveals a face not wrinkled, but smooth as wax, and she always keeps her eyes downcast.*

The STEPDAUGHTER, *18 years of age, is arrogant and shameless. Very beautiful, she too is dressed in mourning, but with a gaudy elegance. She shows contempt for the timid, distressed and almost bewildered manner of her little brother (a gloomy* YOUNG BOY *of 14 who is also dressed in black) and, on the other hand, a lively tenderness for her little sister, a* CHILD *of four dressed in white with a black silk sash around the waist.*

The SON, *22 years old, tall and rigid in his severe attitude of contempt for the* FATHER, *with a sullen indifference towards the* MOTHER, *wears a violet-coloured overcoat with a long green scarf around his neck.*]

USHER [*with hat in hand*]: Excuse me, sir.

DIRECTOR [*quick and rude*]: And now what?

USHER [*timidly*]: There are some people here asking for you.

[*The* DIRECTOR *and the* ACTORS *are amazed as they look down from the stage into the audience.*]

DIRECTOR [*again in a rage*]: But this is a rehearsal. And certainly you know that during rehearsals no one is allowed in. [*Addressing himself to the rear:*] Who are you, please? What can I do for you?

FATHER [*coming forward, followed by the others, as far as one of the two staircases*]: We are here in search of an author.

DIRECTOR [*confused and angry*]: An author? What author?

FATHER: Any author, sir.

DIRECTOR: But there's no author here. We are not rehearsing a new play.

STEPDAUGHTER [*vivaciously rushing up the staircase*]: All the better, so much the better, sir. We can be your new play.

AN ACTOR [*amid the lively comments and laughter of the others*]: Oh, listen to that!

FATHER [*following the* STEPDAUGHTER *onto the stage*]: Yes, but if there is no author! [*To the* DIRECTOR:] Unless you would like to be . . .

[*The* MOTHER, *holding the* CHILD *by the hand, and the* YOUNG BOY *climb a few steps and remain there waiting. The* SON, *who is upset, stays below.*]

DIRECTOR: You people must be joking.

FATHER: No, what on earth are you saying, sir? On the contrary, we bring you a serious and painful play.

STEPDAUGHTER: We could be your good fortune.

DIRECTOR: Would you please do me a favour and leave. We have no time to waste on crazy people.

FATHER [*in a hurt and mellifluous tone*]: Oh, sir, you must be well aware that life is full of endless absurdities which, bold-faced as they may be, do not even have to appear plausible, since they are true.

DIRECTOR: What the hell is he saying?

FATHER: I say that it may well be considered a madness, yes sir, a madness, to force the opposite process; that is, to create credible situations so that they may appear true. But allow me to make the observation that, if this is madness, it is the only reason for the existence of their profession.

[*The* ACTORS *become nervous and offended.*]

DIRECTOR [*rising and looking him up and down*]: So then, our profession is for crazy people, according to you?

FATHER: Sure, to make what is not true appear true without a need to do so: a kind of game. Isn't your job to give life on stage to characters created by one's fantasy?

DIRECTOR [*giving voice to the rising anger of his* ACTORS]: I beg you to believe, my dear sir, that the acting profession is a very noble one indeed. If today, as things go, their highnesses, the new playwrights, manage to give us nothing but silly comedies to put on stage and puppets instead of real men to present, I'll have you know that we can still boast of having given life to immortal works of art here on these very boards!

[*The* ACTORS, *satisfied, approve and applaud the* DIRECTOR.]

FATHER [*interrupting furiously*]: There you are. Exactly, to living people more alive than those who breathe and wear clothes: less real, perhaps, but more true! We are precisely of the same opinion.

[*The* ACTORS *look at one another in amazement.*]

DIRECTOR: What do you mean, if before you were saying . . .

FATHER: No, I beg your pardon, I meant it for you, sir, who just shouted at us that you had no time to waste on crazy people, while no one could know better than yourself that nature serves as instrument of the human fantasy in order to pursue creation at a higher level.

DIRECTOR: OK, fine, but where does all this get us?

FATHER: Nowhere. It shows merely that one is born to life in many ways and in many forms: as a tree, or as a stone, as water, as butterfly ... or as a human. And one can also be born as a character.

DIRECTOR [*with feigned ironic amazement*]: And so you and all those people around you were born as characters?

FATHER: Precisely, sir, and as alive as you see us here.

[*The* DIRECTOR *and* ACTORS *burst into laughter as if at a joke.*]

FATHER [*hurt*]: I am sorry that you laugh like this, because inside us we carry a drama full of pain, as you can deduce from this woman veiled in black.

[*Saying this, he reaches out his hand to the* MOTHER *in order to help her up the last few steps, and, continuing to hold her hand, he leads her with a certain tragic solemnity to the other side of the stage, which is immediately illuminated by a strange light. The* CHILD *and the* YOUNG BOY *follow the* MOTHER; *then there is the* SON *separated from the rest to the rear; then, the* STEPDAUGHTER, *also on her own, towards the front and leaning on the proscenium arch. The* ACTORS, *at first amazed and then appreciative of this development, break out in applause as if they were the audience at a play.*]

DIRECTOR [*shocked and then indignant*]: Enough, let's have some quiet. [*Turning to the* CHARACTERS:] And you, remove yourselves from here. [*To the* PROPERTY MAN:] For God's sake, get them out of here!

PROPERTY MAN [*coming forward, he then stops as if held back by a strange feeling*]: Out! Get out!

FATHER [*to the* DIRECTOR]: No, you see, we ...

DIRECTOR [*shouting*]: Look here. We have to get to work now.

LEADING MAN: It's not right to be made fun of this way.

FATHER [*determined, coming forward*]: I'm surprised at your incredulity. Perhaps you gentlemen are not used to seeing characters created by an author spring to life up here one after another. Perhaps because there is [*he points to the* PROMPTER'*s box*] no script that contains us?

STEPDAUGHTER [*moving towards the* DIRECTOR, *smiling and alluring*]: Believe me, sir, we are really six characters, and very interesting ones, even though we are lost.

FATHER [*dismissing her*]: Yes 'lost', that's the right word! [*To the* DIRECTOR *without pausing:*] In the sense, you see, that the author who, once having created us alive, then no longer wished, or was he able, to put us materially into a work of art. And this, sir, was a real crime, because he who has the luck to be born a live character can even laugh at death. He will never die. The one who will die is the man, the writer, the instrument of the creation. The creation never dies. And for it to live for ever, it need not have exceptional talent or the ability to work miracles. Who was Sancho Panza? Who was Don Abbondio? And yet they live eternally, because, being live germs, they had the good fortune to find a fertile matrix, a fantasy that knew how to raise and nourish them, to make them live for eternity!

DIRECTOR: All this is fine. But what is it that you want here?

FATHER: We want to live, sir!

DIRECTOR [*ironically*]: For eternity?

FATHER: No sir, only for a moment . . . in them.

AN ACTOR: Well, will you listen to that!

LEADING LADY: They want to live in us!

YOUNG ACTOR [*pointing to the* STEPDAUGHTER]: I have no problem with that, as long as I get that one.

FATHER: Look, look! The play has to be made. [*To the* DIRECTOR:] But if you wish, and your actors are willing, we can soon work it out among ourselves.

DIRECTOR [*annoyed*]: What do you want to work out? We don't do workouts here. Here we do plays: dramas and comedies!

FATHER: Precisely. We have come to you precisely for that.

DIRECTOR: And where is the script?

FATHER: It's inside of us!

[*The* ACTORS *laugh.*]

Drama is in us; we are it; and we are anxious to play it – the passion in us drives us to this.

STEPDAUGHTER [*scornful, with perfidious graciousness loaded with impudence*]: My passion, sir, if you only knew. My passion . . . for him! [*She points to the* FATHER *and she makes a gesture to embrace him, but then bursts out into strident laughter.*]

FATHER [*in a fit of anger*]: You behave yourself – for the time being. And I beg you not to laugh that way!

STEPDAUGHTER: No? Then, allow me if you will – I, who am an

orphan of just two months – to show you gentlemen how I dance and sing. [*With a malicious smile she begins to sing 'Prends garde à Tchon-Tchin-Tchon' by Dave Stamper, fox-trot or one-step arrangement by Francis Salabert. She dances as she sings the first verse:*]

> Les chinois sont un peuple malin,
> De Shangai à Pekin,
> Ils ont mis des écriteaux partout:
> Prenez garde à Tchon-Tchin-Tchon.

[*The* ACTORS, *especially the young ones, while she is singing and dancing, are attracted to her as to a strange charm and begin to move towards her as they raise their arms as if to capture her. She slips away, and when the* ACTORS *burst into applause, she becomes, at the reprehension of the* DIRECTOR, *abstract and distant.*]

ACTORS AND ACTRESSES [*laughing and applauding*]: Bravo! Excellent! Well done!

DIRECTOR [*angrily*]: Silence! Where do you think you are, at a piano-bar? [*Taking the* FATHER *aside and in consternation:*] Can you tell me, is she mad?

FATHER: No, not mad. It's worse!

STEPDAUGHTER [*quickly rushing up to the* DIRECTOR]: Worse! Worse! Much more. Let us stage this drama at once! And you will see that at a certain point I – when this little angel here [*she takes the* CHILD, *who is next to the* MOTHER, *by the hand and leads her to the* DIRECTOR], you see how pretty she is – [*picks her up and kisses her*] darling! darling! [*puts her down and, almost unwillingly, adds in an emotional tone:*] well, when God all of a sudden decides to take this little angel from this poor mother, and this imbecile here [*pushing the* YOUNG BOY *forward, and grabbing him roughly by the sleeve*] does the stupidest thing, stupid as he is [*giving him a push towards the* MOTHER], then you will see me take off. Yes sir, take off. Take off and I can't wait! Believe me, I can't wait! Because after that intimate scene that took place between him and me [*indicates the* FATHER *with a horrible wink*], I can't stay any longer with these people, to witness the pain of this mother here for that creep [*indicates the* SON]. Just look at him. Look at him. Indifferent, cold he is, because he is the legitimate son. Full of spite for me, for that one there [*indicates the* YOUNG BOY] for this little creature, because we are bastards – do you understand, bastards! [*Goes to the* MOTHER *and embraces her.*] And this poor mother, who is the common mother of us all, he refuses to recognize as his own mother. And he looks down on her as if she were only the mother of us three bastards. The coward! [*She says all this rapidly and with great excitement, and, arriving at the final word 'coward', her voice having swelled at the word 'bastard', she pronounces it slowly, almost spitting it out.*]

MOTHER [*in great anguish to the* DIRECTOR]: Sir, for the sake of these two poor little creatures, I beg you ... [*She feels faint, starts to fall.*] Oh my God ...

FATHER [*rushing to hold her up together with all the* ACTORS *who are amazed and dismayed*]: For pity's sake, a chair, a chair for this poor widow.

ACTORS [*rushing to help*]: Is it really true then? Is she really fainting?

DIRECTOR: Quick, a chair, here.

[*One of the* ACTORS *offers a chair; the others gather around her showing concern. The* MOTHER, *now seated, tries to prevent the* FATHER *from lifting up the veil that hides her face.*]

FATHER: Look at her, sir, look at her ...

MOTHER: No, please, God, stop it!

FATHER: Let them see you! [*He lifts the veil.*]

MOTHER [*getting up and putting her hands over her face in desperation*]: Oh, sir, I beg you to prevent this man from carrying out his plan – it is horrible for me!

DIRECTOR [*overwhelmed and dumbfounded*]: I don't understand at all what's going on or where we are! [*To the* FATHER:] Is this your wife?

FATHER [*quickly*]: Yes sir, my wife!

DIRECTOR: So then, how come she's a widow if you are alive?

[*The* ACTORS *relieve all their astonishment with roaring laughter.*]

FATHER [*hurt, with bitter resentment*]: Don't laugh! Don't laugh that way, for God's sake! This is precisely what her drama is, sir. She had another man. Another man who should be here.

MOTHER [*with a scream*]: No! No!

STEPDAUGHTER: Fortunately for her, he is dead. Two months ago, as I told you. We are still in mourning as you see.

FATHER: But he's not here, you see, and it's not because he's dead. He's not here because – look at her, sir, please, and you will understand immediately! Her drama could not consist in the love for two men, for whom she, unable to feel anything except, perhaps, a bit of gratitude (not for me but for the other one). She is not a woman, she is a mother! And her drama – a powerful one, sir, powerful! – consists entirely, in fact, in these four children she has had by two men.

MOTHER: I had them? You have the courage to say that it was I who had them, as if I wanted them. It was him, sir! He forced me. He gave me that other man and forced me, forced me to go away with him!

STEPDAUGHTER [*suddenly, indignantly*]: It's not true!

MOTHER [*astonished*]: What do you mean it's not true?

STEPDAUGHTER: Not true! It's not true!

MOTHER: How would you know about it?

STEPDAUGHTER: It's not true. [*To the* DIRECTOR:] Don't believe it! You know why she says that? For him, that one over there. [*Points to the* SON.] That's why she says it! Because she tortures herself, she languishes in the indifference of that son over there – she wants him to believe that if she abandoned him when he was two years old, it was because he [*points to the* FATHER] forced her to.

MOTHER: [*vigorously*]: He forced me. He forced me, and I call God as my witness! [*To the* DIRECTOR:] Ask him [*points to the* FATHER] if it isn't true! Make him tell you himself . . . She [*pointing to the* DAUGHTER] can't possibly know anything about it.

STEPDAUGHTER: I know that as long as my father was alive you lived happily and in peace. Deny it, if you can!

MOTHER: I don't deny it, no . . .

STEPDAUGHTER: Always full of love and kindness for you! [*To the* BOY, *with anger:*] Isn't it true? Speak up. Why don't you say something, you fool?

MOTHER: Leave this poor boy alone! Why do you want me to appear ungrateful, daughter? I don't want to offend your father. I

17

told him that it was not my fault nor was it for my pleasure that I abandoned his house and my son!

FATHER: It is true, sir. It was my doing.

[*Pause.*]

LEADING ACTOR [*to his companions*]: What a show this is!

LEADING LADY: They are performing for us!

YOUNG ACTOR: For once!

DIRECTOR [*he begins to get really interested*]: Let's listen to them! Let's listen! [*And, saying this, he goes down one of the staircases and remains standing in front of the stage as if, like a spectator, to capture the impression of the scene.*)

SON [*without moving from his place, cold, flat and ironic*]: Sure. Let's listen to this bit of philosophical reasoning now! He will talk to you about the Demon of *Proof*.

FATHER: You are a cynical fool. And I've told you so a hundred times. [*To the* DIRECTOR *already in the audience:*] He makes fun of me, sir, because of this phrase which I have found as my excuse.

SON [*contemptuously*]: Phrases.

FATHER: Phrases! Phrases! As if it were not everybody's consolation: faced by a fact that cannot be explained or by some ill that consumes us, to find a word that says nothing but in which we find tranquillity.

STEPDAUGHTER: Even when it comes to remorse. Certainly! Above all in that case.

FATHER: Remorse? It's not true. It was not only with words that I pacified the remorse in me.

STEPDAUGHTER: Yes, and also with a bit of money; sure, with a little bit of money. There was that hundred lire that he was about to offer me as payment, gentlemen!

[*The* ACTORS *are horrified.*]

SON [*with contempt for the* STEPDAUGHTER]: This is despicable.

STEPDAUGHTER: Despicable? There it was on a little mahogany table in a light blue envelope in the back of Madame Pace's shop. You know what I'm talking about, sir, you know what I mean. One of those women who, with the excuse of selling 'Robes et Manteaux', attract girls who are poor and from good families.

SON: And he thinks he has bought the right to tyrannize all of us

with that hundred lire he was about to pay and which, fortunately
– take note of this – he had no motive to do.

STEPDAUGHTER: Ah, but we were on the verge of doing it, you
know. [*Bursts out laughing.*]

MOTHER [*protesting*]: Shame on you, daughter, shame!

STEPDAUGHTER [*in an outburst*]: Shame? This is my revenge! I'm
thrilled; thrilled with the desire to live that scene! The room . . .
Here the store window-case with capes on display; there the sofa-
bed; the looking-glass; a screen; and there in front of the window
the little mahogany table with the light blue envelope containing
the hundred lire. I see it! I could pick it up! But you, gentlemen,
should turn your backs now: I am almost in the nude! I'm no
longer blushing, because he is blushing now! [*To the* FATHER:]
But I assure you he was very pale, very pale at the moment! [*To
the* DIRECTOR:] Believe me, sir!

DIRECTOR: I don't understand a thing!

FATHER: No wonder you don't when it's put that way. Get things
in order here and let me speak. Don't listen to her infamous
remarks which she, this person here, so ferociously would have
you believe about me without the required explanation.

STEPDAUGHTER: You can't tell a story here. Not here. No
narration.

FATHER: I'm not narrating! I want to explain to him.

STEPDAUGHTER: Ah, sure, that's nice! Explain in your own way!

[*The* DIRECTOR *at this point gets back on stage in order to get things
in order.*]

FATHER: But can't you see that all the trouble lies here! In the
words! All of us have a world full of things inside of us, each of
us his own world of things! And how can we understand one
another, sir, if in the words I speak I put the meaning and the
value of things as I myself see them, while the one who listens
inevitably takes them according to the meaning and the value
which he has in himself of the world he has inside of *himself*. We
think we understand each other; we never understand one another. You see: my pity, all the pity I have for this woman [*points
to the* MOTHER] she has taken as the most ferocious form of
cruelty.

MOTHER: But if you drove me out.

FATHER: There, did you hear that? Drove out! It seems to her that I drove her out!

MOTHER: You know how to talk; I don't . . . But believe me, sir, that after having married me . . . who knows why? . . . I was a poor, simple woman . . .

FATHER: But precisely for this, for your simplicity that I loved in you, I married you, believing . . . [*He stops speaking when she shows signs of contradicting him; he opens his arms in an act of desperation seeing how impossible it was to be understood by her, and he turns to the* DIRECTOR.] No, you see she says no. Frightening, isn't it, sir, believe me, frightening [*he strikes his forehead*] her deafness, mental deafness. Heart, yes, for her children. But deaf, deaf in the brain, deaf, sir, to the point of desperation.

STEPDAUGHTER: Fine, but have him tell now how lucky we were to have the help of his intelligence.

FATHER: If a person could only foresee all the bad that can come from the good that we think we are doing!

[*At this point the* LEADING LADY, *who is desolate at seeing the* LEADING MAN *flirting with the* STEPDAUGHTER, *comes forward and asks the* DIRECTOR:]

LEADING LADY: Excuse me, sir, are we planning to go on with the rehearsal?

DIRECTOR: But of course. Certainly. But let me hear this first.

YOUNG ACTOR: It's such a strange case!

YOUNG ACTRESS: Extremely interesting.

LEADING LADY: For those interested in such matters! [*She gives the* LEADING MAN *a dirty look.*]

DIRECTOR [*to the* FATHER]: But you will have to explain yourself very clearly. [*He sits down.*]

FATHER: Well then. You see, sir, I had working for me at one time a poor man, a subordinate of mine, my secretary who was totally devoted to her. They got along splendidly and understood each other perfectly [*indicates the* MOTHER] without the slightest trace of malice, you understand – he was a good and simple person like her, both of them not only incapable of doing anything wrong but even of entertaining the thought of doing so!

STEPDAUGHTER: So instead he thought of it for them — and he did it!

FATHER: It is not true. It was my intention to do what was good for them, and also for me — I confess! I had reached the point, sir, where I could not say a word to either one of them without their immediately exchanging glances and looks of mutual understanding, where one did not quickly seek the eyes of the other — in search of counsel on how to take my words so as not to make me angry. This was enough, you understand, to keep me in a constant rage, in a state of intolerable exasperation!

DIRECTOR: I beg your pardon, but why didn't you just throw him out, that secretary of yours?

FATHER: Exactly! I did, in fact, throw him out, sir! But then I had to watch this poor woman wandering around the house as if lost, like an animal without its master that one takes in out of pity.

MOTHER: No wonder!

FATHER [quickly turning towards her as if to forestall her]: About the son, though, it's true, isn't it?

MOTHER: First of all, he took my son away from me, sir.

FATHER: But not to be cruel. I did it so that he would grow up healthy and strong by living out in the country.

STEPDAUGHTER [pointing to him, ironically]: You can see how it shows!

FATHER: Is it my fault if he turned out this way? I sent him to a wet nurse in the country, a peasant girl because she didn't seem to me to be strong enough, even though she did come from humble origins. And that was the reason, in fact, that I had married her. Crazy as it sounds, but what can you do? I always had these odious aspirations towards a certain solid moral sanity.

[At this point the STEPDAUGHTER again roars with laughter.]

Please make her stop. It's intolerable.

DIRECTOR: Stop laughing and let me listen for God's sake.

[Immediately, once again, in the middle of a laugh, she becomes, at the DIRECTOR's reprimand, distant and immersed in thought. The DIRECTOR gets down from the stage again in order to get an impression of the scene.]

FATHER: I could never imagine this woman next to me again.

21

[*Points to the* MOTHER.] But it's not so much, believe me, the tedium, the feeling of suffocation – real suffocation – as much as it is the compassion, the anguishing compassion that I felt for her.

MOTHER: And he sent me away.

FATHER: And well provided for, to that man, yes sir, to free her of me.

MOTHER: And to free himself.

FATHER: Yes sir, myself as well – I admit it. And great harm has come from it. But I did it with good intentions . . . and more for her than for me. I swear it! [*Crosses his arms on his chest; then, all of a sudden, turning to the* MOTHER:] Did I ever lose sight of you, tell me, did I ever lose sight of you; not until that other man took you away one day without my knowing it to another town, stupidly misunderstanding my pure interest in you – yes sir, pure, believe me, without any ulterior motive in it. I watched with incredible tenderness the new family she was raising. She too can attest to it. [*Points to the* STEPDAUGHTER.]

STEPDAUGHTER: Oh, yes, and how! I was just a little thing, so high, with braids over my shoulders and underpants longer than my skirts. Just so high! I would see him in front of the school whenever I would come out. He used to come to see how I was growing up . . .

FATHER: This is malicious. Disgraceful.

STEPDAUGHTER: No, why?

FATHER: Shameful! Shameful! [*Quickly and with agitation to the* DIRECTOR *in an explanatory tone:*] After she left my home, sir [*indicating the* MOTHER], it seemed, all of a sudden, empty. She was my nightmare, but she filled my house. All alone I found myself in those rooms like a headless fly. That one over there [*indicates the* SON] brought up away from home – I don't know – when he came back, he no longer seemed to be mine. With no mother between him and me, he grew up on his own, alone, with no relationship, either emotional or intellectual, with me. And then (it may sound strange, sir, but that's the way it is), first drawn by curiosity, gradually, I became attracted towards that little family of hers which due to me had come into being: the thought of it began to fill the emptiness that I felt around me. I needed, I really needed to believe that she had found peace, completely absorbed in the daily cares of life, fortunate because she was far away from the complications that torment my soul. And to have proof of this, I would go to see that little girl when she would leave school.

STEPDAUGHTER: Yes, that's right. He would follow me down the street, smile at me, and when I reached home, wave at me – like this! I would give him a cross look. I didn't know who he was. I told my mother. And she must have understood immediately who it was. [*The* MOTHER *nods her head in agreement.*] At first she didn't want to send me to school any more, not for many days. When I did go back, I saw him again at the school exit – looking funny – with a big bundle of paper in his hands. He came up to me, caressed me, and out of all that paper he took a big, beautiful, Florentine straw hat surrounded by tiny May roses – all for me!

DIRECTOR: But all this is narrative, dear sirs.

SON [*disdainfully*]: Of course. It's literature, literature.

FATHER: What do you mean, 'literature'! This is life, sir! Passion.

DIRECTOR: It may well be. But it can't be played out!

FATHER: I agree, sir. This is only the background that leads up. I am not saying that this should be staged. As you can see, in fact, she [*indicates the* STEPDAUGHTER], she is no longer that little girl with braids on her shoulders – with her underpants showing below her skirt! Now, sir, comes the drama: new and complex.

STEPDAUGHTER [*sombre, proud, coming forward*]: As soon as my father died –

FATHER [*quickly, so as not to give her a chance to talk*]: The misery, sir. They came back here without my knowing it. Because of her stupidity. [*Points to the* MOTHER.] She can barely write. But she could have had her daughter write me, or that boy, that they were in need!

MOTHER: You tell me, sir, how was I to guess all that he was feeling?

FATHER: This is precisely your mistake: never having guessed any of my feelings!

MOTHER: After being apart so many years, and all that had happened . . .

FATHER: And so is it my fault if this fellow carried you off the way he did? [*Turning to the* DIRECTOR:] I mean, all of a sudden . . . because he found some job or another. It was not possible for me to find them; and then, of course, after so many years my interest in them faded. But the drama explodes, sir, unforeseen and violent, on their return, when I, unfortunately, led by the wretched needs of the flesh, still alive . . . Ah, wretchedness, true wretchedness for a lonely man who had no taste for degrading relationships; not yet old enough to do without a woman and no longer young enough comfortably to look for one without shame. Wretched? What am I saying? It's a horror, horror, because no woman can give him love any more. And when one realizes this, one should do without . . . It's easy to say, sir, but each of us – on the outside, in front of others – dresses in dignity, but inside himself he is well aware of these unconfessible things that pass through the secrecy of his heart. A man gives in, concedes to temptation only to rise again right afterwards with great eagerness to rebuild his dignity whole and solid like a tombstone on a grave that buries and hides from our very eyes every sigh and the memory itself of that shame. It's the same for everyone! What's lacking is the courage to admit, to say these things!

STEPDAUGHTER: Everyone appears, though, to have the courage to do them.

FATHER: Yes, everyone! But in secret. And therefore it takes more courage to say these things. Because all one has to do is say these things – and that's it – they brand you a cynic. But it isn't true, sir; he is like all the others, better, even better, because he is not afraid to reveal with the light of intelligence the redness of shame there in human bestiality to which others always close their eyes so as not to see it. Woman, for example, take the case of a woman. She looks at you with provocation, invitingly. You grab her! No sooner is she caught than she immediately closes her eyes. It is the sign of her surrender, the sign which tells the man: 'I am blind, now blind yourself!'

STEPDAUGHTER: And when she can no longer close them? What about when she no longer feels the need to close her eyes and hide from herself the redness of her shame, and now, dry-eyed and impassive, sees only that of the man who has blinded himself without love? Ah, how disgusting; these intellectual complications make me sick, sick of all this philosophy that reveals the beast in us and then wants to save him, to excuse . . . I can't listen to it any more, sir! Because when you are forced to 'simplify' life – this way, bestially – throwing away all 'human' encumbrance, every chaste aspiration, all pure sentiment, idealism, duty, modesty and shame, then nothing is more contemptible and nauseous than certain kinds of remorse – crocodile tears!

DIRECTOR: Let's get to the point. Let's get to the event, ladies and gentlemen. This is only discussion.

FATHER: Of course, yes sir! But the event is like a sack: when empty it will not stand up. In order for it to stand up, one must first fill it with reason and feelings which are the cause of its existence. I could not know that, once that man died and they returned here in poverty, she [*indicates the* MOTHER], in order to support her children, had got work as a dressmaker . . . and in a place like Madame Pace's!

STEPDAUGHTER: A real fine dressmaker, if you gentlemen are interested in knowing. Apparently she serves the high-class ladies, but in such a way that these high-class ladies then serve her purpose . . . without prejudice to the other, let's say, so-so ladies.

MOTHER: Believe me, sir, when I tell you that never once, even vaguely, did the doubt pass through my mind that the old witch gave me work because she had her eyes on my daughter.

STEPDAUGHTER: Poor Mamma! Do you know, sir, what that woman would do as soon as I brought back the work done by my mother? She would show me those things she had given my mother to sew and which she had done badly. And she would deduct and deduct, so that, you see, I was the one who was paying while that poor woman believed she was sacrificing herself for me and for those two, sitting up even at night sewing those things for Madame Pace.

[*Movement and exclamations of disdain from the* ACTORS.]

DIRECTOR [*quickly*]: And there, in that place, one day, you met –

STEPDAUGHTER [*pointing to the* FATHER]: – him, yes sir, him! An old client. Wait till you see what a scene that is to play! Superb!

FATHER: With the arrival of her, the mother –

STEPDAUGHTER [*quickly, treacherously*]: – almost in time! –

FATHER [*shouting*]: – no, in time, in time! Because, fortunately, I recognized her in time! And I took the whole family back with me, sir! Just imagine her situation and mine, now face to face; she as you see her here; and I who cannot look her in the eye.

STEPDAUGHTER: That's very funny! But is it possible, sir, that I be expected – 'after that fact' – to be a modest young lady, well brought up and virtuous, in accordance with his damned aspirations 'for a solid, moral sanity'?

FATHER: The drama for me, sir, lies all in this: in the conscience I have, which every one of us has – you see – we think we are 'one' with 'one' conscience, but it is not true: it is 'many', sir, 'many' according to all the possibilities of being that are in us: 'one' with this, 'one' with that – all very different! So we have the illusion of always being at the same time 'one for everyone' and always 'this one' that we believe we are in everything we do. It is not true! It is not true! We see this clearly whenever, in something we do, under very unfortunate circumstances, we are all of a sudden caught, as if suspended on a hook; we realize, I mean to say, that all of our self is not in that act, and that, therefore, it would be an atrocious injustice to pass judgement on us by that single action: to hold us fixed, hooked and suspended for our entire existence, as if our existence were all summed up in this one act! Now do you understand the wickedness of this girl? She took me by surprise acting in a place where she was not supposed to know me, just as I was not supposed to be for her, and she wants to give me a reality which I could never have expected to have assumed for her, in a fleeting shameful moment of my life. This, it is this, sir, that I feel above all. And you will see that from this fact the drama will acquire great importance. But, there is the situation of the others. His ... [*Indicates the* SON.]

SON [*shrugging his shoulders disdainfully*]: Leave me out of it! I have nothing to do with it!

FATHER: What do you mean you have nothing to do with it?

SON: I've got nothing to do with it, and I don't want to have anything to do with it, because, as you well know, I wasn't made to be involved with all of you here.

STEPDAUGHTER: We are just common folk! – He's refined! But have you noticed, sir, how often I fix my eyes on him with a look of contempt and how many times he lowers his eyes? It's because he knows the harm he caused me.

SON [*hardly looking at her*]: I?

STEPDAUGHTER: You, you! It's to you, my dear, I owe my street-walking! To you!

[*The* ACTORS *show horror.*]

Did you or did you not with your behaviour deny us – I won't go as far as to say the intimacy of a home – but that kindness which makes a guest feel that he is less of a bother? We were the intruders who were coming to invade the kingdom of your 'legitimacy'. I wish you could see, privately that is, certain little scenes between him and me! He says that I tyrannized everybody. Do you see? It was precisely this behaviour of his that made me make use of the reason which he calls 'vile', the reason for which I came into his house with my mother – who is also his mother – that is, to be head of the household.

SON [*slowly coming forward*]: It's easy for all of them, sir, to take sides against me. I ask you to try to picture a son who, one fine day, while sitting peacefully in his home, has to witness the arrival, all cocky – such 'haughty eyes' – of a young lady who asks for his father, who wants to discuss who knows what with him; and then he has to witness her return, always with the same arrogant manner, accompanied by that little one over there; and finally, he has to see his father treated – who knows why? – in a most ambiguous and 'curt' fashion, asking him for money in a tone of voice that makes one think that he *must* pay, because he is thoroughly obliged to do so.

FATHER: But I do, in fact, truly have such an obligation – to your mother!

SON: How was I supposed to know? When did I ever see her, sir? When did I ever hear her name mentioned? I see her show up one day with her [*indicates the* STEPDAUGHTER], with that boy, and with that child; they say to me: 'Oh, you know, this is your mother too.' I get an idea from the way she acts [*again he indicates the* STEPDAUGHTER] what the motive was for their coming home all of a sudden ... Sir, what I am going through, what I am feeling, I cannot, nor do I wish to, express. At best I might confess it in secret, but I wouldn't even care to tell it to myself. And so you see no action can arise because of me. Believe me, believe me, sir. I am not a character that has been 'realized' dramatically, that is; and I feel bad, very bad, in their company. Please leave me alone!

FATHER: What? Look! If it's precisely because you are that way –

SON [*with violent exasperation*]: How do you know what I am like? When did you ever care about me?

FATHER: Granted, granted. But isn't this also a situation? This isolation of yours which is so cruel to me and for your mother who, returning home, sees you almost for the first time, so grown-up, and doesn't know you, but she knows you are her son. [*Pointing at the* MOTHER *for the* DIRECTOR:] There she is! Look, she's crying.

STEPDAUGHTER [*with anger, banging her feet*]: Like a fool.

FATHER [*too quickly pointing to her for the* DIRECTOR]: And she can't stand him, obviously. [*Referring again to the* SON:] He says he has nothing to do with it, but he is practically the pivot-point of the action. Look at that boy who always stays close to his mother, bewildered and humiliated ... he's like that because of him! Perhaps his situation is the most painful of all. He feels like a stranger more than the others; and he feels, poor thing, mortified and anguished at being taken into a home out of charity. [*In confidence:*] He is just like his father, humble and silent.

DIRECTOR: Ah, but this isn't a very good idea. You have no idea what trouble boys can cause on stage.

FATHER: Oh, but he will relieve you of the trouble immediately. And also that little girl who is, by the way, the first to go ...

DIRECTOR: Yes, fine. And I assure you that all this interests me, it really interests me. I sense there is material here to put together a good play.

STEPDAUGHTER [*trying to intrude*]: Especially with a character like myself!

FATHER [*chasing her away, all excited to hear the* DIRECTOR's *decision*]: You be quiet!

DIRECTOR [*continuing without paying attention to the interruption*]: New material, yes . . .

FATHER: Ah, very new, sir!

DIRECTOR: It takes quite a bit of nerve, however – I mean to come and present it to me this way . . .

FATHER: After all, sir, born as we are for the stage!

DIRECTOR: Are you amateur actors?

FATHER: No, I say born for the stage because . . .

DIRECTOR: Come on, you must have acted before.

FATHER: No, we have not, sir. The only acting we do is in that role for which each of us has been cast or which others have given us in life. In my own case, it is passion itself, you see, as often happens, that becomes on its own – as in everyone – as soon as it is exalted, a bit theatrical . . .

DIRECTOR: Let's drop it, let's just drop it! You understand, dear sir, that without an author . . . I could put you in contact with someone, an author who . . .

FATHER: No, no. Look here: you're the one!

DIRECTOR: Me? You don't know what you're saying!

FATHER: Yes, you! You! Why not?

DIRECTOR: Because I have never been an author before!

FATHER: I beg your pardon, but I don't see why you can't do it now! It doesn't take much. A lot of people do it. And your job would be facilitated by the fact that all of us are already here, alive, right in front of you.

DIRECTOR: But that's not enough.

FATHER: What do you mean it's not enough? When you can actually see us living out our drama . . .

DIRECTOR: That's fine! But you still need someone who will write it.

FATHER: No – What's needed, in case, is someone who will copy it down, since he would have it all here in front of him – in action – scene by scene. It would be enough just to sketch it out, at first, just a rough copy – then we try it out!

DIRECTOR [*climbing back on stage, and tempted*]: Well, you know, I'm almost tempted. Why not, just for fun . . . Why not give it a try?

FATHER: Of course, sir. Wait till you see what scenes come out of it. I can show you some immediately.

DIRECTOR: It's tempting . . . I'm tempted. Let's give it a try. Come with me to my dressing-room. [*Addressing the* ACTORS:] You all take a short break. But don't wander off too far. In a quarter of an hour, twenty minutes, everybody back here. [*To the* FATHER:] Let's see . . . let's see. Perhaps something really extraordinary could come out of all this.

FATHER: But without a doubt. Don't you think it would be better if they came too? [*Indicating the other* CHARACTERS.]

DIRECTOR: Yes, all of you come. Come along. [*Moves away, but then turns back to the* ACTORS.] Please be punctual, OK? In a quarter of an hour.

[*The* DIRECTOR *and the* SIX CHARACTERS *cross the stage and disappear. The* ACTORS *remain, looking at one another in astonishment.*]

LEADING MAN: Is he serious? What is he going to do?

YOUNG ACTOR: This is outright madness!

THIRD ACTOR: He expects us to improvise a play – just like that!

YOUNG ACTOR: Sure, like in the 'Commedia dell'Arte'!

LEADING LADY: Ah, if he thinks I'm going along with a joke like this . . .

YOUNG ACTRESS: I'm not playing his game either!

FOURTH ACTOR: I'd like to know who those people are [*alluding to the* CHARACTERS].

THIRD ACTOR: They are either insane or they are charlatans.

YOUNG ACTOR: And he bothers to listen to them?

YOUNG ACTRESS: Vanity. The vanity of appearing as an author!

LEADING MAN: But this is unheard of. If theatre has come to this, ladies and gentlemen . . .

FIFTH ACTOR: I'm having fun!

THIRD ACTOR: Who knows? After all; well let's see what comes of all of this.

[*And conversing with each other this way, the* ACTORS *leave the stage, some going out the little door at the back of the stage, others returning to their dressing-rooms. The curtain remains up. The play is interrupted for about twenty minutes.*]

ACT TWO

The theatre bell rings to announce that the play is starting again.

From the dressing-rooms, from the door and also from the orchestra come the ACTORS, *the* STAGE MANAGER, *the* TECHNICIAN, *the* PROMPTER, *the* PROPERTY MAN *and, at the same time, the* DIRECTOR *and the* SIX CHARACTERS *from his dressing-room.*

Once the theatre lights are out, the stage is lit as it was before.

DIRECTOR: OK, let's go, ladies and gentlemen. Are we all here? Pay attention. Attention now. We're beginning. Technician!

TECHNICIAN: Here I am.

DIRECTOR: Quick, get the parlour scene ready. Two wings and a drop with a door will do. Quickly, please.

[*The* TECHNICIAN *quickly runs to do it, and while the* DIRECTOR *is discussing the upcoming show with the* STAGE MANAGER, *the* PROPERTY MAN, *the* PROMPTER *and the* ACTORS, *he prepares the indicated setting: two wings and a drop with a door with pink and gold stripes.*]

DIRECTOR [*to the* PROPERTY MAN]: Go and see if there isn't a divan in wardrobe.

PROPERTY MAN: Yes sir, there's the green one.

STEPDAUGHTER: No, no. Not green. It was yellow with a floral design made of 'peluche' – very big and very comfortable.

PROPERTY MAN: Ah, we don't have one like that.

DIRECTOR: It makes no difference. Use what you've got.

STEPDAUGHTER: What do you mean it makes no difference? And what about Madame Pace's famous chaise-longue?

DIRECTOR: We're just trying it out for now! Please don't interfere. [*To the* STAGE MANAGER:] See if you can find a shop window that's rather long and low.

STEPDAUGHTER: The little table, the little mahogany table for the light blue envelope.

STAGE MANAGER [*to the* DIRECTOR]: There's that little one with the gold colour.

DIRECTOR: OK, get that one.

FATHER: A big mirror.

STEPDAUGHTER: And the screen! Don't forget, we need a screen. Otherwise what will I do?

STAGE MANAGER: Yes, miss. Don't worry, we've got plenty of those.

DIRECTOR [to the STEPDAUGHTER]: Also, some clothes hangers, don't we?

STEPDAUGHTER: Yes, a lot of them. Lots.

DIRECTOR [to the STAGE MANAGER]: See how many we've got and have them brought here.

STAGE MANAGER: Yes sir, I'll see to it.

[The STAGE MANAGER also rushes off to do this, and while the DIRECTOR continues talking to the PROMPTER and also with the CHARACTERS and the ACTORS, he has the indicated props brought by STAGE HANDS and places them where he thinks they should be.]

DIRECTOR [to the PROMPTER]: Now you sit down. Look here: here's an outline of the scenes, act by act. [He hands him some sheets of paper.] Now you're going to have to do something unusual.

PROMPTER: Write in shorthand?

DIRECTOR [happily surprised]: Ah, excellent! You know shorthand?

PROMPTER: I may not know prompting, but shorthand . . .

DIRECTOR: But that's even better! [Turning to a STAGE HAND:] Go and get paper in my dressing-room – a lot; get a lot, as much as you can find.

[The STAGE HAND rushes off and shortly after returns with a good amount of paper which he hands to the PROMPTER.]

DIRECTOR [continuing to the PROMPTER]: Follow the scenes as we play them little by little and try to get down the dialogue, or at least the major points. [Then, turning to the ACTORS:] Clear the stage, ladies and gentlemen. Here you go. Everyone to this side [indicates the left] and pay close attention.

LEADING LADY: I beg your pardon, but we . . .

DIRECTOR [anticipating her]: Don't worry. You won't have to improvise!

LEADING MAN: And what are we supposed to do?

DIRECTOR: Nothing. For now, just listen carefully and watch. Then each of you will have his own written part. It's just a try-out now. They're going to do it [*indicating the* CHARACTERS].

FATHER [*as if fallen from the clouds into the confusion on stage*]: We? Excuse me, but what do you mean 'try-out'?

DIRECTOR: A try-out. A rehearsal for them! [*Indicates the* ACTORS.]

FATHER: But if we are the characters . . .

DIRECTOR: All right then 'the characters'. But here, my dear sir, the characters do not act. Here the actors act. The characters stay there in the script [*points to the* PROMPTER's *box*] – when there is a script!

FATHER: Exactly! Since there is none and you people have the good fortune to have here in front of you, alive, the characters . . .

DIRECTOR: Oh, that's great! You would like to do it all on your own then: to act, to present yourselves before the public?

FATHER: Certainly. Just the way we are.

DIRECTOR: Ah, I can assure you it would be some show!

LEADING MAN: So what are we doing here anyway?

DIRECTOR: They couldn't possibly think that they know how to act, could they? What a laugh that is!

[*The* ACTORS, *in fact, laugh.*]

There, you see, they're laughing. But, by the way, we have to cast the parts. Oh, it's easy: they cast themselves. [*To the* SECOND ACTRESS:] You, madame, play the mother. [*To the* FATHER:] We'll have to find her a name.

FATHER: Amalia, sir.

DIRECTOR: But that's the name of your wife. We don't want to call her by her real name!

FATHER: And why not, if that is her name . . . But, still, if that lady is going to be . . . [*With a slight movement of his hand he indicates the* SECOND ACTRESS:] I see this woman [*indicates the* MOTHER] as Amalia, sir. But do as you please . . . [*He gets more and more confused.*] I don't know what else to say to you . . . I am beginning now to . . . I don't know, hear my own words ringing false, ringing with a different sound.

34

DIRECTOR: Well, don't you worry about it; don't worry about it. Leave it to us to find the right tone! And as far as the name is concerned, if you want 'Amalia' then Amalia it is, or we can find another name. For the time being let's call the characters this way. [*To the* YOUNG ACTOR:] You are the son. [*To the* LEADING LADY:] You, young lady, of course are the stepdaughter.

STEPDAUGHTER [*excitedly*]: What, what? I am that woman there? [*She bursts out laughing.*]

DIRECTOR [*angrily*]: What are you laughing at?

LEADING LADY [*insulted*]: No one ever dared to laugh at me! I expect to be respected, otherwise I'm leaving.

STEPDAUGHTER: I'm sorry but I'm not laughing at you.

DIRECTOR [*to the* STEPDAUGHTER]: You should be honoured to be played by –

LEADING LADY [*at once, indignantly*]: – 'that woman there'.

STEPDAUGHTER: But I wasn't referring to you, believe me. I was speaking of myself, whom I cannot see at all in you. That's it. I don't know, no . . . you're not in any way like me.

FATHER: Sure, that's it. You see, sir, our expression, our way of being?

DIRECTOR: What about your expression! Do you really think you have it in you, your expression? Nothing doing!

FATHER: What! We don't have our own expression?

DIRECTOR: Not at all. Your expression becomes material here to which the actors give body and form, voice and gesture, my actors – for your information – were capable of giving expression to much greater material; whereas yours is so little that, if it should manage to hold up on stage, the merit, you can believe me, belongs entirely to my actors.

FATHER: I don't dare to contradict you, sir. But believe me, it is horribly painful to be the way we are, the way you see us, with this body, with this look.

DIRECTOR [*cutting him off, losing patience*]: But this can be taken care of with make-up, the make-up will remedy that, my dear man, as far as the look is concerned.

FATHER: OK, but the voice, the gestures –

35

DIRECTOR: Oh, after all, here you cannot exist as your real self! Here it is the actor that represents you. And that's the end of it!

FATHER: I understand, sir. But now I think I also see why our author, who conceived of us so alive, no longer wanted to put us on stage. I have no intention of offending your actors. God forbid. But when I think of myself being represented – I don't know by whom . . .

LEADING MAN [*with pride, getting up and going towards him followed by the happy young actresses who are laughing*]: By me, if you don't mind!

FATHER [*humble and smooth*]: It will be a great honour, sir. [*He bows.*] Still, I think that, no matter how much this gentleman may try with all his good will and all of his artistic ability to make himself into me . . . [*Losing his train of thought.*]

LEADING MAN: Finish what you're saying. Finish!

[*The* ACTRESSES *laugh.*]

FATHER: Ah, I mean, the performance he will give, even doing his best to look like me with make-up . . . I mean, with his height . . .

[*All the* ACTORS *laugh.*]

it will be difficult to play me as I really am. It will be more like – apart from how I look – it will be more like how he plays the way I am, how he feels like me – if he does feel like me – and not how I myself feel inside of me. And it seems to me that, concerning this matter, whoever is expected to judge us should keep this in mind.

DIRECTOR: Now you're worried about the judgements of the critics? Let the critics say what they like, and let's concentrate more on getting this play into shape, if we possibly can! [*Moving to one side and looking around.*] Come on. Let's go. Is the stage set? [*To the* ACTORS *and* CHARACTERS:] Move away, move out of my way. Let me see. [*Gets down from the stage.*] Let's not lose any more time! [*To the* STEPDAUGHTER:] Do you think the set is OK as it is now?

STEPDAUGHTER: Hmm. I really don't see myself in this place.

DIRECTOR: Here we go again! You don't expect us to construct for you here the back shop of Madame Pace, exactly as it was,

exactly the way you know it. [*To the* FATHER:] You told me it
was a small room with floral designs?

FATHER: Yes, sir. White.

DIRECTOR: It's not white. It's striped. But it doesn't matter much.
As for the furniture, more or less, I think we've got it! That little
table, bring it a bit further front!

   [*The* STAGE HANDS *follow instructions.*]

[*To the* PROPERTY MAN:] In the meantime you find an envelope, if possible light blue, and give it to the gentleman. [*Indicates
the* FATHER.]

PROPERTY MAN: Envelope for a letter?

FATHER: For a letter. For a letter.

PROPERTY MAN: Immediately. [*Exits.*]

DIRECTOR: Let's go. Let's go. First scene is the young lady's.

   [*The* LEADING LADY *comes forward.*]

No, no, you wait. I was speaking to the young lady. [*Indicates
the* STEPDAUGHTER.] You will watch –

STEPDAUGHTER [*quickly adding*]: – how I live it!

LEADING LADY [*offended*]: Don't worry, once I get into it, I'll know
how to live it too.

DIRECTOR [*with hands to his head*]: Ladies and gentlemen, that's
enough talk. Now then, the first scene is the young lady with
Madame Pace. Oh, [*he looks around as though lost and gets back up
on stage*] and this Madame Pace of yours?

FATHER: She is not with us, sir.

DIRECTOR: Then what do we do now?

FATHER: But she's alive; she's alive too!

DIRECTOR: Sure! But where is she?

FATHER: Wait, let me speak. [*Turning to the* ACTRESSES:] If
you ladies would be so kind as to give me your hats for a
moment.

ACTRESSES [*somewhat surprised and laughing slightly, in chorus*]:
What?
Our hats?
What does he mean?
Why?
Ah, look!

DIRECTOR: What do you want to do with the ladies' hats?

[*The* ACTORS *laugh.*]

FATHER: Oh, nothing really. I just want to put them on these clothes pegs for a moment. And would one of the ladies also be so kind as to remove her wrap.

ACTORS [*as above*]: A wrap too?

And what else?

He's got to be mad!

ACTRESSES [*as above*]: But why?

Just one wrap?

FATHER: To hang up here, just for a moment. Please be so kind, won't you?

ACTRESSES [*removing their hats, and one of them her wrap, they continue to laugh as they go around hanging them on the racks*]: And why not?

There you are.

This is really funny.

Do we put them on display?

FATHER: That's right. Precisely, yes ma'am, just like that, on display.

DIRECTOR: Do you mind telling me the reason for this?

FATHER: You see, sir, perhaps by preparing the scene appropriately for her, attracted by the very objects of her trade, who knows, she could appear among us ... [*Inviting everyone to look at the exit backstage:*] Everybody look! Look!

[*The rear door opens and* MADAME PACE *takes a few steps forward. She is an enormously fat old hag wearing a voluminous carrot-coloured wig made of wool with a flaming-red rose to one side – Spanish style; all dolled up, dressed in a clumsily elegant gown of gaudy red silk with a fan of feathers in one hand, and the other hand raised, holding between two fingers a lit cigarette. With her appearance the* ACTORS *and the* DIRECTOR *rush from the stage with a shout of fear and head for the stairs as if to flee down the aisle. The* STEPDAUGHTER, *instead, runs towards* MADAME PACE; *she appears submissive, as towards a mistress.*]

STEPDAUGHTER [*rushing*]: Here she is! She's here!

FATHER [*radiant*]: It's her. Didn't I tell you? Here she is!

DIRECTOR [*overcoming his amazement and with indignation*]: What kind of a trick is this?

LEADING MAN [*almost at the same time*]: What's going on here anyway?

YOUNG ACTOR [*as above*]: Where did she come from?

YOUNG ACTRESS [*as above*]: They were holding her in reserve!

LEADING LADY [*as above*]: They'rea bunch of thimbleriggers!

FATHER [*in control of the protests*]: Excuse me, but why would you want to ruin, in the name of a commonplace sense of truth, this miracle of a reality that is born, evoked, attracted and formed by the stage itself and which has more right to live here than all of you, because it is much truer than you? Which one of you will play the part of Madame Pace? Well, Madame Pace herself is right over there! You do agree with me that the actress that will act her will be less true than this one here – who is herself in person! Look, my daughter has recognized her and she immediately went to her side. Let's see; let's watch the scene.

[*With hesitance the* DIRECTOR *and* ACTORS *go back up on stage. But already, while the protest of the* ACTORS *and the reply of the* FATHER *is taking place, the scene between the* STEPDAUGHTER *and* MADAME PACE *has begun. It takes place in undertones, very quietly, that is to say naturally – in a way that would be impossible to present on stage. So when the* ACTORS, *called to attention by the* FATHER, *turn around to look and see* MADAME PACE, *who has placed her hand under the* STEPDAUGHTER's *chin in order to raise her head, they are for a moment captivated, but when they hear them speak in a completely unintelligible way, they quickly become deluded.*]

DIRECTOR: Well?

LEADING MAN: What is she saying?

LEADING LADY: You can't hear a thing.

YOUNG ACTOR: Louder! Louder!

STEPDAUGHTER [*leaving* MADAME PACE, *who has an unusual smile on her face, and moving towards the group of* ACTORS]: 'Louder'. You're joking! What louder? These aren't things you can say out loud! I could say them out loud in order to shame him [*indicates the*

FATHER] and get my revenge. But for madame it is another matter, gentleman. It could mean prison!

DIRECTOR: Oh, that's great! Just beautiful! But here you've got to make yourself heard, my dear. We can't even hear you and we are on stage! You can imagine what it would be like for a theatre audience! The scene has got to be done. And in any case you can certainly speak louder to each other, since we will not be here, as we are now, to hear you. Make believe that you are alone in a room in the back of the shop where no one can hear you.

[*The* STEPDAUGHTER *gracefully and with a slightly malicious smile makes a gesture indicating 'no' with her finger several times.*]

DIRECTOR: What do you mean, 'no'?

STEPDAUGHTER [*sotto voce, mysteriously*]: There is someone who will hear us, sir, if she [*indicates* MADAME PACE] speaks out loud.

DIRECTOR [*very dismayed*]: Is somebody else about to appear out of the blue?

[*The* ACTORS *pretend to run from the stage again.*]

FATHER: No, no sir. She is alluding to me. I have to be there behind that door waiting, and madame knows this. In fact, with your permission, I'll go right now so that I will be ready. [*He makes a move to go.*]

DIRECTOR [*stopping him*]: No, no, wait! The requirements of the theatre have to be respected. Before you are ready . . .

STEPDAUGHTER [*interrupting him*]: Yes, right away! Right now! I'm dying, I tell you, with the urge to live it, to see this scene played out. If he's ready right now, I'm more than ready!

DIRECTOR [*shouting*]: But first the scene between you and the lady over there [*indicates* MADAME PACE] must be played out clearly. Do you understand?

STEPDAUGHTER: Oh, for God's sake, sir, she's just told me what you already know: that Mamma's work is badly done again; the material is ruined; and that I have to be patient if I want her to keep on helping us in our misery.

MADAME PACE [*coming forward with an air of great importance*]: Eh cià, señor, watta for becausa I no wanna taka advantaciò . . . pusha myself ahead.

DIRECTOR [*almost terrified*]: What, what? She speaks like that?

[*All the* ACTORS *burst out laughing.*]

STEPDAUGHTER [*also laughing*]: Yes, sir, she speaks just like that, in an odd, garbled mixture of languages.

MADAME PACE: Ima tink you noa do very nica tink you laugh a me I trying speaka as a good I can English, señor!

DIRECTOR: No, no, on the contrary. Speak like that. Speak exactly that way, madame! It's a sure thing! It couldn't be better! Sure. It provides some humour to break up the harshness of the situation a bit. Yes, speak, speak just like that! It's great!

STEPDAUGHTER: It's great! Of course it is! To hear yourself proposi-tioned in such a language, it's a sure thing for an effect, because it sounds almost like a joke, sir. You have to laugh when you hear that a 'viècho señor' wants to 'amusarse con migo'. Isn't that true, madame?

MADAME PACE: Olda, sura tink! Olda, baby, but is better for a you if he non giva you fun, he giva you, howa you say, security.

MOTHER [*rising up amid the amazement and consternation of all the* ACTORS, *who were not paying any attention to her and who now, when they hear her shout, jump up laughing in order to restrain her, while she in the meantime will have ripped the wig off* MADAME PACE's *head and thrown it on the floor*]: Witch, old witch! You murderess! My daughter!

STEPDAUGHTER [*rushing to restrain the* MOTHER]: No, no, Mamma! For God's sake, no!

FATHER: [*also rushing over at the same time*] Calm down now! Calm yourself and sit down!

MOTHER: But get her out of my sight, then!

STEPDAUGHTER [*to the* DIRECTOR, *who has also run there*]: It isn't possible; my mother musn't be here!

FATHER [*also to the* DIRECTOR]: They cannot be together. It's for this reason, you see, that woman there was not with us when we came. If they are together, you understand, the whole thing is of course given away!

DIRECTOR: It doesn't matter! No matter! For now it's just a first draft. Everything is useful — just to get the various elements of the scene together, even in a confused way! [*Turning to the*

MOTHER *and leading her back to her chair:*] Come along now, good lady, calm yourself, and sit down now.

[*Meanwhile the* STEPDAUGHTER, *moving again to the middle of the set, turns to* MADAME PACE.]

STEPDAUGHTER: Come on, let's start now, madame.

MADAME PACE [*offended*]: Much tanks you, I do nottin witta you mother she's righta here!

STEPDAUGHTER: Don't be ridiculous! Bring in the 'viècho señor, porqué se amusi con migo'! [*Turning imperiously towards everyone:*] This scene has to be done, doesn't it! Let's go on with it. [*To* MADAME PACE:] You can leave!

MADAME PACE: Ah, Ima go now. Mi go for sure!

[*She exits in a fury, picking up her wig and looking fiercely at the* ACTORS *who applaud her, giggling.*]

STEPDAUGHTER [*to the* FATHER]: Make your entrance. You don't have to walk around. Come straight here. Make believe you've already come in. There we are: I stand here with my head bent – modest like. And now, come on, speak up! Say to me in a fresh voice, like someone who has just come in from the outside: 'Good morning, miss . . .'

DIRECTOR [*already off the stage*]: Will you look at that! Do you mind telling me, are you directing or am I? [*To the* FATHER, *who looks uncertain and perplexed:*] Yes, do it: go to the back there without going out, and then come forward again.

[*The* FATHER *follows the instructions, looking bewildered. He is very pale, but once he is affected by the reality of his created life, he smiles as he approaches from the rear, as if he were still alien to the drama about to engulf him. The* ACTORS *immediately become intent on the scene which is unfolding.*]

DIRECTOR [*softly and quickly to the* PROMPTER *in his box*]: You, now see that you're ready to write.

[*The scene:*]

FATHER [*coming forward with a new tone of voice*]: Good morning, miss.

STEPDAUGHTER [*head lowered, with repressed disgust*]: Good morning.

FATHER [*briefly looking at her face almost entirely covered by her little hat and, noticing how young she is, exclaiming as if to himself, partly out of pleasure and partly out of fear of compromising himself in a risky adventure*]: Ah . . . But . . . it's not the first time, is it? I mean that you are coming here.

STEPDAUGHTER [*as above*]: No, sir.

FATHER: Have you been here other times? [*And after the* STEP-DAUGHTER *nods 'yes':*] More than once? [*He waits a bit for the answer; peeks again at her under the little hat; he smiles, then says:*] Well then . . . you needn't be this way . . . Allow me to remove this little hat.

STEPDAUGHTER [*quickly, anticipating him, with unrestrained disgust*]: No, sir, I'll take it off myself. [*She removes it quickly and nervously.*]

> [*The* MOTHER, *who watches the scene with the* SON *and the other two, who are littler and more her own and who remain constantly at her side, isolated on the opposite side from the* ACTORS, *is on tenterhooks as she accompanies with various expressions of grief, contempt, anxiety, horror, the words and behaviour of those other two. At times she hides her face and at times she moans.*]

MOTHER: Oh God! Oh my God!

FATHER [*at the sound of her moans he freezes for a long moment, then answers in the same tone as before*]: Here we are, let me have it. I'll put it down. [*He takes the hat from her hand.*] Come now, a dear pretty little head like yours should have a hat that is more worthy of it. So would you like to help me choose one, then, from Madame Pace's stock? Wouldn't you?

YOUNG ACTRESS [*interrupting him*]: Hold on there. These are our hats you know!

DIRECTOR [*quickly, in anger*]: Quiet for Christ's sake! Don't try to be witty! This is the scene! [*To the* STEPDAUGHTER:] Begin again, please, miss.

STEPDAUGHTER [*continuing*]: No thank you, sir.

FATHER: Ah, come now, don't refuse me. Won't you please accept it? I'll feel bad if you don't. There are some lovely ones here. Look. And it would make madame happy too. She puts them on display here for that very reason, you know.

STEPDAUGHTER: Oh no, sir. You see, I couldn't possibly wear it.

FATHER: You say this, perhaps, because of what they might think at home when they see you come in with a new hat? Ah certainly, you know how these things go. You must know how to handle these matters at home.

STEPDAUGHTER [*agitated, at her wit's end*]: No, it's not that, sir. I couldn't wear it, because I am ... as you can see ... you might have already noticed ... [*She shows her black dress.*]

FATHER: ... in mourning, of course, I'm so sorry. It's true, I see. I beg your pardon. Believe me when I say I am truly mortified.

STEPDAUGHTER [*forcing herself to gather courage to overcome her contempt and her nausea*]: No, stop, please stop, sir! I should be thanking you and you should not feel mortified or allow yourself to suffer. Pay no attention, I beg you, to what I told you. I, too, you understand ... [*Forces herself to smile, then adds:*] I really shouldn't be thinking about it: that I am dressed this way.

DIRECTOR [*interrupting, turns towards the* PROMPTER *in his box and climbs back on stage*]: Wait! Hang on there! Don't write it! Leave it out! Leave out that last remark. [*Turning to the* FATHER *and the* STEPDAUGHTER:] It's going fine! Very fine! [*Then only to the* FATHER:] And right here then you go on the way we decided to before. [*To the* ACTORS:] Quite charming, this scene with the hat, don't you agree?

STEPDAUGHTER: Ah, but the best is yet to come! Why aren't we going on?

DIRECTOR: Be patient for a moment. [*Turning again to the* ACTORS:] It has to be handled rather lightly, of course.

LEADING MAN: With a certain kind of easiness to be sure.

LEADING LADY: Sure. It won't take much effort! [*To the* LEADING MAN:] Why don't we try doing it right now?

LEADING MAN: Ah, as far as I'm concerned ... OK, here we go: I'm turning to make my entrance! [*He goes out and prepares to re-enter by the door in the backdrop.*]

DIRECTOR [*to the* LEADING LADY]: And so now then you see, the scene between you and Madame Pace is finished – I'll get it written up later on. You stay here ... No, where are you going?

LEADING LADY: Wait, I'll put my hat on again ...

[*She does so after taking her hat from the rack.*]

DIRECTOR: Ah, of course, excellent! Now then, you remain here with your head bowed.

STEPDAUGHTER [*amused*]: But she's not dressed in black!

LEADING LADY: I shall be dressed in black, and much more appropriately than you!

DIRECTOR [*to the* STEPDAUGHTER]: Be quiet, please and watch! You can learn from this! [*Clapping his hands.*] Come on! Let's go! Entrance!

[*And he gets down from the stage again to get an impression of the scene. The door at the rear of the stage opens and the* LEADING MAN *comes forward in a lively manner with the roguishness of an old gallant. The way the* ACTORS *render the scene will seem from the very first words something quite different, without having, nevertheless, the slightest air of parody; it will seem more like a good copy of the original. The* STEPDAUGHTER *and the* FATHER, *of course, unable to recognize themselves at all in the* LEADING LADY *and* LEADING MAN, *and hearing their very own words pronounced, will express by various means, at times with gestures, at times by smiling, or in open protest, the impression they get, whether it be surprise, amazement, pain, etc., as will be seen later on. The voice of the* PROMPTER *can be heard clearly from his box.*]

LEADING MAN: 'Good morning, miss . . .'

FATHER [*instantly, unable to control himself*]: No, no!

[*The* STEPDAUGHTER, *seeing the* LEADING MAN *enter in such fashion, bursts out laughing.*]

DIRECTOR [*furious*]: Silence everybody! And you stop that laughing once and for all! We can't go on this way!

STEPDAUGHTER [*coming from front of stage*]: I'm sorry, sir, but it's the most natural thing. That young lady [*indicating the* LEADING LADY] is standing there stiff and composed; but I can assure you that if it were me standing there and I heard someone say to me 'good morning' in that way and with that tone of voice, I would have burst out laughing exactly the way I just did!

FATHER [*he too coming slightly forward*]: That's it! Of course! The manner, the tone . . .

DIRECTOR: What are you talking about manner! Tone! Stand aside now and let me see the rehearsal.

LEADING MAN [*coming forward*]: If I have to act the part of an old man who comes to a house of questionable repute . . .

DIRECTOR: Yes, OK! Don't listen to them, for Heaven's sake! Pick it up; pick it up from there. It's going beautifully! [*Waiting for the* LEADING MAN *to start again:*] Well, then?

LEADING MAN: 'Good morning, miss . . .'

LEADING LADY: 'Good morning . . .'

LEADING MAN [*imitating the* FATHER'S *gesture of peeking under her hat, but then expressing very distinctly first the pleasure and then the fear*]: 'Ah . . . But . . . I mean, it couldn't be the first time, I hope . . .'

FATHER [*correcting, unable to resist*]: Not 'I hope', but 'is it true?', 'is it true?'

DIRECTOR: He says 'is it true' – question mark.

LEADING MAN [*nodding at the* PROMPTER]: I heard 'I hope!'

DIRECTOR: Yes, yes. It's all the same: 'is it true' or 'I hope'. Go on, go on with it. Yes, that's it: lighten it up a bit. Here, I'll do it for you. Watch me . . . [*Gets back on stage, then, acting the part starting from the entrance:*] 'Good morning, miss . . .'

LEADING LADY: 'Good morning.'

DIRECTOR: 'Ah, but . . . I mean . . .' [*Addressing himself to the* LEADING MAN *to show him the way he should look at the* LEADING LADY *under her hat:*] Surprise . . . fear and satisfaction . . . [*Then, going on, addressing the* LEADING LADY:] 'It couldn't be the first time, is it true; that you come here . . .' [*Again addressing the* LEADING MAN *with a knowing look:*] Have I made myself clear? [*To the* LEADING LADY:] And then you say: 'No, sir.' [*Again to the* LEADING MAN:] I don't know; how can I explain it? With ease! [*Gets off the stage again.*]

LEADING LADY: 'No, sir . . .'

LEADING MAN: 'Have you been here other times? More than once?'

DIRECTOR: No, no, wait. Wait for her to nod 'yes' first. [*Indicates the* LEADING LADY.] 'Have you been here other times?'

[*The* LEADING LADY *raises her head slightly painfully half-closing her eyes out of disgust, and then with a 'Down!' from the* DIRECTOR, *she lets her head drop twice.*]

STEPDAUGHTER [*unable to resist*]: Oh, my God! [*And she quickly puts her hand on her mouth to stop herself from laughing.*]

DIRECTOR [*turning round*]: What's the matter?

STEPDAUGHTER [*quickly*]: Nothing! Not a thing!

DIRECTOR [*to the* LEADING MAN]: It's your line! Go on!

LEADING MAN: 'More than once? Well ... then, you needn't be this way ... will you allow me to remove this little hat?'
[*The* LEADING MAN *says this last line in such a tone and accompanies it with such a gesture that the* STEPDAUGHTER, *who still has her hand over her mouth, no matter how hard she tries, is unable to contain her laughter which bursts forth irresistibly and resounds from between her fingers.*]

LEADING LADY [*indignant, returning to her place*]: Ah, I'm not going to stay here and be made a fool of by her!

LEADING MAN: And neither am I! That's it for me!

DIRECTOR [*to the* STEPDAUGHTER, *shouting*]: That's enough! Stop it now!

STEPDAUGHTER: You're right. Forgive me! I'm sorry.

DIRECTOR: You're rude and uncivilized. That's what you are: very presumptuous!

FATHER [*trying to intervene*]: Yes, sir, it's true, true. But you must forgive her ...

DIRECTOR [*getting back on stage*]: How can I forgive her! It's disgusting!

FATHER: Yes, sir, but believe me, believe me, all this gives you such a strange feeling –

DIRECTOR: – strange? What strange? Why strange?

FATHER: I admire, sir, admire your actors: that gentleman there [*points to the* LEADING MAN], this young lady here [*points to the* LEADING LADY], but certainly ... you see, they are not us!

DIRECTOR: Of course they're not! How could they possibly be 'you', if 'they' are the actors?

FATHER: Exactly, they're actors. And both of them act our parts very well. But, believe me, for us it's a different thing – something that would like to be the same, but at the same time is not!

DIRECTOR: What do you mean 'is not'? What is it, then?

FATHER: Something that . . . becomes part of them, and is no longer ours.

DIRECTOR: But it has to be this way! I've told you this already.

FATHER: Yes, I understand, I understand . . .

DIRECTOR: Well, then, let's put an end to it! [*Turning to the* ACTORS:] So we will have to have the rehearsals on our own, the way they should be done. It's always been my curse to rehearse with the author present. They're never satisfied! [*Turning to the* FATHER *and the* STEPDAUGHTER:] OK, let's try it again with them. And let's try and see if you can keep from laughing.

STEPDAUGHTER: I won't laugh; I won't laugh again! The best part for me is coming up right now. Wait and see.

DIRECTOR: So then, when you say: 'Pay no attention, I beg you, to what I told you. I, too, you understand! . . .' [*Turning to the* FATHER:] you come in quickly with 'Ah, I understand, I understand . . .' and then immediately you ask her –

STEPDAUGHTER [*interrupting*]: How? What?

DIRECTOR: The reason for your mourning.

STEPDAUGHTER: Not at all, sir. Look, when I told him that I shouldn't be concerned with how I was dressed, do you know how he answered me? 'Ah, that's fine! So then, let's take this little dress off immediately!'

DIRECTOR: Beautiful! Perfect! A great way to knock the audience out of their seats!

STEPDAUGHTER: But it's the truth.

DIRECTOR: What truth, don't make me laugh! This is the theatre! The truth goes just so far!

STEPDAUGHTER: Excuse me, what do you want to do then?

DIRECTOR: You'll see. You'll see. Leave it to me now.

STEPDAUGHTER: No, sir! Am I wrong to think what you would like to do is to make out of all of this, out of my nausea, out of all the reasons, one more cruel and more vile than the other, which make me what I am – 'this person' and 'like this' – a nice little messy sentimental romantic scene with him asking me the reason for my mourning and with me answering in tears that two months ago my papa died? No, sir, no, my dear sir! He has to tell me what he really told me: 'So then, let's take this little dress off immediately!' And I, with all that mourning of barely two months in my heart, went over there, you see, there behind that screen, and with these fingers that tingle with shame, I, shivering with disgust, undid my corset, my dress . . .

DIRECTOR [*running his hands through his hair*]: For God's sake, what are you saying?

STEPDAUGHTER [*shouting in a frenzy*]: The truth. The truth, sir!

DIRECTOR: Of course, I don't deny it, it may well be the truth; and I understand, I understand all your horror, miss. But you have to understand too that all this cannot be done on stage!

STEPDAUGHTER: Cannot be done? Well then, thank you very much, but this is not for me!

DIRECTOR: Now wait, you see . . .

STEPDAUGHTER: It's not for me! I'm not staying! What can be done on stage the two of you decided together back there, thank you. I know very well what's going on! He wants to get straight to his scene [*with emphasis*] of great spiritual torment! But I want to act out my own drama. My own!

DIRECTOR [*upset, with a vehement shrug of the shoulders*]: Oh, so there's just your part. I'm sorry to have to tell you that yours is not the only part. There are also the others: his part [*points to the* FATHER], your mother's. You can't have a character invading the scene and becoming so dominant that he overpowers the others. All of them have to be contained in a harmonious framework and then act out what is actable. I too am well aware of the fact that everyone has his own interior life which he would like to bring out into the open. But the difficulty is precisely this: to bring out into the open only what is important in reference to the others; and at the same time reveal through that little bit all of that unrevealed interior life! Ah, it would be too easy if a character could in a nice monologue or . . . better yet . . . in a lecture dish out to the public all that is boiling in his part! [*In a kind and conciliating tone:*] You have to control yourself, my dear young lady. Believe me, it is in your own interest, because you might give a very bad impression of yourself, I'm warning you, all this fury tearing you apart, this exasperating disgust when you yourself, you know, have confessed to having been with others before you went with him at Madame Pace's – and more than once!

STEPDAUGHTER [*lowering her head, in a deep voice, after pausing to get herself together*]: It's true. But remember all of those others for me mean him.

DIRECTOR [*not understanding*]: What do you mean, the others?

STEPDAUGHTER: For the one who falls into error, sir, the person responsible for all the errors that follow is not always the one who first determined the downfall. For me he is the one responsible, and he was so even before I was born. Just look at him and see if it isn't true!

DIRECTOR: All well and good, but does the weight he bears of so much remorse really seem light to you? Give him a chance to act it out!

STEPDAUGHTER: But how, I beg you, tell me how could he act out all these 'noble' remorses of his, all of his 'moral' torments, if you decide to spare him the horror of finding himself one fine day, after having invited someone to remove her dress, a dress of recent mourning, in the arms of a woman, a fallen woman, that same little girl, sir, that little girl he used to go and watch coming out of school? [*She says these final words in a voice trembling with emotion.*]

[*The* MOTHER, *hearing these words, overcome by a rush of unbearable pain, which she expresses first with a few suffocating sobs, finally breaks into inconsolable weeping. Everyone is overcome with emotion. A long pause.*]

STEPDAUGHTER [*as soon as the* MOTHER *gives signs of quieting down adds gravely and resolutely*]: We are still here among ourselves now, still unknown to the public. Tomorrow you will give a performance of us as you choose, using us as you like. But how would you like to see real drama exploding for real, the way it was?

DIRECTOR: Of course I would. I couldn't ask for anything better – this way I can get as much out of it as possible from now on.

STEPDAUGHTER: OK, then, have the mother come out.

MOTHER [*rising from her tears to a shout*]: No, no! Don't allow it, sir. Don't allow it!

DIRECTOR: But it's only so that we can see it, madame!

MOTHER: I can't! I can't!

DIRECTOR: But if everything has already happened. Forgive me, but I don't understand.

MOTHER: No, it's happening now. It happens all of the time! My anguish is not over, sir! I am alive and present all the time and in every moment of my anguish which renews itself, alive and always present. But those two little ones over there, have you heard them speak? They can no longer, sir! They are still here and continue to cling to me in order to keep my anguish alive and present. But for themselves they do not exist; they are no longer. And this one [*indicating the* STEPDAUGHTER], sir, she has fled, she has run away from me and she is lost, lost . . . And if now I see her here it is still for this, and only for this, always, forever, in order to renew always, alive and present, the anguish that I suffer for her as well.

FATHER [*solemn*]: The eternal moment, as I told you, sir! She [*indicates the* STEPDAUGHTER] is here to catch me, fix me, hold me hooked and suspended for eternity in the stocks, for that one fleeting and shameful moment of my life. She cannot give it up! And you, sir, cannot in truth spare me from it.

DIRECTOR: Oh yes, I don't mean not to act it out; in fact, it will form the nucleus of the entire First Act right up until we get to her surprise [*indicates the* MOTHER] –

FATHER: – That's it! Yes! Because this is my condemnation, sir: the passion of all of us which must culminate in that final cry of hers.

STEPDAUGHTER: I still have it here in my ears! It has driven me mad, that cry! You can present me on stage in any way you like sir. It doesn't matter to me! Even dressed, so long as you allow me to have at least one arm bare – just the arm – because – now look – standing like this [*she goes up to the* FATHER *and puts her head on his chest*] with my head resting this way and my arms around his neck so, I could see pulsating here, in my arm, here, a vein; and then as if that live vein and nothing else had filled me with horror, I shut my eyes tight, this way, like this, and let my head sink into his chest. [*Turning towards the* MOTHER:] Cry out, Mamma, cry out! [*She lets her head sink onto the* FATHER's *chest, and with her shoulders raised as if not to hear the cry, she adds in a voice suffocated with anguish:*] Cry out! The way you cried out then!

MOTHER [*moving forward to separate them*]: No, my daughter, oh my daughter! [*And after pulling her away from him:*] Beast! You beast! She's my daughter! Can't you see she is my daughter?

DIRECTOR [*at the cry he backs up as far as the footlights amidst the bewilderment of the* ACTORS]: Excellent, yes excellent! And then curtain. Curtain.

FATHER [*rushing towards him, excited*]: Yes, of course, because it truly happened that way, sir.

DIRECTOR [*pleased and convinced*]: Yes, right here, curtain. No doubt about it: curtain!

[*At the repeated shouts of the* DIRECTOR *the curtain drops, leaving in front of it, before the footlights, the* DIRECTOR *and the* FATHER.]

DIRECTOR [*looking up with his arms raised*]: What an idiot! I say, 'curtain', meaning that this is where the Act must end, and they actually go and drop the curtain on me! [*To the* FATHER, *as he lifts an edge of the curtain in order to re-enter on stage:*] Yes, yes, excellent! Excellent! The effect's a sure thing! This is the way to end it! I promise the First Act is a sure thing!

[*When the curtain goes up again the audience will notice that the* TECHNICIAN *and* STAGE HANDS *have removed the first bit of scenery and replaced it with a small garden pool.*

To one side of the stage the ACTORS *are seated in a line and on the other side are the* CHARACTERS. *The* DIRECTOR *is standing in the middle of the stage with one hand closed in a fist over his mouth as if he were meditating.*]

DIRECTOR [*stirring after a brief pause*]: Well then, let's get to the Second Act! Leave it to me, just the way we decided earlier. Leave it to me and it'll go just fine!

STEPDAUGHTER: It's our coming into his home [*indicates the* FATHER] and to his resentment [*indicates the* SON]!

DIRECTOR [*losing patience*]: OK, but let me handle it, I tell you!

STEPDAUGHTER: Just so long as his resentment is made quite clear!

MOTHER [*from her side shaking her head*]: For all the good that came of it . . .

STEPDAUGHTER [*turning towards her suddenly*]: It makes no difference! The more harm done us, the more remorse for him!

DIRECTOR [*losing his patience*]: I understand! I understand! I will keep this in mind especially in the beginning. So don't worry!

MOTHER [*imploring*]: But make it very clear, sir, I beg you, for the sake of my conscience, that I tried in every possible way . . .

STEPDAUGHTER [*interrupting with indignation as she continues the* MOTHER's *speech*]: . . . to pacify me, to advise me not to be spiteful towards him. [*To the* DIRECTOR:] Satisfy her! Make her happy, because it's true. In the meantime I'm enjoying it very, very much, as you can see: the more imploring she is, the more she tries to get at his heart, all the more distant, the more 'absent' he becomes! How I relish it!

DIRECTOR: Well then, do we or do we not want to start this Second Act?

STEPDAUGHTER: I won't say another word. But I warn you that it isn't possible to have it all take place in the garden as you would like to!

DIRECTOR: Why is it not possible?

STEPDAUGHTER: Because he [*indicates the* SON *again*] is always closed up in his room, isolated. Besides this, there is also the whole part of the boy over there that has to be played inside the house – that bewildered child over there, as I have already told you.

DIRECTOR: Could be, but on the other hand you have to understand, we can't put signs up or openly change the scenery three or four times in the same Act!

LEADING MAN: They used to do it once . . .

DIRECTOR: Sure, perhaps when the public was as old as that little girl over there!

LEADING LADY: It's the easiest kind of illusion.

FATHER [*alarmed, jumping up*]: For God's sake, illusion! Don't use that word – for us it is an especially cruel word.

DIRECTOR [*stunned*]: Do you mind telling me why not?

FATHER: But yes, cruel. It's cruel! You ought to be able to understand that.

53

DIRECTOR: What are we supposed to say then? The illusion that must be created here for the audience –

LEADING MAN: – with our performance –

DIRECTOR: – the illusion of reality!

FATHER: I understand you, sir, but perhaps you don't understand us. Forgive me, but you see, here, for you and your actors it is only a matter – and this is only right – of playing a game.

LEADING LADY [*interrupting, offended*]: What do you mean a game? We're not a bunch of kids! We take our acting seriously here!

FATHER: I don't deny it. And, what I mean, in fact, is the game of their art, which must render precisely – as the gentleman says – a perfect illusion of reality.

DIRECTOR: That's it, precisely!

FATHER: Now, if you consider that we as we are [*indicates himself and, summarily, the other five* CHARACTERS] have no other reality besides this illusion!

DIRECTOR [*amazed, looking at his* ACTORS *also in a state of shock and bewilderment*]: What are you trying to say?

FATHER [*after having observed them with a pale smile*]: But of course, gentlemen. What other do we have? What for you is an illusion that must be created, is for us, instead, our only reality. [*Brief pause; takes a few steps towards the* DIRECTOR, *and adds:*] But not only for us, however, I'll have you know. Think carefully about it. [*He looks him in the eyes.*] Can you tell me who you are? [*He keeps his finger pointed at him.*]

DIRECTOR [*upset, half-smiling*]: What? Who am I? I'm me!

FATHER: And if I were to tell you that it isn't true, because you are me?

DIRECTOR: I would tell you that you are crazy!

[*The* ACTORS *laugh.*]

FATHER: They are right to laugh, because here we are all playing a game [*to the* DIRECTOR:] and you, then, could allege that it is only part of the game that the gentleman over there [*indicating the* LEADING MAN] who is 'himself' has to be 'me', who, on the contrary, am myself. You see, how I've caught you in a trap?

[*The* ACTORS *start laughing again.*]

DIRECTOR [*annoyed*]: But we said all this a little while ago. Are we going to start all over again?

FATHER: No, no. This is not really what I meant to say. I would like, rather, to invite you to step out of this game [*looking at the* LEADING LADY *as if to anticipate her*] of art! of art! which you are accustomed to playing here with your actors and seriously reconsider the question: who are you?

DIRECTOR [*turning, astonished as well as irritated, to the* ACTORS]: Well if this doesn't take some nerve! Someone who is trying to pass himself off as a character comes and asks me who I am!

FATHER [*with dignity but not arrogance*]: A character, sir, can always ask a man who he is. Because a character truly has a life of his own, marked by his own characteristics, because of which he is always 'someone'. On the other hand, a man – I'm not saying you at this moment – a man in general, can be 'nobody'.

DIRECTOR: OK. But you are asking me, the director, the head man! Do you understand?

FATHER [*Almost soundlessly, with mellifluous modesty*]: All I wanted to know, sir, is if you, as you are now, can truly see yourself . . . as you see, for example, in the distance of time, what you were at one time, with all the illusions that you had back then, with all those things in and around you as they seemed to you then – and which were actually real to you – well then, sir, if you think back to those illusions which now you no longer have, to all those things which now no longer 'seem' to be for you what they 'were' at one time, don't you feel – not necessarily the boards of this stage – but the ground, the very ground beneath your feet give way – when you deduce that in the same way 'this', the way you feel right now, all the reality of today, the way it is, is destined to seem an illusion to you tomorrow?

DIRECTOR [*not having understood well and astounded by the specious argument*]: And so what? And what are we supposed to conclude from all this?

FATHER: Oh, not a thing, sir. It was merely to show you that if we [*again he indicates himself and the other* CHARACTERS] have no other reality beyond the illusion, it would be also a good idea for you not to trust in your own reality, the one you breathe and feel today within yourself, because – like that of yesterday – it is destined to reveal itself as an illusion tomorrow.

DIRECTOR [*turning to make fun of him*]: Ah, very good indeed! You actually would go so far as to say that this play that you have come to act out here is more true and more real than I am!

FATHER [*in all seriousness*]: But there is no doubt about it, sir.

DIRECTOR: Ah, really?

FATHER: I thought you had understood this from the very beginning.

DIRECTOR: More real than me?

FATHER: But if your reality can change from one day to the next . . .

DIRECTOR: But we know it can change! Of course it can! It keeps on changing like anyone else's.

FATHER [*with a shout*]: But ours does not, sir! You see, the difference is this: it does not change, it cannot change, nor can it be another, because it is fixed – this way – this is it – for ever – it's a terrible thing, sir! Immutable reality – it should make you shudder to be near us!

DIRECTOR [*leaping up as an idea occurs to him all of a sudden*]: I would like to know, however, when has anyone ever seen a character come out of the part he is playing and begin preaching the way you are now, and even to propose the very idea as well as explain it. Can you tell me? I've never seen it happen before!

FATHER: You never saw it before, sir, because authors usually hide the workings of their creation. When characters are alive, truly alive before their author, he has only to follow them in their words and actions which they precisely suggest to him, and he has no other choice except to want them to be the way they want themselves to be. And he's in for trouble if he doesn't! When a character is born, he immediately assumes so much independence, even from his own author, that he can be imagined by everybody in a number of other situations in which the author never thought of putting him, and sometimes he even acquires a meaning the author never dreamed of giving him!

DIRECTOR: Yes, I know this.

FATHER: Well then, what's so surprising about us? Just imagine what it is like for a character whose misfortune I mentioned before — that is to be born alive from the fantasy of an author who then denies him life — and then tell me if this character left this way, alive and without life, has every right to do what we are doing at this moment, here in front of you, after having done the same thing over and over again — believe me — in front of him, trying to persuade him, to urge him; sometimes I would appear to him, other times she [*indicates the* STEPDAUGHTER] and at times that poor mother . . .

STEPDAUGHTER [*coming forward as if lost in reverie*]: It's true. I did it too, sir. I tried to tempt him many times while he was at his desk feeling melancholy around twilight or when he would abandon himself to his armchair, unable to decide whether or not to turn on the lights, allowing the shadows to invade the room, shadows that were swarming with our presence, coming to tempt him . . . [*As if she could still see herself there by that desk and was annoyed by the presence of all those* ACTORS:] If all of you would only go away! If you would leave us alone! The mother there with that son — with that child — that boy there always alone — and then I with him [*barely indicating the* FATHER] — and then I all alone, I alone — in those shadows. [*Suddenly she makes a startled movement as if in the vision she has of herself, alive and vivid in those shadows, she is attempting to capture herself.*] Ah, my life! What scenes, what scenes we proposed to him! I, I was the one who tempted him more than any of the others.

FATHER: Yes. But perhaps it was your fault, precisely because of your excessive insistence and lack of restraint.

STEPDAUGHTER: Not true! He was the one who wanted me that way [*approaching the* DIRECTOR *to speak to him confidentially*]. I think, sir, that it was more out of disappointment or contempt for the theatre that today's public is used to seeing and wanting to see . . .

DIRECTOR: Let's get on with it, let's go on, for God's sake, let's get to the action, ladies and gentlemen.

STEPDAUGHTER: I beg your pardon, but it seems to me that you've even got too much action with our moving into the house of this

ates the FATHER]! You said before you couldn't put up
iange the scene every five minutes!

Of course not! But precisely. Combine the scenes,
m into one simultaneous and tight action, and not the
way you expect it to be done: first you want to see your little
brother returning from school and wandering like a ghost through
the rooms of the house, hiding behind doors and meditating
some plan which – how did you put it? –

STEPDAUGHTER: – He sucks himself up, sir, completely sucks himself
up!

DIRECTOR: I've never heard that expression before! OK, then, 'only
his eyes grow larger' – is that true?

STEPDAUGHTER: Yes, sir. There he is [*indicating him near the* MOTHER].

DIRECTOR: Isn't that nice? And then, at the same time, you also
want that little girl to be playing, innocently, in the garden. One
in the house, the other in the garden, is that the case?

STEPDAUGHTER: Ah, yes sir, in the sun, happy! It's my only
reward: her happiness, her rejoicing in that garden, removed
from the misery, from the squalor of a horrible room where all
four of us would sleep together – and I with her – me, just think,
with my vile and contaminated body next to hers as she held me
tight, very tight, with her innocent and loving little arms. As
soon as she would see me in the garden she would run and take
me by the hand. She couldn't see the tall flowers, so she would
go instead in search of all those 'teeny teeny' ones. She loved to
show them to me; she loved doing it so much!

[*Saying this, tortured by the memory, she breaks into long and
desperate weeping, her head falls into her arms abandoned on the
little table. Everyone is overcome with emotion. The* DIRECTOR
*approaches her in a paternal manner and says in order to comfort
her:*]

DIRECTOR: We will have the garden scene. Don't you worry,
we'll have it in the garden. You're going to be happy with the
way it turns out. We'll group all the scenes around the garden.
[*Calling by name one of the* STAGE HANDS:] Yeh! Drop a few
tree pieces here: two little cypress trees here in front of this
pool!

[*Two little cypress trees are lowered to the stage from above. The* TECHNICIAN, *running, nails down the two bases.*]

DIRECTOR [*to the* STEPDAUGHTER]: It's just to give an idea now of what it's going to be like. [*Calls by name the* STAGE HAND *again:*] Hey, now give me a little bit of sky.

STAGE HAND [*from above*]: What?

DIRECTOR: A bit of sky! A backdrop, lower it here behind this pool.

[*A white cloth drops from above the stage.*]

DIRECTOR: No, not white! I said sky! Never mind, leave it; I'll take care of it. [*Calling:*] Hey, electrician, all lights out and give me a bit of atmosphere . . . some moon . . . blue, blue on the rack lights and blue on the drop with the reflectors . . . Like that! OK, enough!

[*At his orders, a mysterious moonlight scene is created which induces the* ACTORS *to speak and move as if it were nighttime in a garden beneath the moon.*]

DIRECTOR [*to the* STEPDAUGHTER]: Here you are, you see. And now the young boy, instead of hiding behind the doors of a room, can wander around here in the garden and hide behind the trees. But you must understand that it's not going to be easy to find a little girl who will do a good job in that scene with you – you know, when she shows you the little flowers. [*Turns to the* YOUNG BOY:] Come, you come forward, up here. Let's see if we can't get this scene in order. [*And because the* BOY *does not move:*] Come on, come along. [*Then pulling him forward and trying to make him hold his head up, which he lets drop every time:*] Ah, I tell you we've got another problem here with this boy . . . But what's the matter . . . For God's sake, he's certainly got to have a few words to say . . . [*He approaches him, puts a hand on his shoulder and takes him behind the trees.*] Come on, come along now. Let me see now. Hide yourself here . . . this way . . . Now stick your head out a bit as if you were spying on someone . . . [*He backs up in order to get the effect, and, as soon as the* YOUNG BOY *completes the action to the amazement of the* ACTORS *who are very impressed:*] Ah, excellent, very good indeed. [*Turning to the* STEPDAUGHTER:] And what if the little girl were to surprise him while he was spying and run over to him, so perhaps we could get a word or two out of him this way.

STEPDAUGHTER [*getting to her feet*]: There's no hope he'll ever speak as long as that one there is present. [*Indicates the* SON.] You have to send him away first.

SON [*moving resolutely towards one of the two stairways*]: But immediately! And most happily! I couldn't ask for anything better!

DIRECTOR [*quickly stopping him*]: No! Where are you going? Wait!

[*The* MOTHER *gets up alarmed and pained by the thought that he might be truly leaving, and instinctively she raises her arms as if attempting to hold him back without, however, moving from her place.*]

SON [*to the* DIRECTOR *who stops him as he reaches the footlights*]: I have absolutely nothing to do with what is going on here. I do not. Let me go, I beg you. Please allow me to leave.

DIRECTOR: What do you mean you have nothing to do with it?

STEPDAUGHTER [*calmly, with irony*]: Don't keep him from leaving. He won't go, anyway.

FATHER: He has to act out the terrible scene in the garden with his mother!

SON [*suddenly, resolutely, vehemently*]: I shall act out nothing. And this I have said from the very start! [*To the* DIRECTOR:] Please leave me alone.

STEPDAUGHTER [*rushing to the* DIRECTOR]: Will you allow me, sir? [*Makes him lower his arms with which he is holding back the* SON.] Release him! [*Then, addressing him as soon as the* DIRECTOR *has released him:*] Well then, go!

[*The* SON *remains fixed in an attempt to move towards the stairway, but, as if bound by a mysterious power, he cannot go down the stairs; then, to the amazement and uneasy bewilderment of the* ACTORS, *he moves slowly along the footlights in the direction of the other stairway going down from the stage. But once he arrives there he remains fixed and unable to descend. The* STEPDAUGHTER, *whose eyes have followed him with a look of defiance, bursts out laughing.*]

You see, he can't. He can't do it! He has to stay here, he's forced to, bound indissolubly to the chain. If I who will take flight, sir, when what has to happen happens – precisely because of the hatred I bear for him, precisely in order not to have to see him any more – well then, if I am still here and can put up with his face and with his presence, do you suppose that he has the right to leave, he who has really to remain here with that wonderful father of his and that mother there whose only son he is . . . [*Turning to the* MOTHER:] Come on, Mamma, get up. Come along . . . [*Turning to the* DIRECTOR *and pointing her out:*] You see, she was getting up, she was getting up to hold him back . . . [*To the* MOTHER, *as if magically attracting her2:*] Come, come . . . [*Then, to the* DIRECTOR:] Imagine the courage she must have to show your actors here what she is feeling. But so great is her desire to get close to him that – there you are – you see? She is willing to live out her scene!

[*In fact, the* MOTHER *comes up to him and as soon as the* STEP-DAUGHTER *has pronounced her last words, she opens her arms to show her willingness.*]

SON [*quickly*]: Ah no, not I. I won't. If I cannot leave, then I shall stay here. But I repeat: I am acting out nothing!

FATHER [*to the* DIRECTOR, *seething with rage*]: But you can force him to, sir.

SON: No one can force me! No one!

FATHER: I shall force you!

STEPDAUGHTER: Wait, wait! First the child at the pool! [*She runs to get the child, kneels before her and holds her little face between her hands.*] Poor little darling, you look lost with those pretty, big eyes of yours; I wonder where you think you are! We're on a stage, my love! And what is a stage? Don't you see? A place where one plays, but seriously, where you act a play. And we are going to do the play. But really, you know. You too . . . [*She embraces her, holding her tight as she rocks for a moment.*] Oh my love, my little darling, what a horrible play for you! What a horrible part has been thought up for you! The garden, the pool . . . It's fake you know. And that's the trouble, my love: it's all fake here! Ah, but then again, my child, perhaps you prefer a fake pool to a real one. You could play in it, couldn't you? But no, for the others it's only a plaything, but not for you, unfortunately, because you are real, my darling, and you are really playing in a real pool. It's nice and big and green, with lots of shady bamboo that reflects in the water and lots and lots of ducks swimming around breaking the shade. And you want to catch one of these little ducks ... [*With a scream that frightens everyone:*] No, Rosetta, no! Your mother isn't looking after you because of that no-good son over there! And I, my head full of crazy thoughts. And that one over there ... [*Leaves the child and turns with her usual harsh look to the* YOUNG BOY:] What are you doing here always with that miserable look of yours? It's going to be your fault too if that little one there drowns. Because of this attitude of yours, as if I, bringing you all into the house, didn't have to pay the price for everyone. [*Grabbing him by the arm, forcing him to take his hand out of his pocket:*] What have you got there? What are you hiding? Take out that hand! [*She pulls his hand out of his pocket, and to everyone's horror, she discovers that he is holding a revolver. She looks at him a moment almost with satisfaction, then she says in a gloomy way:*] Ah, where, how did you get hold of this? [*And since the* YOUNG BOY, *shocked, always with his eyes wide open and looking empty, does not answer:*] You fool, if I had been you, I would have killed one of those two, or even both of them: father and son, instead of myself!

[*She pushes him back behind the little cypress from where he had been spying. Then she takes the* CHILD *and puts her in the pool, laying her down so that she remains hidden. Finally, she gives in with her face in her arms, leaning on the edge of the pool*].

DIRECTOR: Very good indeed! [*Turning to the* SON:] And at the same time ...

SON [*with contempt*]: What do you mean at the same time? It is not true, sir. There was never a scene between me and her! [*Indicating the* MOTHER:] Have her tell you directly how it happened.

[*Meanwhile the* SECOND ACTRESS *and the* YOUNG ACTOR *have separated themselves from the group of* ACTORS *and one of them has begun observing with great care the* MOTHER, *who is in front of her, and the other the* SON, *in order to play their parts later on.*]

MOTHER: Yes it's true, sir, I had gone into his room.

SON: Into my room. Did you understand? Not into the garden!

DIRECTOR: But that's not important. As I told you before, you have to group the action.

SON [*noticing the* YOUNG ACTOR *who is observing him*]: Is there something you want?

YOUNG ACTOR: No, nothing. Just observing you.

SON [*turning to the other side, to the* SECOND ACTRESS]: Ah, ha, and here you are. To re-enact her role. [*Indicates the* MOTHER.]

DIRECTOR: Precisely! Precisely so! And it seems to me that you should be grateful for the interest they take in you!

SON: Oh, really! Thanks so much. Somehow you still do not seem to understand that you cannot put on this play. We are not inside of you, and you actors are looking at us from the outside. Is it possible that we have to live in front of a mirror which, as if it were not enough, is not satisfied to freeze us in the image of our very own expression, but rather gives it back to us as an unrecognizable grimace of ourselves.

FATHER: This is true. It's the truth. Believe it!

DIRECTOR [*to the* YOUNG ACTOR *and the* SECOND ACTRESS]: All right. Move away.

SON: It's no use. I'm not getting involved.

DIRECTOR: Be quiet now and let me hear what your mother has to say. [*To the* MOTHER:] OK, then, you had already entered, no?

MOTHER: Yes, sir, into his room, because I couldn't stand it any more. In order to empty my heart of all the anguish that oppresses me. But as soon as he saw me come in –

SON: – no scene! I left there. I left in order not to make a scene. Because I have never made a scene. Never. Is that clear?

MOTHER: It's true. That's it! That's the way it is!

DIRECTOR: This scene, nevertheless, must be done between you and him. It's indispensable!

MOTHER: I'm here and ready, sir. If only you could give me a way to be able to speak to him for a moment, to be able to tell him all that is in my heart.

FATHER [*approaching the* SON *in a fierce way*]: You are going to do it for your mother. Do it for your mother!

SON [*determined more than ever*]: I am not doing a thing!

FATHER [*grabbing him by the chest and shaking him*]: For God's sake,

63

do it! Do it! Don't you hear the way she speaks to you? Don't you have the heart of a son?

SON [*also grabbing him*]: No, no! Stop it once and for all!

[*General commotion. The* MOTHER, *who is frightened, tries to intervene and separate them.*]

MOTHER [*as before*]: For the love of God! For the love of God!

FATHER [*without releasing him*]: You must obey! You must obey!

SON [*coming to blows with him and finally throwing him to the floor near the stairway, to everyone's horror*]: What is this mad rage that's come over you? Has she no dignity to display her shame and ours here in front of everyone? I will have nothing to do with it! I will not be a part of it! And in so doing I represent the will of the one who refused to put us on stage.

DIRECTOR: But you have come here.

SON [*pointing to the* FATHER]: He, not I.

DIRECTOR: But aren't you here too?

SON: He was the one who wanted to come, dragging all of us along with him, and who was even willing to put together the scene in the other room with her, using not only what really happened but, as if that wasn't enough, what never actually took place!

DIRECTOR: Now you tell me, at least tell me what happened! You can tell me. You left your room without saying anything?

SON [*hesitating a moment*]: Not a thing. Precisely in order not to make a scene.

DIRECTOR [*urging him on*]: OK, fine, and then? What did you do next?

SON [*amid the painful attention of all, taking a few steps on the stage*]: Nothing . . . Walking across the garden . . . [*He interrupts himself, gloomy, absorbed.*]

DIRECTOR [*continuing to urge him to say more, impressed by his restraint*]: Well then, walking across the garden?

SON [*exasperated, hiding his face with his arm*]: But why do you want me to talk about it, sir? It's horrible.

[*The* MOTHER, *trembling all over, with stifled laments, looks towards the pool.*]

DIRECTOR [*slowly, observing that look, turns towards the* SON *with increasing apprehension*]: The child?

SON [*looking ahead of himself, into the audience*]: There, in the pool.

FATHER [*still on the floor, pointing compassionately at the* MOTHER]: And she was following him, sir.

DIRECTOR [*to the* SON, *anxiously*]: And then you . . .

SON [*slowly, continuing to look straight ahead*]: I ran. I rushed over to pull her out . . . But then all of a sudden I stopped, because behind those trees I saw something that made my blood run cold: the boy, the boy standing over there fixed, with a crazy look in his eyes staring into the pool at his little sister, drowned.

[*The* STEPDAUGHTER, *still bending over the pool to hide the child, responds like an echo from the deep, sobbing desperately. Pause.*]

I started to move towards him, and then . . .

[*He goes back behind the trees where the* YOUNG BOY *remains hidden; a shot from the revolver. With a cry of anguish, the* MOTHER *runs in that direction, together with the* SON *and all the* ACTORS *amid the general turmoil.*]

MOTHER: My son! My son! [*And then amid the confusion and pandemonium of cries from the others:*] Help! Help!

DIRECTOR [*amid the cries, trying to make his way, while the* YOUNG BOY *is lifted up by the head and feet and carried off behind the white backdrop*]: Is he wounded? Is he really wounded?

[*Everyone, except for the* DIRECTOR *and the* FATHER, *who is still on the floor near the stairway, disappears behind the backdrop that serves as the sky, and they remain there a while, painfully chatting. Then, from both sides of the drop, the* ACTORS *return on stage.*]

LEADING LADY [*re-entering from the right, full of sorrow*]: He's dead! Poor boy! He's dead! Oh, how awful!

LEADING MAN [*re-entering from the left, laughing*]: What, dead? It's make-believe. He is just pretending! Don't believe it.

OTHER ACTORS [*from the left*]: No, make-believe. It's make-believe.

FATHER [*getting up and shouting among them*]: What make-believe! Reality, sir, reality! [*And he too disappears in desperation behind the backdrop.*]

DIRECTOR [*no longer able to put up with it all*]: Make-believe! Reality! You can all go to Hell, every last one of you! Lights! Lights! Lights!

[*All of a sudden the entire stage and theatre hall flashes with the brightest possible light. The* DIRECTOR *takes a deep breath as if released from a nightmare, and everyone looks at each other, uncertain and dumbfounded.*]

I don't know, but nothing like this has ever happened to me before. They made me lose the whole day! [*Looks at his watch.*] Go, go on. There's nothing more we can do today. It's too late to pick up the rehearsal. Until tonight! [*And as soon as the* ACTORS *have left saying goodbye to him:*] Hey, electrician, put out all the lights.

[*No sooner is this said than the theatre for an instant sinks into the depths of blackness.*]

Oh, Christ! At least give me enough light to see my feet!

[*Immediately, behind the backdrop, as if because of a bad electrical contact, a green spotlight turns on and projects large and clear the outlines of the* CHARACTERS *except for the* YOUNG BOY *and the* CHILD. *When the* DIRECTOR *sees them, he is terrified and jumps from the stage. At the same time the spotlight behind the backdrop goes out and the stage returns to the night-blue colour it was before. Slowly, from the right side of the curtain, there comes forth first the* SON *followed by the* MOTHER, *with her arms stretching out for him; then from the left the* FATHER. *They come to a stop at centre stage and remain fixed there like shapes in a dream. Coming out last from the left is the* STEPDAUGHTER, *who runs towards one of the stairways. She stops for a moment on the first step to look at the other three, bursts into shrill laughter, then rushes down the stairway, and runs down the main aisle between the seats; again she stops and laughs once more as she looks at the three left up there on stage; she vanishes from the theatre hall, and again from out in the lobby there comes that laughter. Shortly after, the curtain falls.*]

HENRY IV

LIST OF CHARACTERS

HENRY IV
THE MARCHESA MATILDA SPINA
FRIDA *her daughter*
CARLO DI NOLLI *the young Marquis*
THE BARON TITO BELCREDI
DOCTOR DIONYSIUS GENONI
LANDOLPH (LOLO)
HAROLD (FRANCO) *the four make-believe*
ORDULPH (MOMO) *secret counsellors*
BERTHOLD (FINO)
JOHN *the old servant*
TWO PAGES *in costume*

A solitary villa in the Umbrian countryside in our own day.

ACT ONE

The great hall in the villa, scrupulously decorated in such a way as to look like the throne-room of Henry IV in the imperial residence at Goslar. Among the antique furnishings two large, modern, life-size oil paintings clearly stand out, mounted against the back wall, slightly raised from the floor and on a carved wooden pedestal running the entire length of the wall. (It is wide and protruding enough to sit on like a long bench.) One painting is on the left, the other on the right side of the throne which is mid-way along the wall, interrupting the wooden pedestal into which is inserted the imperial chair with its low baldacchino.

The two portraits are of a gentleman and a lady, both young, disguised in carnival costumes; one dressed as 'Henry IV' and the other as 'Matilda of Tuscany'. Exits to the right and left.

When the curtain goes up, the two PAGES, *as if surprised, jump down from the pedestal-bench on which they are lying and take their positions with their halberds at the foot of the throne, one on either side, as if they were statues. After a short time, from the second exit, right, enter* HAROLD, LANDOLPH, ORDULPH *and* BERTHOLD, *all young men paid by the* MARQUIS CHARLES DI NOLLI *to play the role of 'Secret Counsellors' and royal vassals from the lower aristocracy at the court of Henry IV; therefore, they are dressed like German knights of the eleventh century. The last one,* BERTHOLD, *whose real name is Fino, is just starting his job there for the first time. His three companions are filling him in on his duties and at the same time enjoying themselves as they tease him. The whole scene must be played with unusual vitality.*

LANDOLPH [*to* BERTHOLD *as if he were explaining something*]: And this is the throne-room.

HAROLD: At Goslar.

ORDULPH: Or, should you prefer, at the castle in the Hartz.

HAROLD: Or at Worms.

LANDOLPH: Depending on the scene we are presenting, you jump around with us, sometimes here, sometimes there.

ORDULPH: In Saxony.

HAROLD: In Lombardy.

LANDOLPH: On the Rhine.

ONE OF THE PAGES [*without moving except for his lips*]: Pst, pst.

HAROLD [*turning towards the sound*]: What is it?

FIRST PAGE [*remaining like a statue*]: Is he or isn't he coming in? [*He alludes to* HENRY IV.]

ORDULPH: No, no, he's asleep. Relax.

SECOND PAGE [*releasing his pose, along with the other* PAGE, *starting to breathe again and returning to lie down on the pedestal-bench*]: For God's sake, you could have told us!

FIRST PAGE [*going over to* HAROLD]: Do you have a match, please?

LANDOLPH: Hey, no pipe in here.

FIRST PAGE [*while* HAROLD *offers him a lit match*]: No, I'm smoking a cigarette. [*He lights up and also goes to lie down on the bench while he smokes.*]

BERTHOLD [*who has been observing between amazement and bewilderment, looking around the room and then at his costume and that of his companions*]: Excuse me, but this room, these costumes . . . What Henry IV? I don't really get it. Is he or isn't he the one from France?

> [*At this question* LANDOLPH, HAROLD *and* ORDULPH *burst out laughing.*]

LANDOLPH [*still laughing, and pointing out* BERTHOLD *to his companions, who also keep on laughing, as if inviting them to make even more fun of him*]: The French one, he says!

ORDULPH: He thought it was the French one.

HAROLD: Henry IV of Germany, my dear boy! Of the Salian dynasty.

ORDULPH: The great and tragic Emperor.

LANDOLPH: He of Canossa. Every day, right here, we carry on the terrible war between Church and State, let me tell you!

ORDULPH: Empire against Papacy, I tell you.

HAROLD: Anti-popes against the Pope.

LANDOLPH: Kings against anti-kings.

ORDULPH: War against the Saxons!

HAROLD: And all the rebel princes!

LANDOLPH: Against the very sons of the Emperor!

BERTHOLD [*protecting his head with his hands against this avalanche of information*]: I understand! I understand! That's why I didn't catch on at first: me dressed this way and walking into this hall! I was right, then: this is not the way people dressed in the fifteen-hundreds!

HAROLD: What fifteen-hundreds?

ORDULPH: Right now we're somewhere between the eleventh and twelfth centuries!

LANDOLPH: You can figure it out for yourself: if on 25 January 1071 we are before Canossa. . . .

BERTHOLD [*more bewildered than ever*]: My God, what a mess this is!

ORDULPH: That's for sure. Especially if you thought you were at the French Court!

BERTHOLD: And all that historical preparation I did . . .

LANDOLPH: We are, my dear friend, four hundred years earlier than you! For us you're just a kid!

BERTHOLD [*getting angry*]: They could have told me, for God's sake, that it was about the German one and not Henry IV of France! During the past fifteen days that they gave me to prepare myself, you can't imagine how many books I went through!

HAROLD: Forgive me for asking, but didn't you know that here poor Tito was Adalbert of Bremen?

BERTHOLD: What Adalbert! I didn't know a damned thing!

LANDOLPH: No, don't you see how it works? When Tito died, the Marquis Di Nolli . . .

BERTHOLD: It was really him, the Marquis? It wouldn't have taken much for him to tell me . . .

HAROLD: Perhaps he thought you already knew.

LANDOLPH: He didn't want to hire anyone else to take his place. The three of us who remained seemed to him to be enough. But then he started shouting: 'Now that Adalbert has been driven out . . .' because, you see, for him poor Tito was not dead; for him Tito had been driven out of the Court by the rival Bishops of Cologne and Mayence.

BERTHOLD [*grabbing his head and holding it with both hands*]: I tell you, I can't make head nor tail out of all this business!

ORDULPH: Well then, my good friend, you're in real trouble!

HAROLD: And the problem is that we don't even know who you are!

BERTHOLD: Not even you? You mean you don't know who I'm supposed to be?

ORDULPH: Hum! 'Berthold'.

BERTHOLD: But who is this Berthold? And why Berthold?

LANDOLPH: 'They have driven out Adalbert? Well then I shall have Berthold. I want Berthold!' This is what he started to shout.

HAROLD: The three of us looked each other in the eyes. Who could this Berthold possibly be?

ORDULPH: And here you are, 'Berthold', my dear friend.

LANDOLPH: And you're going to do a great job!

BERTHOLD [*objecting and about to leave*]: Ah, but I'm not going to do it! Thanks a lot! I'm out of here! I'm off!

HAROLD [*restraining him together with Ordulph amid the laughter*]: No, relax, take it easy.

ORDULPH: You're not by any chance that Berthold in the fairy tale, are you?

LANDOLPH: And don't feel too bad, since none of us really know who we are, either! He's Harold; he's Ordulph; I'm Landolph. That's what he calls us. By now we're used to it. But who are we really? Just names of the period. And yours, too, is a name of the period: 'Berthold'. Only one of us, poor Tito, had a great part assigned to him, a part you find in history: the Bishop of Bremen. He was like a real bishop. Oh, magnificent he was, poor Tito!

HAROLD: Sure, at least he had a part he could prepare for well from the history books, he could!

LANDOLPH: He even managed to order His Majesty about; he would take charge, he guided him like a tutor and counsellor. As far as that goes, we, too, are 'secret counsellors', but in name only, because we know from the history books that Henry IV was hated by the upper aristocracy for surrounding himself at Court with young men of the lower classes.

ORDULPH: That's us.

LANDOLPH: That's right, insignificant regal vassals, devoted, a bit
dissolute, good-humoured . . .

BERTHOLD: I have to be good-humoured, too?

HAROLD: And how! Just like us.

ORDULPH: And it's not easy, you know.

LANDOLPH: It's really a pity! Because, as you can see, we've got all
the fittings. With the wardrobe we've got, we would make a fine
showing in this historical reconstruction, the kind that everybody
goes for in today's theatre. And what material, oh yes, there's
enough material in the story of Henry IV to get many a play out
of! Ah, the four of us here, and those two poor wretches over
there [*pointing to the* PAGES] standing stiff as a board, are . . . well,
we are just here with no one to give us content or to give us a
scene to act out. It's as though . . . how can I put it? The form is
there but the content is missing. We're worse off than the real
secret counsellors of Henry IV, because, of course, no one gave
them a part to play either, but they, at least, didn't feel that they
had to play a part. They played their part because they played
their part: in other words it was not a part, it was their life. They
looked out for themselves at the expense of others; they sold
investitures and who knows what else. We, on the other hand,
are stuck here, in costumes like these, and in this splendid court
. . . for what? Nothing . . . like six puppets hanging on the wall
waiting for someone to come and take them and make them
move this way or that way and to make them say something.

HAROLD: Ah no, my dear fellow, I beg your pardon, but you have
to give him the right answer. You have to answer to the point.
You're in trouble if he speaks to you and you are not ready with
the answer he expects from you!

LANDOLPH: Exactly. That's right; yes, it's true.

BERTHOLD: Well, you've said a mouthful! How am I supposed to
give him the right answer if I've prepared for Henry IV of
France, and all of a sudden, right here and now, a Henry of
Germany pops up!

[LANDOLPH, ORDULPH *and* HAROLD *start laughing again.*]

HAROLD: You've got to take care of this right away!

ORDULPH: Don't worry, we'll help you.

HAROLD: We've got lots of books over there. A quick review of the subject will be enough to start out with.

ORDULPH: You must have some general idea . . .

HAROLD: Look [*he turns him around and shows him the portrait of the Marchesa Matilda on the back wall*] – who, for example, would you say that is?

BERTHOLD [*looking*]: Her? Eh, I'm sorry, but it seems to me, just to begin with, that she's terribly out of place! Two modern paintings here in the midst of all this respectable antiquity.

HAROLD: You're right. And, in fact, they weren't there before. There are two niches behind those paintings. Two statues carved in the style of the period were supposed to be placed there. They remained empty, and then they were covered by those two canvases over there.

LANDOLPH [*interrupting and continuing*]: They certainly would be out of place if they really were paintings.

BERTHOLD: So what are they? Aren't they paintings?

LANDOLPH: Yes, if you go and touch them, they are paintings. But for him [*pointing mysteriously to the right, alluding to* HENRY IV] who does not touch them . . .

BERTHOLD: No? And so what are they for him?

LANDOLPH: Oh, I'm just guessing, you know, but I think on the whole I'm right. They are images, images like, well, like the ones a mirror reflects. Am I making myself clear? There, that one over there [*points to the portrait of* HENRY IV] represents himself, alive as he is in this throne-room, which is also as it should be, in the style of the period. Forgive me, but what do you find so surprising? If you were to stand in front of a mirror, wouldn't you see yourself alive, here and now, dressed up this way in ancient garb? Well, it's as if there were two mirrors over there that reflect living images here in the midst of a world which, you'll see, don't worry, you'll see for yourself after living with us, will also totally come to life too!

BERTHOLD: Oh, I warn you, I have no intentions of going crazy here!

HAROLD: What do you mean go crazy? You're going to have a great time.

BERTHOLD: Uh, tell me, how is it that all of you have become so wise?

LANDOLPH: My good man, you don't go back over 800 years of history without accumulating a bit of experience.

HAROLD: Come on, come on! You'll see how quickly you'll get with it.

ORDULPH: And in a school like ours you'll become wise too!

BERTHOLD: Yes, but for God's sake, give me some help right away! At least give me the basic facts.

HAROLD: Leave it to us. We'll all chip in.

LANDOLPH: We'll put your strings on and turn you into the best and most accomplished of puppets. Let's go. Come on.

[*He takes him by the arm to lead him off.*]

BERTHOLD [*stopping and looking in the direction of the portrait on the wall*]: Hold it. You haven't told me who she is over there. The Emperor's wife?

HAROLD: No. The wife of the Emperor is Bertha of Susa, sister of Amadeus II of Savoy.

ORDULPH: And the Emperor, who wants to be one of our young group, cannot stand her and is thinking of getting rid of her.

LANDOLPH: That is his most fierce of enemies: Matilda, the Marchesa of Tuscany.

BERTHOLD: Ah yes, I know: the one who played host to the Pope . . .

LANDOLPH: At Canossa, precisely.

ORDULPH: Pope Gregory VII.

HAROLD: He's our bugbear! Come on, let's get going.

[*All four of them move towards the right exit through which they entered, when from the left exit there enters the old servant* JOHN *in evening dress.*]

JOHN [*quickly, with impatience*]: Oh! Pst! Franco! Lolo!

HAROLD [*stopping and turning around*]: What do you want?

BERTHOLD [*surprised at seeing him enter the throne-room in evening dress*]: Oh! What's this all about? What's he doing in here?

LANDOLPH: A twentieth-century man! Away with you!

[*They run over to him together with the two* PAGES, *pretending to threaten him and throw him out.*]

ORDULPH: Messenger of Gregory VII, be gone with you!

HAROLD: Be gone! Get out!

JOHN [*defending himself, annoyed*]: Come on now, that's enough of this!

ORDULPH: No! You are not allowed to set foot in here!

HAROLD: Out! Get out!

LANDOLPH: [*to* BERTHOLD]: Magic, you know. He's a demon conjured up by the Magician of Rome. Draw, draw your swords!

　　[*He, too, makes a move to draw his sword.*]

JOHN [*shouting*]: Stop it, I tell you. Stop fooling around with me! The Marquis has arrived with his group of friends . . .

LANDOLPH [*rubbing his hands together*]: Ah, good! Are there any ladies?

ORDULPH: Old? Young?

JOHN: There are two gentlemen.

HAROLD: But the ladies! Who are the ladies?

JOHN: The Marchesa with her daughter.

LANDOLPH [*surprised*]: Oh! What's that?

ORDULPH: Did you say the Marchesa?

JOHN: The Marchesa, the Marchesa!

HAROLD: And the gentlemen?

JOHN: I don't know.

HAROLD [*to* BERTHOLD]: They're coming to give us our content, you see?

ORDULPH: All of them ambassadors of Gregory VII! What fun!

JOHN: Are you or are you not going to let me speak?

HAROLD: Speak! Speak up!

JOHN: It seems that one of those two gentlemen is a doctor.

LANDOLPH: Oh, I get it, another one of the usual doctors!

HAROLD: Good for you, Berthold! You bring us luck!

LANDOLPH: Watch how we work this doctor of ours!

BERTHOLD: I think I'm about to find myself in a nice mess, and soon!

JOHN: Listen to me, will you? They want to come in here.

LANDOLPH [*surprised and puzzled*]: What! Here? The Marchesa is here?

78

HAROLD: Well then, this is really going to be content – and content with a vengeance!

LANDOLPH: This is the birth of a real tragedy!

BERTHOLD: Why? Why?

ORDULPH [*pointing to the portrait*]: But don't you see, she's the one over there.

LANDOLPH: The daughter is the fiancée of the Marquis.

HAROLD: But what did they come for? Would someone mind telling me?

ORDULPH: There'll be trouble if he sees her!

LANDOLPH: Perhaps by now he won't recognize her any more!

JOHN: You'll have to keep him over there if he wakes up.

ORDULPH: Sure! Are you joking? And how do we do that?

HAROLD: You know what he's like!

JOHN: By God, even if you have to use force! These are my orders. So go now. Go on.

HAROLD: Yes, yes, because he may already be awake by now.

ORDULPH: Let's go. Let's go.

LANDOLPH [*starting off with the others, to* JOHN]: Then you'll explain it all to us later on!

JOHN [*shouting after them*]: Close that door over there and hide the key. Also this door [*pointing to the other exit to the right*].

[LANDOLPH, HAROLD *and* ORDULPH *go off through the second exit to the right.*]

JOHN [*to the two* PAGES]: Out! You get out, too. Over there [*points to the first exit to the right*]! Close the door behind you and get rid of the key!

[*The two* PAGES *leave through the first exit to the right.* JOHN *goes to the left exit and opens the door to let in the* MARQUIS DI NOLLI.]

DI NOLLI: Have you made my orders clear?

JOHN: Yes, my Lord. You may rest assured.

[DI NOLLI *goes out again for a moment and then proceeds to invite the others in. First the* BARON TITO BELCREDI *and* DR DIONYSIUS GENONI *enter and then* LADY MATILDA SPINA *and the young Marchesa,* FRIDA. JOHN *bows and exits.* LADY MATILDA SPINA *is about 45 years old, still beautiful and shapely, even though there are too many signs of her attempts to repair the inevitable damage of age with a strong but intelligent use of make-up, giving her head the wild look of a Walkyrie. Her make-up assumes a prominence which contrasts with and severely perturbs her sorrowful and very beautiful mouth. A widow for many years, she has as her friend the* BARON TITO BELCREDI, *whom neither she nor anyone else has ever taken seriously — or at least it would seem so. And then what* TITO BELCREDI *really means to her, only he alone knows, and so he can laugh if his friend feels she has to pretend not to know; he can always laugh in response to the laughter which the jokes made by the* MARCHESA *at his expense give rise to in the others. Slim, prematurely grey, a bit younger than she, he has a strange bird-like head. He would be a very lively person if his supple agility (which made him a most feared swordsman) were not sheathed in an Arab-like, sleepy laziness, which reveals itself through his strange voice, which is somewhat nasal and drawn-out.* FRIDA, *the daughter of the* MARCHESA, *is 19 years old. Overshadowed by her imperious and over-conspicuous mother, she is affected by the facile gossip that the latter provokes as much against her as against herself. Fortunately, however, she is engaged to the* MARQUIS CARLO DI NOLLI, *a rigid young man, very indulgent towards others, but closed and fixed in what he believes he amounts to in the world, even though, perhaps, down deep, he himself does not know. And, in any case, he is dismayed by all the responsibilities he feels weighing down on him and feels that everybody else, yes, they can talk (God bless them) and enjoy themselves, but not him, and not because he wouldn't like to, but because he is truly unable to do so. He is dressed in strict mourning for the recent death of his mother.* DR DIONYSIUS GENONI *has a nice, kind of impudent face, rubicund and satyr-like, with bulging eyes, a short and pointed little beard (shiny as silver), good manners and nearly bald. They enter looking perturbed, as if afraid, looking curiously around the room (except* DI NOLLI); *and at first they speak in low voices.*]

BELCREDI: Ah, magnificent! Magnificent!

DOCTOR: Very, very interesting. Even in the surroundings insanity is perfectly taken into account. Magnificent, ah yes, yes, magnificent.

LADY MATILDA [*her eyes searching for her portrait and discovering it, she moves closer to it*]: Ah, there it is! [*Admiring it from the proper distance, mixed feelings stir within her.*] . . . Yes, yes . . . Oh, look . . . My God . . . [*Calls her daughter:*] Frida, Frida . . . Look . . .

FRIDA: Ah, your portrait?

LADY MATILDA: No! Look! It's not me, it's you there!

DI NOLLI: Yes, it's true. I told you so.

LADY MATILDA: But I never would have believed such a resemblance. [*Shaking as if from a chill down her spine:*] God, what a feeling! [*Then looking at her daughter:*] Come now, Frida. [*She pulls her close to her, putting an arm around her waist.*] Here now! Don't you see yourself in me, there?

FRIDA: Umm, I, in all truth . . .

LADY MATILDA: Don't you think so? But how can you not think so? [*Turning to* BELCREDI:] You look at it, Tito! You be the judge.

BELCREDI [*without looking*]: Ah no; I will not look. For me, *a priori*, the answer is no!

LADY MATILDA: How silly of you! You think you are paying me a compliment. [*Turning to* DR GENONI:] Do say something, speak up, Doctor.

[*The* DOCTOR *is about to move closer to the portrait.*]

BELCREDI [*with his back turned, pretending secretly to call him back*]: Pst! No, Doctor! For the love of God, don't get involved!

DOCTOR [*bewildered and smiling*]: And why shouldn't I?

LADY MATILDA: Don't pay any attention to him. Come now. He's insufferable!

FRIDA: Didn't you know, he's the professional fool.

BELCREDI [*to the* DOCTOR *as he sees him going over*]: Watch your feet, be careful of your feet, Doctor! Your feet!

DOCTOR: Feet? Why should I?

BELCREDI: You're wearing heavy shoes!

DOCTOR: I am?

BELCREDI: Yes, sir. And you're about to step on four delicate, little glass feet.

DOCTOR [*laughing loudly*]: Not at all! I would think – after all – there's nothing surprising about a daughter resembling her mother . . .

BELCREDI: Ca boom! That's it! It's all over with!

DOCTOR [*innocently*]: Isn't that so?

BELCREDI [*answering the* MARCHESA]: He said that there's nothing to be surprised at, and you are quite surprised. And why are you, then, may I ask, if the thing is so natural for you now?

LADY MATILDA [*even more angry*]: You fool! Fool! Precisely because it is so natural. Because it is not my daughter who is there. [*Points to the canvas:*] That is my portrait. And to find my daughter there instead of myself amazed me, and my amazement, I beg you to believe me, was sincere, and I forbid you to cast doubts on it!

[*After this violent outburst of anger, a moment of awkward silence for everyone.*]

FRIDA [*softly, annoyed*]: My God, always the same . . . Over every little thing an argument.

BELCREDI [*also in a low voice, as if with his tail between his legs, in an apologetic tone*]: I am not casting doubt on anything. I simply noticed that from the very beginning you did not share your mother's amazement; or, if something did amaze you, it was because the resemblance between you and that portrait seemed so close.

LADY MATILDA: Of course. Why can't she recognize herself in me, the way I was at her age while I, there, can easily recognize myself in her, the way she is now?

DOCTOR: Perfectly true! Because a portrait is there fixed in a moment of time, far away and without memories for the young Marchesa, while for the Marchesa herself it can bear memories of everything: movements, gestures, glances, smiles, and so many other things that are not even in there . . .

LADY MATILDA: There you are! Precisely!

DOCTOR [*continuing, turned towards her*]: You, naturally enough, can see them there alive now in your daughter.

LADY MATILDA: He always has to go and ruin even the tiniest bit of pleasure I get from my most spontaneous sentiments, and just for the delight he takes in irritating me.

DOCTOR [*dazzled by the light he has shed on the matter, he adopts his usual professional tone; turned to Belcredi*]: The resemblance, my dear Baron, often stems from imponderable things. And in point of fact it is for this reason that one explains that –

BELCREDI [*in order to interrupt the lecture*]: – that someone might also find a certain resemblance between you and me, my dear professor!

DI NOLLI: Let's drop the subject. Enough now, please. [*He points to the two exits to the right as a warning that someone might be listening from over there.*] We've had enough fun, coming . . .

FRIDA: Of course! When he's around [*indicating* BELCREDI] . . .

LADY MATILDA [*quickly*]: That's precisely why I didn't want him to come.

BELCREDI: But if you've had so many good laughs at my expense! Such ingratitude!

DI NOLLI: Please, that's enough! Tito! We have the Doctor here, and we have come for a very serious reason, and you know how important it is for me.

DOCTOR: Exactly so. Let's try first to get some facts clear. This portrait of yours, excuse me, Marchesa, how did it get here? Was it a gift from you then?

LADY MATILDA: No, no. For what reason would I have given it to him? At that time I was like Frida, and not even engaged. I gave it to him three or four years after the accident. I gave it to him at the obvious insistence of his mother [*points to* DI NOLLI].

DOCTOR: Who was his sister, yes? [*Indicating the exits at the right, alluding to* HENRY IV.]

DI NOLLI: Yes, Doctor. It is a debt – that is, our coming here – paid to my mother who passed away a month ago. Instead of being here, she [*indicating* FRIDA] and I should be on a trip . . .

DOCTOR: And thinking about other things altogether. I understand.

DI NOLLI: Hmm! She died with the firm conviction that this brother of hers, whom she adored, was on the verge of being cured.

DOCTOR: And can you tell me, if you would, from what signs did she deduce this?

DI NOLLI: It would seem to have come from certain strange remarks that he made to her shortly before mother died.

DOCTOR: Remarks? Ah . . . you see . . . it would be very helpful, extremely helpful, to know what they were. It certainly would!

DI NOLLI: Ah, but I have no way of knowing. I do know that my mother returned from her last visit with him in a very upset state.

It seems that he displayed unusual tenderness in a way that almost served as a forecast of her approaching death. On her death-bed she made me promise never to neglect him, that I would have him checked and visited . . .

DOCTOR: All right. That's fine. Let's see now, let us see first . . . Many times the least causes . . . this portrait, then . . .

LADY MATILDA: Good Heavens, Doctor, I really don't think we should exaggerate its importance. It struck me only because I hadn't seen it in many years.

DOCTOR: Please, please . . . just a minute . . .

DI NOLLI: Of course! It's been there for around fifteen years.

LADY MATILDA: More! More than eighteen by now!

DOCTOR: Please, I beg your pardon, but you have yet to find out what I wish to know! I attach much importance, a good deal, to these two portraits, executed, I would imagine, before the famous and most unfortunate cavalcade. Isn't that the case?

LADY MATILDA: Eh, yes, that's true.

DOCTOR: And, therefore, when he was in complete control of his senses — that's exactly what I've been trying to say. Was it he who suggested to her that the portraits be done?

LADY MATILDA: No, no, Doctor. A number of us who took part in the cavalcade had them done as a remembrance of the event.

BELCREDI: I had mine done, too: mine was 'Charles of Anjou'!

LADY MATILDA: As soon as the costumes were ready.

BELCREDI: Because, you see, it was suggested that all our portraits be collected and hung in an art gallery as a kind of souvenir, in one of the rooms of the villa where the cavalcade took place. But then everyone decided to keep his own.

LADY MATILDA: And mine here, as I already told you, I gave to him — without, in fact, much regret — since his mother . . . [*Once again she indicates* DI NOLLI.]

DOCTOR: You are not aware whether or not it was he who requested it?

LADY MATILDA: I'm afraid I don't know. Perhaps . . . Or his sister, in order to encourage the love affair . . .

DOCTOR: Another thing, one other thing! Was the idea of having a cavalcade his?

BELCREDI [*quickly*]: No, no, it was mine! I had the idea!

DOCTOR: Please . . .

LADY MATILDA Pay no attention to him. The idea was poor
Belassi's.

BELCREDI: What's this about Belassi?

LADY MATILDA [*to the* DOCTOR]: Count Belassi who died, poor
thing, two or three months later.

BELCREDI: But if Belassi wasn't even there when . . .

DI NOLLI [*annoyed by the threat of another discussion*]: I beg your
pardon, Doctor, is it absolutely necessary to establish whose idea
it was?

DOCTOR: Eh, yes, it would help me . . .

BELCREDI: But the idea was all mine! This is incredible! I beg your
pardon, but I have nothing to be proud of in coming up with this
idea, considering how it all turned out. Look here, Doctor, I
remember it well, it was one night at the beginning of the month
of November at the club. I was looking through an illustrated
magazine, a German one – I was looking only at the pictures,
you understand, since I do not read German. In one of the
pictures there was the Emperor in some university town or other
where he had been a student.

DOCTOR: Bonn, Bonn.

BELCREDI: Right, Bonn. Dressed up, on horseback, in one of those
strange traditional costumes worn by the ancient student guilds in
Germany. He was followed by a procession of other students of
the nobility, they, too, on horseback and in costume. That's
where I got the idea, from that picture. You see, the club was
thinking of putting on a grand pageant for the coming carnival
season. I proposed we have this historical cavalcade – historical in
a manner of speaking, more Tower of Babel-like. Each of us was
supposed to choose a character from this or that century to
impersonate: king or emperor or prince, and alongside him on
horseback his lady, queen or empress. The horses, of course,
were decked out in the fittings of the period. And my proposal
was accepted.

LADY MATILDA: I received my invitation from Belassi.

BELCREDI: Embezzlement is what it is, if he told you the idea was

85

his! I tell you he wasn't even there at the club that night when I made the proposal. And, in fact, neither was he! [*Alluding to* HENRY IV.]

DOCTOR: And so he chose the character of Henry IV?

LADY MATILDA: Because I — allowing my own name to make the choice — not giving the matter much consideration, said that I wanted to be the Marchesa Matilda of Tuscany.

DOCTOR: No . . . I don't fully understand the relationship.

LADY MATILDA: Ah, you know, neither did I at first when he told me that from then on he would be at my feet like Henry IV at Canossa. True, I did know something about Canossa, but to tell the truth, I didn't have the history well in mind; and I had a strange impression as I reviewed the history, in order to prepare myself to play my part, and discovered I was the very faithful and extremely zealous friend of Pope Gregory VII, who was in fierce conflict with the Emperor of Germany. Then, since I had chosen to play the part of that character, who was his implacable enemy, it became clear to me why he wanted to be at my side in that cavalcade as Henry IV.

DOCTOR: Ah, perhaps because . . .

BELCREDI: Doctor, my God! It was because he was madly courting her and she [*indicating the* MARCHESA] naturally . . .

LADY MATILDA [*pointedly, with fire*]: Naturally, exactly, just so! And then more than ever 'naturally'!

BELCREDI [*pointing her out*]: There you are! She couldn't stand him!

LADY MATILDA: But that is not true. I did not find him unlikable. On the contrary! But all I need is someone who wants to be taken seriously and . . .

BELCREDI [*continuing*]: That someone provides you with the brightest proof of his stupidity.

LADY MATILDA: No, my dear, not in this case, because he was not at all as stupid as you are.

BELCREDI: I never tried to make myself be taken seriously!

LADY MATILDA: Ah, how well I know it! But with him, however, there was no joking! [*In a different tone, turning to the* DOCTOR:] One of the many misfortunes that happen to us ladies, my dear Doctor, is to find ourselves now and again before two eyes that look at us with a contained and intense promise of everlasting devotion! [*She breaks out in high-pitched laughter.*] There is nothing more ridiculous. If men could only see themselves with that everlasting devoted look of theirs. I have always laughed about it – then more than ever! But I must confess: I can do so now after twenty and more years. When I laughed at him this way, it was also out of fear, because one, perhaps, could have believed in a promise like that from those eyes. But it would have been very dangerous.

DOCTOR [*with great interest, concentrating*]: I see, yes, this – this I find most interesting indeed. Very dangerous, you say.

LADY MATILDA [*light-heartedly*]: Simply because he wasn't like the others. And then since I am also . . . yes, well, I am a bit like that . . . more than just a little bit, to be quite honest . . . [*looking for a simple word*] intolerant, that's the word, intolerant of all that is formal and so boring! But at that time I was too young – you understand, and a woman: I had to control myself! It would have taken the kind of courage that I did not feel I had. I, too, laughed at him. With remorse, however, in fact, with a true feeling of disgust towards myself, for I saw that my laughter was mixed up with that of all the others – all those fools – who were making fun of him.

BELCREDI: The same case as mine, more or less.

LADY MATILDA: You always make people laugh with that affected look of humiliation you put on, my dear, while he, on the contrary! There is quite a difference! And then, in your case, people laughed in your face.

BELCREDI: Ah, well, let me tell you, it's better than being laughed at behind your back!

DOCTOR: Let's return to our subject. Let us go back to what we were talking about at first. And so, then, he was already somewhat eccentric from what I seem to understand!

BELCREDI: Yes, but in a very strange way, Doctor.

DOCTOR: And how would that be?

BELCREDI: Let me see, you might say . . . cold-bloodedly . . .

LADY MATILDA: What, cold-bloodedly? He was what he was, Doctor. A bit strange, certainly, but because he was full of life: he was original!

87

BELCREDI: I don't mean to say that he was faking his eccentricity; quite the contrary, he was often genuinely eccentric. But, Doctor, I could swear that he was acutely aware of himself in acting out his eccentricity. And I think this must have been the case even in his most spontaneous actions. Furthermore, I am certain he must have suffered because of it. Sometimes he would go into the funniest kinds of angry fits with himself!

LADY MATILDA: That is true.

BELCREDI [to LADY MATILDA]: And why? [To the DOCTOR:] As far as I could tell, because that instant lucidity that comes from acting a part suddenly excluded him from any kind of intimacy with his own feelings, which seemed to him to be not exactly false – because they were sincere – but rather like something he immediately had to give the value of – what can I say? – of an act of intelligence, to make up for the lack of that sincere and cordial warmth that he felt was missing. And so he would improvise, exaggerate, let himself go – that's it – in order to forget his troubles and to see himself no longer. He would appear changeable, fatuous and ... yes, to tell the truth, also, at times, ridiculous.

DOCTOR: And, tell me, unsociable?

BELCREDI: No, not at all! He was with it! He was famous for organizing such things as *tableaux vivants*, dances, benefit recitals – all for the fun of it, you understand. But he was a very good actor, you know.

DI NOLLI: With his madness he became a magnificent and terrible actor.

BELCREDI: But even at the start! You can just imagine, when the accident happened, after he fell from the horse ...

DOCTOR: He hit his head, did he not?

LADY MATILDA: Oh, how awful. He was by my side. I saw him there between the hoofs of the horse as it was rearing ...

BELCREDI: But at first we had no idea at all that he had seriously hurt himself. It's true, there was a bit of confusion in the cavalcade and things came to a halt. People wanted to know what had happened, but he had already been picked up and taken to the villa.

LADY MATILDA: Nothing at all, you realize. Not. even a scratch! Not even a drop of blood.

BELCREDI: We thought he had merely fainted . . .

LADY MATILDA: And when, about two hours later . . .

BELCREDI: That's right, when he appeared again in the main room of the villa – yes, that's what I wanted to say . . .

LADY MATILDA: Ah, the look on his face! I realized it immediately!

BELCREDI: No, no. Not at all! None of us realized it, Doctor, believe me!

LADY MATILDA: Of course not! All of you were acting like crazy people!

BELCREDI: Everyone was having fun playing his own part. It was a real Babel!

LADY MATILDA: You can imagine, Doctor, what a shock it was, when we realized that he, instead, was taking his part seriously.

DOCTOR: Ah, because he, too, then . . .

BELCREDI: Really! He appeared in the midst of us. We thought he was his old self again and that he had started acting along with the rest of us . . . better than the rest of us, because, as I told you before, he was an excellent actor, he was. In other words, we thought he was joking!

LADY MATILDA: They began to make fun of him . . .

BELCREDI: And then . . . he was armed as a king would be – he drew his sword and was brandishing it around at two or three of us. It was a terrifying moment for all of us.

LADY MATILDA: I shall never forget that scene: all of our faces masked, gross and distorted, there in front of that terrifying mask of his face that now was no longer a mask but rather madness itself!

BELCREDI: Behold! Henry IV. He was that very Henry IV in person, and in a moment of rage!

LADY MATILDA: I think that the obsession he had with that masquerade, Doctor, must have affected him, the obsession he created for himself for over a month and more. He would always make it a part of everything he did, that obsession of his!

BELCREDI: How he studied to prepare himself for it! All the particulars, down to the slightest detail . . .

DOCTOR: Ah, it's elementary! A momentary obsession became a fixation with the fall and blow to the head resulting in cerebral damage. It became fixed in perpetuity. You can become mentally deficient, you can become insane.

BELCREDI [*to* FRIDA *and* DI NOLLI]: You see what tricks life has in store for us, my little ones? [*To* DI NOLLI:] You were four or five years old. [*To* FRIDA:] Your mother seems to think that you have taken her place there in that portrait, when, at the time, the last thing she had on her mind was the possibility of bringing you into the world. My hair is already grey, and he – look at him there [*points to the portrait*]. Boom! One bang on the head, and he never moved again from where he is: Henry IV.

DOCTOR [*who was immersed in thought, spreads his hands before his face, as if to draw the attention of the others, and prepares to give his scientific explanation*]: Well then, you see, ladies and gentlemen, it comes down to this . . .

[*But all of a sudden the first exit to the right opens, the one closest to the footlights, and* BERTHOLD, *whose face is completely transformed, enters.*]

BERTHOLD [*rushes in like someone no longer able to contain himself*]: Forgive me. I beg your pardon.

[*He stops short, however, when he sees what confused amazement his appearance causes in the others.*]

FRIDA [*with a terrified shout, seeking protection*]: Oh God! There he is!

LADY MATILDA: [*backing away in fear, with one arm raised in order not to see him*]: Is it he? Is it?

DI NOLLI [*quickly*]: No! Of course not! Calm down.

DOCTOR [*amazed*]: Who is this?

BELCREDI: One of our runaway masqueraders.

DI NOLLI: He is one of the four young men that we employ here to assist him in his madness.

BERTHOLD: I beg your pardon, Marquis . . .

DI NOLLI: Damn your pardon! I gave orders for all the doors to be kept locked and for no one to enter here!

BERTHOLD: Yes sir! But I can't take it any more! And I request your permission to leave this place.

DI NOLLI: Ah, I see, you're the one who was to begin working here this morning?

BERTHOLD: Yes sir, and I'm telling you I can't stand . . .

LADY MATILDA [to DI NOLLI with real dismay]: Well then, he's not as calm as you said he was!

BERTHOLD [quickly]: No, no, Madame! It's not him! It's my three companions. You say 'assist him', Marquis. There's no assisting going on! They don't assist. They are the real madmen! I walk in here for the first time, and instead of helping me, Your Lordship . . .

[LANDOLPH and HAROLD make an excited and sudden appearance at the same right exit but stop on the threshold before entering.]

LANDOLPH: With your permission?

HAROLD: With your permission, Marquis?

DI NOLLI: Come in! What is going on here? What are you doing?

FRIDA: Oh, my God! I'm frightened! I'm leaving! I'm going to run away! [She starts to move towards the left exit.]

DI NOLLI [holding her back at once]: No, don't, Frida!

LANDOLPH: My lord, this fool here . . . [Points to BERTHOLD.]

BERTHOLD [protesting]: Ah, no. No, thanks, my friends. I have no intention of staying under such circumstances. I'm not staying!

LANDOLPH: What do you mean, you're not staying?

HAROLD: He ruined everything, my Lord, running off here!

LANDOLPH: He made him furious! We can't keep him in the other room over there any longer! He gave orders to have him arrested, and he wants to 'pronounce sentence' on him from the throne right now! What do we do?

DI NOLLI: Close the door! Go and close that door!

[LANDOLPH goes to close it.]

HAROLD: Ordulph won't be able to hold him back all on his own . . .

LANDOLPH: Perhaps, my Lord, if we could announce your visit at once in order to distract him. Have the gentleman considered under which guise they wish to be presented?

DI NOLLI: Yes, yes, everything has been thought out. [To the DOCTOR:] If you, Doctor, think it wise to examine him immediately . . .

FRIDA: Not me, not me, Carlo. I'm going. And you too, Mother, for the love of God, come, too. Come with me!

DOCTOR: You don't think . . . He's not armed by any chance, is he?

DI NOLLI: Of course he's not armed. What nonsense, Doctor! [*To* FRIDA:] I'm sorry, Frida, but this fear of yours is really childish. You did want to come . . .

FRIDA: Not I, I beg your pardon. It was Mother.

LADY MATILDA [*with resolution*]: And I'm ready! So then, what do we do?

BELCREDI: Excuse me, but is it absolutely necessary to disguise ourselves in that way?

LANDOLPH: Indispensable, absolutely indispensable, sir! Ah, unfortunately, as you can see [*shows his costume*], there would be trouble if he were to see you ladies and gentlemen like this in modern dress!

HAROLD: He would think it was some kind of diabolical disguise.

DI NOLLI: The way these men appear disguised to you, so in like fashion we appear to him to be disguised in the clothes we are wearing.

LANDOLPH: And perhaps it wouldn't matter much at all, my Lord, if he didn't suppose it to be the work of his mortal enemy.

BELCREDI: Pope Gregory VII?

LANDOLPH: Exactly so. He says he's 'a pagan'!

BELCREDI: The Pope? That's a good one!

LANDOLPH: Yes, sir. And that he can call back the dead! He accuses him of practising all the diabolical arts. He is terribly afraid of him.

DOCTOR: A persecution complex!

HAROLD: He would become furious!

DI NOLLI [*to* BELCREDI]: Actually, it is not necessary for you to be there, don't you agree? We'll move over there. All that is needed is for the Doctor to see him.

DOCTOR: Are you saying . . . I, alone?

DI NOLLI: But they are here! [*Indicating the three young men.*]

DOCTOR: No, no . . . I mean, if the Marchesa . . .

LADY MATILDA: Yes, of course. I want to be present, too. I want to be there, too. I want to see him again!

FRIDA: But why, Mamma? I beg you . . . Come with us!

LADY MATILDA [*imperiously*]: Let me be! It is for this reason that I have come! [*To* LANDOLPH:] I shall be 'Adelaida', the mother.

LANDOLPH: Yes, very good indeed. The mother of the Empress Bertha – excellent. Well then, the only thing Your Ladyship need do is to wear the ducal crown and put on a mantle to hide her clothes. [*To* HAROLD:] Go on, off you go, Harold!

HAROLD: Wait. What about the gentleman? [*Indicating the* DOCTOR.]

DOCTOR: Ah, yes . . . We decided, if I remember correctly, the Bishop . . . yes, the Bishop Hugh of Cluny.

HAROLD: Does the gentleman mean the Abbot? Excellent. Hugh of Cluny.

LANDOLPH: He has been here many times before . . .

DOCTOR [*amazed*]: What's that? Been here?

LANDOLPH: No need to worry. What I mean is, since it is such an easy disguise.

HAROLD: We made use of it on other occasions.

DOCTOR: But . . .

LANDOLPH: There's no chance of his remembering it. He pays more attention to the costume than to the person.

LADY MATILDA: Well, then, this will work in my favour as well.

DI NOLLI: We're going. Frida. Come, come with us, Tito.

BELCREDI: Eh, no. If she stays [*indicating the* MARCHESA], I stay, too.

LADY MATILDA: But I have absolutely no need for you here!

BELCREDI: I'm not saying you need me here. I, too, simply would enjoy seeing him again. Am I not allowed to?

LANDOLPH: Yes, perhaps it would be better if there were three of you.

HAROLD: And now, what about the gentleman?

BELCREDI: Oh, just see if you can find some easy costume for me, too.

LANDOLPH [*to* HAROLD]: Ah yes, something related to Cluny.

BELCREDI: Related to Cluny? What does that mean?

LANDOLPH: Benedictine robes of the Abbey of Cluny. He will appear to be part of Monsignor's following. [*To* HAROLD:] You

can go now. [*To* BERTHOLD:] You too, off you go. And be sure
not to show up here all day! [*But as soon as he sees them coming:*]
Wait now. [*To* BERTHOLD:] Bring the clothes he will give you
here to me. [*To* HAROLD:] And you go at once and announce the
visit of the 'Duchess Adelaida' and 'Monsignor Hugh of Cluny'.
Is that clear?

  [HAROLD *and* BERTHOLD *leave by the first exit to the right.*]

DI NOLLI: So then we should withdraw. [*He leaves with* FRIDA *by
the left exit.*]

DOCTOR [*to* LANDOLPH]: He should, I think, look favourably on
me dressed in the robes of Hugh of Cluny . . .

LANDOLPH: Very much so, rest assured. The Monsignor has always
been received with great respect. You, too, Your Ladyship, may
rest assured. He always remembers that it was due to the interces-
sion of the two of you that after two days of waiting in the
snow, almost frozen to death, he was admitted to the Castle of
Canossa and to the presence of Gregory VII, who did not want
to receive him.

BELCREDI: Excuse me, and I?

LANDOLPH: You remain respectfully to the side.

LADY MATILDA [*irritated, very nervous*]: You would be better off
going away!

BELCREDI: [*in a low voice, irritated*]: You're quite upset . . .

LADY MATILDA [*proudly*]: I am as I am! Leave me in peace!

  [BERTHOLD *comes back with the clothing.*]

LANDOLPH [*seeing him enter*]: Ah, here come the costumes. This
mantle for the Marchesa.

LADY MATILDA: One moment while I take off my hat. [*She does so
and gives it to* BERTHOLD.]

LANDOLPH: Be sure you take it over there. [*Then to the* MARCHESA
as he offers to place the ducal crown on her head:] Allow me.

LADY MATILDA: Oh dear, isn't there a mirror here somewhere?

LANDOLPH: There, over there. [*Points to the left exit.*] If Her Ladyship
would rather do it herself . . .

LADY MATILDA: Yes, yes, I think it better that way. Give it here. I
won't take long.

  [*She takes back her hat and leaves with* BERTHOLD, *who is carrying*

the mantle and crown. In the meantime, the DOCTOR *and* BELCREDI
without help start putting on, as best they can, the Benedictine robes.]

BELCREDI: I never thought, to tell the truth, that one day I would
find myself playing the role of a Benedictine. Oh, by the way,
this crazy business must cost quite a bundle!

DOCTOR: Sure, as do a number of other crazy things.

BELCREDI: When you've got a fortune at your disposal to back it
up . . .

LANDOLPH: Yes sir, we have a complete wardrobe over there: all
period costumes, copied to perfection from old models. This is
my particular responsibility: I buy only from the best theatrical
costumers. It's very expensive.

[LADY MATILDA *returns decked out in mantle and crown.*]

BELCREDI [*at once, admiring her*]: Ah, magnificent! Truly regal!

LADY MATILDA: [*seeing* BELCREDI *and breaking out in laughter*]: Oh
my God! No, never! Take it off! You're impossible! You look
like an ostrich disguised as a monk!

BELCREDI: And look at the Doctor!

DOCTOR: Eh, never mind . . . There's nothing I can do about it.

LADY MATILDA: No, no, there's nothing wrong with the Doctor
. . . You, however, really make me laugh!

DOCTOR: [*to* LANDOLPH]: So then, do you have many receptions
like this here?

LANDOLPH: It depends. Many times he will give orders for this or
that person to appear before him; which means, then, that we
must find someone able to play the part. This goes for women
too . . .

LADY MATILDA [*hurt, and trying to hide the fact*]: Ah, women as
well!

LANDOLPH: Ah, yes, at first . . . Many.

BELCREDI [*laughing*]: Oh, that's a good one! In costume? [*Indicating
the* MARCHESA:] Like that?

LANDOLPH: Eh, you know: women, the kind that . . .

BELCREDI: That lend themselves to . . . I understand. [*Nastily, to
the* MARCHESA:] Be careful, this could become dangerous for
you!

[*The second exit to the right opens and* HAROLD *appears; first, he makes an inconspicuous sign for all conversation in the room to end, and then solemnly announces:*]

HAROLD: His Majesty the Emperor!

[*First, the two* PAGES *enter and take their positions at the foot of the throne. Then, between* ORDOLPH *and* HAROLD, *who remain at a respectable distance behind, there enters* HENRY IV. *He is close to age 50, very pale, and the hair on the back of his head is already grey; however, his hair at the temples and in front appears to be blond, tinted in a child-like and very obvious way; and on his cheeks, in the midst of all that tragic pallor, is a red, doll-like make-up, it, too, very obvious. Over his regal garb he wears a penitent's sack, as at Canossa. In his eyes there is a fixed look of suffering, which is frightening to behold and which is in contrast to the attitude of a person who wishes to be humbly repentant, and is all the more ostentatious, the more he feels his humiliation is undeserved.* OR-DOLPH *with both hands holds the imperial crown and* HAROLD *the sceptre with the eagle and the globe with the cross.*]

HENRY IV [*bowing first to* LADY MATILDA, *then to the* DOCTOR]: My Lady . . . Monsignor . . . [*Then he observes* BELCREDI *and is about to bow also to him, but instead turns to* LANDOLPH, *who has moved closer to him, and with diffidence asks in a low voice:*] Is this Peter Damian?

LANDOLPH: No, Your Majesty, he is a monk of Cluny who is accompanying the Abbot.

[HENRY IV *starts to examine* BELCREDI *again with growing diffidence, and taking notice that* BELCREDI *has turned his attention in an uncertain and embarrassed fashion to* LADY MATILDA *and the* DOCTOR, *as if searching for advice with his eyes, he stands up straight and shouts:*]

HENRY IV: It's Peter Damian. Useless, Father, to look at the Duchess! [*Turning at once to* LADY MATILDA *as if to ward off a danger:*] I swear, I swear to you, my Lady, I have had a change of heart towards your daughter! I confess that if he [*indicates* BELCREDI] had not come to impede me in the name of Pope Alexander, I would have repudiated her! Yes, there were those who were ready to favour the repudiation: the Bishop of Mayence for one and for one hundred and twenty plots of farmland. [*Looks at*

LANDOLPH *a bit perplexed, and says quickly:*] I should not, at this time, be speaking badly about the bishops. [*Returning humbly in front of* BELCREDI:] I am grateful, believe me, when I say that now I am grateful for that impediment. My life is all made of humiliations – my mother, Adalbert, Tribur, Goslar – and now this sackcloth you see me wearing. [*His tone of voice all of a sudden changes and he speaks like a person going over his part in an astute parenthesis.*] It doesn't matter! Clarity of ideas, perspicacity, firm resolution and patience in adverse fortune! [*Then turning to everyone and saying with grave solemnity:*] I know how to correct the errors I have committed, and even before you, Peter Damian, I humble myself! [*He makes a deep bow and remains there curved over before him as if bent by an oblique suspicion that springs up in his mind and forces him to add, as if against his will, in a threatening tone:*] Was it not perhaps from you that the obscene rumour that my holy mother, Agnes, was having illicit relations with the Bishop of Auguste originated?

BELCREDI [*while* HENRY IV *is still bent over, with a threatening finger pointed at him, he puts his hands on his chest, and then denies*]: No, it did not come from me, certainly not!

HENRY IV [*straightening up*]: No, is it not true? Infamy! [*He looks at him awhile and then adds:*] I did not think you capable of it. [*He draws close to the* DOCTOR *and gives his sleeve a quick pull as he winks slyly:*] That's the way 'they' are, Monsignor. Always the same, they are!

HAROLD [*quietly, in a whisper, as if prompting the* DOCTOR]: Eh, yes, those rapacious bishops, yes.

DOCTOR [*trying to maintain his role, turned towards* HAROLD]: Oh, them, of course . . . Those ones . . .

HENRY IV: Nothing is enough for them! Just a poor young lad I was, Monsignor . . . You spend time playing even when, without knowing it, you are a king! Six years old I was and they tore me away from my mother, and against her they used me, who was unsuspecting, against the very power of the Dynasty, they, profaning everything, stealing and stealing, one more greedy than the other . . . Anno more than Stephen, Stephen more than Anno!

LANDOLPH [*in a whisper, persuasively, to rebuke him*]: Your
Majesty . . .

HENRY IV [*turning at once*]: Ah, yes, of course: I must not at this
time speak ill of the bishops. But this infamy against my mother,
Monsignor, surpasses all limits! [*He looks at the* MARCHESA *and
becomes tender:*] And I cannot even mourn for her, my Lady . . .
But I appeal to you who must have a mother's heart. She came to
see me, from her convent, almost a month ago now. They told
me she is dead. [*Long pause, full of emotion; then smiling with a
certain sadness:*] I cannot mourn for her, because if you are here
now and I am like this [*shows the sackcloth he is wearing*], it means
that I am twenty-six years old.

HAROLD [*almost whispering sweetly to comfort him*]: And that she,
therefore, is alive, Your Majesty.

ORDOLPH [*as above*]: Still in her convent.

HENRY IV [*turning to look at them*]: That's right. And I can,
therefore, postpone my grief until another time. [*Almost in a
flirting manner, he shows the* MARCHESA *the tint he has used on his
hair.*] Look at this: still blond . . . [*Then softly, as if in confidence:*]
It's for you! I have no need of it. But some exterior touches do
help out. A question of age. Do I make myself clear, Monsignor?
[*He draws close to the* MARCHESA, *observing her hair:*] Ah, but I see
that . . . you, too, Duchess . . . [*He winks and makes an expressive
gesture with his hand:*] Italian, no? [*As if to say, 'fake', but without
the slightest sign of contempt, but rather with mischievous admiration:*]
God forbid that I should show disgust or surprise! Foolish aspiration! Nobody wants to recognize that certain dark and fatal
power that assigns limits to the will. But, I tell you, if one is born
and one dies! To be born, Monsignor: did you want to be born? I
did not. And between one case and the other, both independent
of our will, so many things happen which all of us wish had not
happened and to which we resign ourselves reluctantly!

DOCTOR [*just to say something while studying him carefully*]: Ah, yes,
alas, unfortunately!

HENRY IV: This is how it is! When we are not resigned, out come
our desires. A woman who wants to be a man . . . an old man
who wants to be young . . . None of us lie or pretend! There's

little doubt about it: in good faith we have fixed ourselves, all of us, in a fine concept of our own selves. Nevertheless, Monsignor, while you hold tight, clinging with both your hands to your holy cassock, there slips away, down your sleeves, like a snake shedding its skin, something you are not aware of: life, Monsignor! And it's a surprise when you see it materialize there all of a sudden in front of you, escaping from you. Spite and anger against yourself, or remorse, also remorse. Ah, if you only knew how much remorse I found before me! With a face that was my very own face, but so horrible, that I could not look at it . . . [*He draws closer to the* MARCHESA.] Did it never happen to you, my Lady? Do you actually remember always being the same, do you? Oh God, but then one day . . . how was it? How was it that you could commit that particular act . . . [*he looks so intensely into her eyes, she almost faints*] yes, that one, precisely that very one! We understand one another, no? Rest assured, I shall reveal it to no one! And that you Peter Damian could ever have been the friend of such a person . . .

LANDOLPH [*as before*]: Your Majesty . . .

HENRY IV [*immediately*]: No, no, I shall not name him! I know how much it bothers him! [*Turning to* BELCREDI *in a fleeting way:*] What's your opinion, hmm? What did you think of him? But all of us, none the less, continue to hold tightly to the concept we have of ourselves, just the way someone growing old will colour his hair. What does it matter if you cannot consider this dyed hair of mine to be its true colour? You, my Lady, certainly do not dye your hair in order to deceive others or yourself; you do it only to deceive a little – just a tiny bit – your own image in front of the mirror. I do it for a laugh; you do it seriously. But I assure you that no matter how seriously you take it, you, too, are masquerading, my Lady; and I am not referring to the venerable crown which adorns your forehead, and to which I pay reverence, nor to your ducal mantle; I am speaking only about that memory of yours which you desire to fix artificially in yourself of your blonde colour which on a certain day you found pleasing – or of your dark colour if you were dark: the fading image of your youth! For you instead, Peter Damian, the memory of what you were, of what you did, appears now to be a recognition of past realities that remain inside you — is it not true? — like a dream. It is the same for me — like a dream — and so many of them, to think about it, inexplicable memories ... Ah, well! Nothing surprising, Peter Damian, it will be the same thing tomorrow with our life of today! [*All of a sudden becoming infuriated, he grabs hold of the sackcloth he is wearing.*] This sackcloth right here!

[*With a kind of ferocious joy he is about to tear it off himself while* HAROLD *and* ORDOLPH, *frightened, run to him in order to stop him.*]

Ah, For God's sake! [*He pulls back and, removing the sackcloth, shouts at them:*] Tomorrow, at Bressanone, twenty-seven bishops, German and Lombard, will put their signatures with mine for the deposition of Gregory VII: No Pope is he, but a false friar!

ORDOLPH [*with the other two imploring him to be silent*]: Majesty, Your Majesty, in the name of God!

HAROLD [*inviting him with gestures to put his sackcloth back on*]: Give heed to what he says!

LANDOLPH: The Monsignor is here, together with the Duchess, to intercede on your behalf! [*And secretly he makes urgent signals to the* DOCTOR *to say something quickly.*]

DOCTOR [*bewildered*]: Ah, that is correct ... yes ... We are here to intercede ...

HENRY IV [*repenting at once, almost frightened, allowing the three to put back the sackcloth on his shoulders, and with convulsed hands pulling it down over himself*]: Forgive me ... yes, oh, yes ... forgive me. Forgive me, Monsignor, forgive me, my Lady. I feel, I swear to you, I feel the whole weight of the anathema. [*He bends over, holding his head between his hands as if in expectation of something about to crush him; and he remains this way for a while, but then with a different voice, but without moving, he says quietly, in confidence to* LANDOLPH, *to* HAROLD *and to* ORDOLPH:] I don't know why, but today I cannot manage to be humble before him over there! [*He indicates, as if secretly,* BELCREDI.]

LANDOLPH [*in a whisper*]: But why, Your Majesty, do you insist on believing that he is Peter Damian, when he is not?

HENRY IV [*looking at him in panic*]: Is he not Peter Damian?

HAROLD: But of course not, Your Majesty, he is a poor monk!

HENRY IV [*sorrowful, with an exasperation of sighs*]: Ah, there is not one of us able to evaluate that which he does, when done out of instinct . . . You, perhaps, my Lady, are better able to understand me than any of the others, because you are a woman.* (This is a solemn and decisive moment. I could, you see, at this very moment, while I speak with you, accept the help of the Lombard bishops and take possession of the Pope, imprisoning him here in the castle; then run to Rome to elect an Anti-pope; extend a hand of allegiance to Robert Guiscard – Gregory VII would be lost! I resist the temptation, and believe me, I am wise in doing so. I can feel the aura of the times and the majesty of one who knows how to be what he must be: a Pope! Perhaps you feel like laughing at me, seeing me like this. You would be very stupid, because it shows that you do not understand what political wisdom it is which counsels me to wear these robes of penitence. I tell you that the roles, tomorrow, could be reversed! And what, then, would you do? Would you, by any chance, laugh at the Pope dressed in prisoner's clothes? – No – we would be even: I masquerading as penitent today; he, as prisoner tomorrow. But Heaven help the one who does not know how to wear his mask, be he king or Pope! Perhaps at this time he is a bit too cruel: this, yes.) Think back, my Lady, when Bertha, your daughter, for whom, I repeat, my feelings have changed, [*all of a sudden he turns around to* BELCREDI *and shouts in his face as if he had said no to him:*] changed, changed because of the affection and devotion of which she gave me proof during that terrible moment. [*He stops, shakes from the outburst of anger, and makes an effort to contain himself with a moan of desperation in his throat; then he turns again with sweet and painful humility to the* MARCHESA:] She came with me, my Lady; she is down in the courtyard; she followed me like a beggar, and she is cold, cold from two nights out in the open under the snow! You are her mother. Does this not stir your insides to pity, to make you want to implore, together with him

---

* The passage in brackets which follows may be omitted to maintain the speed of the action.

[*indicates the* DOCTOR], the Pope for his forgiveness, implore him to receive us?

LADY MATILDA [*trembling, with a feeble voice*]: Oh yes, yes, at once . . .

DOCTOR: We will do it, it shall be done!

HENRY IV: And another thing! One more thing! [*He draws them around him and says in a low tone of voice, very secretively:*] It is not enough that he receive me. You are aware of the fact that he can do 'everything' – I tell you, 'everything' – he can even bring back the dead! [*He strikes his chest.*] Here I am, here! You see me! And there is no magic that is not known to him. Well then, Monsignor, my Lady, my true condemnation is this – or that – you see [*points to his portrait on the wall, with a kind of fear*], never to be able to detach myself from this work of magic! Now I am a penitent and I shall remain so; I swear to you that I shall remain so until he receives me. But then the both of you, once the excommunication has been revoked, must beg the Pope on my behalf to do this which he has power to do: to release me from that, there [*points again to the portrait*], and allow me to live wholly this poor life of mine from which I am excluded . . . One cannot be twenty-six years of age for ever, my Lady! And this I ask you also for your daughter's sake: that I may be able to love her as she deserves to be loved, so well disposed as I am now, full of tenderness as I am now, made so by her pity. There you have it. This. I am in your hands . . . [*He bows.*] My Lady, Monsignor!

[*Bowing this way he starts to withdraw by the exit through which he had entered; however, noticing* BELCREDI, *who has moved somewhat closer in order to hear, turn his face to the rear, and believing that his intentions were to steal the imperial crown, to the amazement and bewilderment of everyone there, he runs to take it and hide it under his sackcloth, and with a very clever little smile in his eyes and on his lips he returns to his continuous bowing, then disappears. The* MARCHESA *is so deeply moved, she drops suddenly into a chair, almost fainting.*]

ACT TWO

Another room in the villa adjoining the throne-room, furnished with austere, antique furniture. To the right, a few feet above the floor, a sort of small choir stall, surrounded by a wooden banister made of small pillars, interrupted to the side and in the front by two access steps. On the choir stall platform is a table and five period chairs, one at the head and two on either side. The main exit to the rear. To the left, two windows that look out to the garden. To the right, a door leading to the throne-room. It is late afternoon of the same day.

On stage are LADY MATILDA, *the* DOCTOR *and* TITO BELCREDI. *They are having a conversation; but* LADY MATILDA *keeps to one side, looking gloomy, apparently annoyed by what the other two are saying; nevertheless, she cannot help listening, because in her agitated state everything is of interest to her in spite of herself and prevents her from concentrating on developing a certain intention stronger than herself that flashes through her mind. Her attention is attracted by what the other two are saying, because instinctively she feels the need to have her attention kept under control at that moment.*

BELCREDI: It may be, it may be as you say, Doctor, but this is my own impression.

DOCTOR: I am not saying you are wrong; but believe me, it is only . . . as I said, an impression.

BELCREDI: I beg your pardon, but he even said it, and very clearly! [*Turning to the* MARCHESA:] Isn't that true, Marchesa?

LADY MATILDA: [*disturbed, turning around*]: What did you say? [*Then, not in accordance:*] Ah, yes . . . But not for the same reason you think.

DOCTOR: He was alluding to the clothes we had on: your mantle [*indicates the* MARCHESA], our Benedictine robes. And all this is childish.

LADY MATILDA [*all of a sudden, turning around in anger*]: Childish? What are you saying, Doctor?

DOCTOR: On the one hand, it is! I beg you to let me explain, Marchesa. But on the other hand, it is much more complicated than you can possibly imagine.

LADY MATILDA: Instead, to me it is absolutely clear.

DOCTOR [*with the indulgent smile a competent person would give those who are incompetent*]: Ah, yes! We must take into consideration that very special psychology of madmen, which allows us to be certain – you see – that they notice things, that they can easily detect someone who is wearing a disguise; and he can recognize it as such; and yes, ladies and gentlemen, at the same time he can believe in it, the way children do, for whom it amounts to a mixture of play and reality. For this reason I said childish. But then, it is extremely complicated in the sense that he has to be perfectly conscious of being an image to himself and for himself: that image of his over there! [*Alluding to the portrait in the throne-room, pointing, therefore, to his left.*]

BELCREDI: He did say that!

DOCTOR: There you are! Perfect! An image before which other images have appeared: our images. Do I make myself clear? Now he, in his delirium – both acute and lucid – was at once able to detect a difference between his image and ours; that is, that in ours, in our images, there was make-believe. All madmen are always armed with a constant and watchful diffidence. But that is all there is to it! And naturally the game we played around his could not seem pitiful to him. And his seemed all the more tragic to us in that he, as if in defiance – am I clear? – and induced by diffidence, wanted to reveal it precisely as the game it was; so it is for his as well, yes, my friends, appearing before us as he did, wearing a bit of dye on his temples and on his cheeks, and telling us that he put it on intentionally, for a laugh!

LADY MATILDA [*bursting out again*]: No. That's not it, Doctor! That's not it! That is not it at all!

DOCTOR: And why is that not it?

LADY MATILDA [*resolute, trembling*]: I am absolutely certain that he recognized me!

DOCTOR: That is not possible . . . not possible . . .

BELCREDI [*at the same time*]: Certainly not!

LADY MATILDA [*still more determined, nearly in a convulsion*]: He recognized me, I tell you. When he came close to me and spoke to me, looking into my eyes, directly into my eyes, he did recognize me!

BELCREDI: But if he was talking about your daughter . . .

LADY MATILDA: It's not true! About me! He was talking about me!

BELCREDI: Yes, perhaps when he said . . .

LADY MATILDA [*at once, without concern*]: About my dyed hair! But didn't you notice how he quickly added 'or the memory of your dark colour, if you were dark'? He remembered perfectly well that 'then' I was dark.

BELCREDI: Ridiculous! Nonsense!

LADY MATILDA [*paying no attention to him, turning to the* DOCTOR]: My hair, Doctor, is, in fact, dark – like my daughter's. And for this reason he began talking about her.

BELCREDI: But if he doesn't even know your daughter! He's never seen her!

LADY MATILDA: Precisely! You are incapable of understanding anything! By my daughter he meant me: me, the way I was then!

BELCREDI: This is catching! It's catching!

LADY MATILDA [*in a low voice, with contempt*]: Catching! You fool!

BELCREDI: I beg your pardon, but were you ever his wife? Were you? Your daughter, in his delirium, is his wife. Bertha of Susa.

LADY MATILDA: That is precisely it! Because I, no longer dark-haired the way he remembered me, but 'this way', blonde, introduced myself to him as 'Adelaida', the mother. My daughter does not exist for him, he has never seen her – you said it yourself. So how would he know whether she is blonde or dark-haired?

BELCREDI: But he said dark-haired speaking in general terms. My God, the way one does when one wants to fix the memory of youth in the colour of the hair, whether it be dark or blonde. And you, as usual, begin to jump to conclusions! Doctor, you said I was the one who should not have come – but it is she who shouldn't have come!

LADY MATILDA [*overcome for a moment by* BELCREDI's *observation, she recovers herself; still absorbed, she is agitated by doubt*]: No, no . . . he was speaking about me . . . He spoke always to me, and with me, and about me . . .

BELCREDI: Goodness gracious! He didn't give me a chance to catch my breath, and you are telling me that he was always talking about you! Unless, of course, you think he was also alluding to you when he was talking to Peter Damian!

LADY MATILDA [*with an air of defiance, almost breaking all the limits of good behaviour*]: Who knows? Are you able to tell me why immediately, from the very start, he showed an aversion for you, and only you?

[*From the tone of the question the answer should appear quite explicitly to be: 'Because he has understood that you are my lover!' BELCREDI senses this as well and for a moment he is caught there with an empty smile of bewilderment.*]

DOCTOR: The reason, if you will allow me, may also be found in the fact that the only visit announced to him was that of the Duchess Adelaida and the Abbot of Cluny. Finding himself in the presence of a third party, whose visit had not been announced to him, at once the diffidence . . .

BELCREDI: There you are, exactly, his diffidence made him see me as an enemy: Peter Damian. But since she has got it into her head that he recognized her . . .

LADY MATILDA: On this particular point there is no doubt! His eyes told me so, Doctor. You know how there can be that certain way of looking that . . . that leaves no possible doubt. It lasted, perhaps, no more than an instant. What more can I say?

DOCTOR: It is not to be excluded: a single lucid moment . . .

LADY MATILDA: That could be it, perhaps! And then his words seemed to me to be full, so full of regret for my youth and for his own – and for the horrible thing that happened to him, and that has held him there, in that masquerade from which he is unable to release himself and from which he wants so much to free himself.

BELCREDI: Of course! So that he can start his love affair with your daughter. Or with you, as you believe, now that he has been made tender by your pity.

LADY MATILDA: Of which there is much, I beg you to believe!

BELCREDI: Clearly so, Marchesa! So much so that even a miracle-worker would most probably attribute it to a miracle.

DOCTOR: Will you allow me to speak now? I do not perform miracles, because I am a doctor and not a magician. I paid strict attention to everything he said, and I repeat that that certain analogical elasticity, common to all systematized delirium, is evidently in his case already very — how shall I put it? — very relaxed. The elements of his delirium, in other words, no longer hold together. It seems to me that now he has difficulty in finding equilibrium with this superimposed personality of his because sudden recollections pull him away — and this is most comforting — not from a state of incipient apathy but rather from a morbid setting for reflexive melancholy, which demonstrates a . . . yes, a considerable amount of cerebral activity. I repeat: very comforting. Now here you have it, if with this violent trick we have devised . . .

LADY MATILDA [turning to the window, with a lamenting tone of one who is ill]: How is it that the car still has not returned? In three and a half hours . . .

DOCTOR [dazed]: What is it you said?

LADY MATILDA: The automobile, doctor! It's been more than three and one half hours!

DOCTOR [taking his watch out and looking at it]: More than four according to this!

LADY MATILDA: It should have been here at least a half hour ago. But, as usual . . .

BELCREDI: Perhaps they can't find the gown.

LADY MATILDA: But I told them exactly where it is! [She is extremely impatient.] Frida, I forgot . . . Where is Frida?

BELCREDI [leaning out of the window a little]: Perhaps she's in the garden with Carlo.

DOCTOR: He will persuade her to overcome her fear . . .

BELCREDI: But it's not fear, Doctor. Don't believe it! The fact is she's fed up with it.

LADY MATILDA: Do me the favour of not even trying to convince her! I know how she is!

DOCTOR: We'll wait patiently. In any case, it will all be done in a moment's time, and it has to be done in the evening. If we succeed in shaking him up, I was saying, and with this violent blow breaking all at once the already loosened threads which still bind him to his fiction, returning to him that which he himself asks for (he said it: 'One cannot always be twenty-six years old, my Lady!'), giving him freedom from this condemnation of his, which even he feels is a condemnation, then there you have it, in short: if we are able to succeed in reacquiring in an instant his sensation of the distance of time . . .

BELCREDI [*at once*]: He'll be cured! [*Then pronouncing every syllable ironically:*] We'll pull him out of it!

DOCTOR: There is hope we can have him back again. He is like a watch that has stopped at a certain hour. Yes, it is as though we were here holding our watches in our hands, waiting for that same hour to strike again – there, one good shake! – and let's hope it starts telling the right time again after having stopped for so long.

[*At this point the* MARQUIS CARLO DI NOLLI *enters through the main door.*]

LADY MATILDA: Oh, Carlo . . . And Frida? Where has she gone?

DI NOLLI: Here she comes. She'll be right here.

DOCTOR: Has the car come?

DI NOLLI: Yes.

LADY MATILDA: Ah, yes? Has the gown arrived?

DI NOLLI: It's been here for quite some time now.

DOCTOR: Oh, very good, then.

LADY MATILDA [*trembling*]: Where is she, then? Where is she?

DI NOLLI [*shrugging his shoulders and smiling sadly, like someone who lends himself reluctantly to a bad joke*]: You'll see . . . [*indicating the main entrance:*] Here she is . . .

BERTHOLD [*appears at the threshold of the entrance and announces solemnly*]: Her Highness the Marchesa Matilda of Canossa!

[*And at once* FRIDA *enters, magnificent and very beautiful, dressed as the 'Marchesa Matilda of Tuscany' in her mother's original gown, and she appears to be the living image copied from the portrait in the throne-room.*]

FRIDA [*passing near* BERTHOLD, *who bows, she says with an imposing air of disdain*]: Of Tuscany, of Tuscany, if you please. Canossa is the name of one of my castles.

BELCREDI [*admiring her*]: Just look at that! Just look! She seems another person!

LADY MATILDA: She looks like me! My God, do you see? Stop there, Frida! Do you see? She is my exact portrait, alive!

DOCTOR: Yes, yes . . . Perfect! Perfect! The portrait!

BELCREDI: Ah yes, there's no arguing . . . she's quite that! Look, look! She's quite something!

FRIDA: Don't make me laugh, or I shall burst. I must say, Mamma, what a tiny waist you had. I had to suck it all in so that I could fit into it!

LADY MATILDA [*nervous, adjusting the gown*]: Wait . . . Stop. These pleats . . . Is it really so tight on you?

FRIDA: I'm suffocating. Please hurry, for Heaven's sake . . .

DOCTOR: Eh, but we must wait until it is evening . . .

FRIDA: No, no I can't resist! I'll never make it till evening!

LADY MATILDA: But why did you put it on so soon?

FRIDA: As soon as I saw it! The temptation! Irresistible . . .

LADY MATILDA: You could have at least called me! Have someone help you . . . It's still all creased, my God . . .

FRIDA: I noticed, Mamma. But they are old creases . . . They will be difficult to get rid of.

DOCTOR: It doesn't matter, Marchesa! The illusion is perfect! [*Then drawing closer and inviting her to step up a little further in front of her daughter without, however, blocking her:*] With your permission. That's it, take your position, there, keep a certain distance – a little further up now . . .

BELCREDI: To produce the sensation of the distance of time!

LADY MATILDA [*turning slightly towards him*]: Twenty years later! A disaster, isn't it?

BELCREDI: Let's not exaggerate now!

DOCTOR [*extremely embarrassed, in order to improve things*]: No, no! I was also saying . . . I meant; I meant the gown . . . I meant in order to see . . .

BELCREDI [*laughing*]: But as far as the gown is concerned, Doctor, twenty years won't do it. It's eight hundred. An abyss! Do you really want to push him into making the jump? [*Pointing first to* FRIDA *then to the* MARCHESA:] From there to here? You'll be collecting his pieces in a basket. My friends, do think about it. I am speaking in all seriousness: for us it is a matter of twenty years, two dresses and a masquerade. But for him, as you say, Doctor, if he has fixed himself in time, if he is living there [*points to* FRIDA] with her, eight hundred years ago, I tell you that the dizziness from the jump will be such that, having dropped into the midst of all of us . . .

[*The* DOCTOR *makes a negative sign with his finger.*]

You think not?

DOCTOR: No. Because life, my dear Baron, goes on. Here – this life of ours will immediately become real for him too, and it will take hold of him at once, quickly tearing from him the illusion and revealing to him that the eight hundred years you talk about are only twenty. It is a kind of trick, you see, similar to the one of jumping into the empty space, for example, belonging to the Masonic rite, which appears to be quite a feat when it actually amounts to going down one stair!

BELCREDI: Oh, what a discovery! But of course! Just look at Frida and the Marchesa, Doctor! Which one is further ahead? We old people, Doctor! Yes, the young ones think they are further ahead. It's not true. We are further along in the sense that time belongs more to us than to them.

DOCTOR: If only we were not so estranged by the past.

BELCREDI: Not at all! Since when? If they [*pointing to* FRIDA *and* DI NOLLI] still have to do what we have already done, Doctor: grow old doing over again more or less the same silly things we did . . . the illusion is this: one enters life ahead of those in front of you! It's not true! No sooner are we born than we begin to die, so that whoever began first is further ahead than the others. And youngest of us all is Adam, our father. Look over there [*indicating* FRIDA], eight hundred years younger than all of us, the Marchesa, **Matilda** of Tuscany. [*And he bows deeply to her.*]

DI NOLLI: I beg you, please, Tito, no more joking.

BELCREDI: Ah, if you think I am joking.

DI NOLLI: Of course, my God ... From the moment you arrived ...

BELCREDI: What do you mean? I even dressed up as a Benedictine ...

DI NOLLI: That's right, and for a serious reason ...

BELCREDI: Eh, let me tell you ... if it has been serious for the others ... There you are, take Frida, now, for example ... [*Then, turning to the* DOCTOR:] I swear to you, Doctor, I still don't understand what it is you want to do.

DOCTOR [*annoyed*]: You shall see. Let me handle it, if you don't mind! If you see the Marchesa still dressed this way ...

BELCREDI: Ah, why, does she also have to ...?

DOCTOR: Of course! Certainly! Wearing a similar gown which is over there, so that he thinks he has the Marchesa Matilda of Canossa standing before him.

FRIDA [*while talking softly to* DI NOLLI, *warning him that the* DOCTOR *is mistaken*]: Of Tuscany! From Tuscany!

DOCTOR [*as above*]: It's the same thing!

BELCREDI: Ah, I understand now! He's going to find two of them standing there in front ...?

DOCTOR: Two, precisely. And then ...

FRIDA [*calling him to one side*]: Do come here, Doctor. Listen!

DOCTOR: I am here! [*He draws close to the two young people and pretends to give them an explanation.*]

BELCREDI [*softly to* LADY MATILDA]: Eh, in the name of God! So, therefore ...

LADY MATILDA [*turning around with a firm look*]: What?

BELCREDI: Are you really as interested as all this? So much so that you will lend yourself to all this? It's an enormous task for a woman!

LADY MATILDA: For an ordinary woman!

BELCREDI: Ah, no, my dear, for all women in this case! It's an abnegation ...

LADY MATILDA: I owe it to him.

BELCREDI: Don't lie. You know you are not degrading yourself.

LADY MATILDA: Well then? What's this abnegation all about?

BELCREDI: Just enough not to degrade you in the eyes of others, but enough to offend me.

LADY MATILDA: Who has you in mind at this moment!

DI NOLLI [*stepping forward*]: All right, that's it, then, yes, yes, we'll do it like that . . . [*Turning to* BERTHOLD:] Oh you, there. Go and call one of those three men over there!

BERTHOLD: At once. [*Exits through main door.*]

LADY MATILDA: But first we must pretend we are leaving.

DI NOLLI: Precisely. That's why I've called him: to see to your departure. [*To* BELCREDI:] You don't have to. Why don't you stay here.

BELCREDI [*nodding his head ironically*]: Sure, I don't care, I needn't bother . . .

DI NOLLI: So as not to arouse his suspicion again, you see?

BELCREDI: Of course. *Quantité négligeable!* That's me.

DOCTOR: We must provide him with the absolute certainty that we have gone away, that we have absolutely left.

[LANDOLPH *followed by* BERTHOLD *enter right exit.*]

LANDOLPH: With your permission?

DI NOLLI: Come in, come in . . . Your name is Lolo, isn't it?

LANDOLPH: Lolo or Landolph, whichever you choose!

DI NOLLI: All right. Pay attention. Now the Doctor and the Marchesa will be leaving . . .

LANDOLPH: Very well. All that needs to be said is that the Pontiff has conceded to the reception. He is there in his rooms moaning and sorry for all that he has said and desperate that he may not be graced with the Pontiff's pardon. Would you be so kind . . . if you would be good enough to put on those robes again.

DOCTOR: Yes, yes, let's go, let's go . . .

LANDOLPH: Just a moment. May I be allowed to suggest something to you? I suggest you add that the Marchesa Matilda of Tuscany also begged with the others that the Pontiff grant him the grace to receive him.

LADY MATILDA: There you are! You see he has recognized me?

LANDOLPH: No. Forgive me. It is only that he fears so much the aversion of the Marchesa who played host to the Pope in her castle. It's strange: in history, as far as I can tell – but then you ladies and gentlemen are certainly in a position to know this better than I – nowhere is it said, in truth, that Henry IV secretly loved the Marchesa of Tuscany.

LADY MATILDA [*at once*]: No, certainly not, not at all. In fact, it's entirely different.

LANDOLPH: There you are, that's what I thought! But he says that he loved her – he's always saying it . . . And now he is afraid that the disdain she has for this secret love may work to his disadvantage with the Pontiff.

BELCREDI: We must make him understand that this aversion no longer exists!

LANDOLPH: Fine. Very good.

LADY MATILDA [*to* LANDOLPH]: Very good, indeed! [*Then to* BELCREDI:] Because history records precisely, in case you were not aware, that the Pope actually did yield to the supplications of the Marchesa Matilda and the Abbot of Cluny. And let me tell you, my dear Belcredi, that back then – during the time of the cavalcade – my intentions were precisely to take advantage of this fact in order to show him that my heart was no longer as hostile towards him as he might have imagined.

BELCREDI: Well then, how surprising, my dear Marchesa. Go on, do go on with the story . . .

LANDOLPH: Well then, in that case, Madame could save herself a double disguise and present herself with the Monsignor [*indicates the* DOCTOR] in the guise of the Marchesa of Tuscany.

DOCTOR [*quickly, with force*]: No, no! For God's sake not that way! It would ruin everything. The impression received from the confrontation must be unexpected and come all of a sudden. No, no, Marchesa, let's go, let's go: you must appear again as the Duchess Adelaida, mother of the Empress. And then we leave. This is more important than anything else: that he knows we have left. Come now, come. We must not lose more time. There is still so much more to be done.

[*The* DOCTOR, LADY MATILDA *and* LANDOLPH *exit right*.]

FRIDA: I am beginning to feel frightened again . . .

DI NOLLI: Not again, Frida!

FRIDA: It would have been better if I had seen him beforehand . . .

DI NOLLI: But believe me, there is nothing to be frightened of!

FRIDA: He's not furious, is he?

DI NOLLI: Certainly not. He's calm.

BELCREDI [*with ironical and sentimental affectation*]: Melancholy! Didn't you hear that he loves you?

FRIDA: Thanks a lot. It's precisely for that reason!

BELCREDI: He has no intention of hurting you . . .

DI NOLLI: It will take but a moment . . .

FRIDA: I know, but there in the dark, with him . . .

DI NOLLI: Just for a single moment, and I will be close by you and the others will all be behind the door, ready and waiting to run in. As soon as he sees your mother there in front of him, you understand, your part is over and you will be finished . . .

BELCREDI: My fear, however, is something else: that we will strike out!

DI NOLLI: Don't start all that again. To me the remedy sounds most effective!

FRIDA: To me too, to me too! I feel it in my insides . . . All of me is trembling.

BELCREDI: But insane people, my dears, (without knowing it, none the less!) have a certain joy which we do not take into account . . .

DI NOLLI [*interrupting, annoyed*]: Now what joy would that be? Come on!

BELCREDI [*with force*]: They do not reason.

DI NOLLI: Excuse me, but what does reason have to do with it?

BELCREDI: What! Isn't it all a kind of reasoning process which he will have to perform, according to us, upon seeing her [*indicates* FRIDA] and seeing her mother. We orchestrated the whole thing!

DI NOLLI: No, not at all. What's this reasoning business? We present him with a double image of his own creation, as the Doctor has said!

BELCREDI [*with a sudden outburst*]: Listen, I have never understood why they get a degree in medicine!

DI NOLLI [*stunned*]: Who?

BELCREDI: The psychiatrists!

DI NOLLI: Oh that's a good one, and in what would you like them to get a degree?

FRIDA: If they are alienists, what else?

BELCREDI: Of course, in law, my dear! It's all talk! And the more one knows how to talk, the better he is! 'Analogous elasticity', 'the sensation of the distance of time'. And meanwhile the first thing they tell you is that they don't perform miracles – when a miracle is what is truly needed. But they know that the more they tell you that they are not miracle-workers, the more others believe in their seriousness. They do not perform miracles, and it is amazing how they always manage to land on their feet!

BERTHOLD [*who had been spying from behind the right exit by looking through the keyhole of the door*]: There they are! There they are! They seem to be coming here . . .

DI NOLLI: Are they?

BERTHOLD: He seems to want to accompany them . . . Yes, yes, here he is; he's here!

DI NOLLI: Let's leave in that case. Let's leave at once! [*Turning to* BERTHOLD *before leaving:*] You remain here!

BERTHOLD: Must I stay?

[*Without answering him,* DI NOLLI, FRIDA *and* BELCREDI *hurry out the main exit, leaving* BERTHOLD *just standing in bewilderment. The door to the right opens and* LANDOLPH *enters first and quickly bows; then* LADY MATILDA *enters with mantle and ducal crown, as in the First Act; then the* DOCTOR *in the robes of the Abbot of Cluny;* HENRY IV *in regal dress is between them; finally* ORDULPH *and* HAROLD *enter.*]

HENRY IV [*continuing with the discourse supposedly begun in the throne-room*]: And I ask you: how can I be astute if you believe me to be stubborn . . .?

DOCTOR: No, no, not stubborn, Heaven forbid!

HENRY IV [*smiling, satisfied*]: Then for you I am truly astute?

DOCTOR: No, no, neither stubborn nor astute!

HENRY IV [*He stops and exclaims in the tone of one who wants to point out in a benevolent way, but doing so ironically, that things cannot remain as they are*]: Monsignor! If stubbornness is not a vice that can be accompanied by astuteness, I was hoping that by denying me the one you would have at least wished to grant me a bit of

astuteness. I can assure you that for me it is most important. But
if you wish to keep it all for yourself . . .

DOCTOR: Ah, what, I? Do you find me to be astute?

HENRY IV: No, Monsignor! What are you saying! You don't seem
to be that at all! [*Cutting off to turn to* LADY MATILDA:] With
your permission, here on the threshold, a word in confidence to
the Duchess. [*He leads her a few steps to the side and asks her
earnestly and in great secret:*] Is your daughter truly dear to you?

LADY MATILDA [*bewildered*]: But of course, certainly . . .

HENRY IV: And is it your wish that I compensate her with all my
love, with all my devotion for the grave wrongs I have done her
– although you should not give credence to all the dissoluteness
of which my enemies accuse me?

LADY MATILDA: No, no. I do not believe it: I never believed in
it . . .

HENRY IV: Well then, is it your wish?

LADY MATILDA: What?

HENRY IV: That I return to loving your daughter. [*He looks at her
and quickly adds in a mysterious tone of warning mixed with alarm:*]
Do not be a friend, do not be a friend of the Marchesa of
Tuscany!

LADY MATILDA: And yet, I tell you again, that she has not begged,
that she has not implored any less than we have in order to obtain
your pardon . . .

HENRY IV [*quickly, softly, trembling*]: Don't tell me that! Don't tell
me about it! For God's sake, my Lady, do you not see the effect it
has on me?

LADY MATILDA [*looks at him, then very softly, as if in confidence*]: Do
you still love her?

HENRY IV [*bewildered*]: Still? How can you say still? You know
then, perhaps? No one knows! And no one must know!

LADY MATILDA: But perhaps she, yes, she knows, if she has begged
so on your behalf.

HENRY IV [*looks at her awhile and then says*]: And you say that you
love your daughter? [*Brief pause. He turns to the* DOCTOR *with a
touch of laughter.*] It's all too true, my discovering, but only
afterwards – too late, too late – that I have a wife. And even

now, yes, I have to have her; and without a doubt I have her. But I could swear to you that hardly ever do I think about her. It may be a sin but I don't feel for her; I don't feel her in my heart. It is amazing, however, that even her mother has no feelings for her in her heart! Admit it, my Lady, you care very little about her! [*Turning to the* DOCTOR *in exasperation:*] She talks to me about that other woman [*becoming more and more excited*] with insistence, with the kind of insistence I cannot understand at all!

LANDOLPH [*humbly*]: Perhaps in order to rid you of a contrary opinion, Majesty, which you may have conceived of the Marchesa of Tuscany. [*And disturbed at having allowed himself to make this observation, he quickly adds:*] I mean, of course, at this moment . . .

HENRY IV: Now you too maintain that she was my friend?

LANDOLPH: Yes, at this moment, yes, Majesty!

LADY MATILDA: There you are, yes, precisely for this . . .

HENRY IV: I understand. What it means, then, is that you do not believe that I love her. I understand. I understand. No one ever believed it; no one ever suspected. All the better this way. Enough. The end. [*Stops short, turning to the* DOCTOR *with heart and face completely different.*] Monsignor, did you see? The conditions upon which the Pope has stipulated for the retraction of my excommunication have nothing, but absolutely nothing, to do with the reason for which he had excommunicated me. Tell Pope Gregory that we shall see each other again at Bressanone. And you, my Lady, if you by chance meet your daughter down in the courtyard of the castle of your friend the Marchesa, what can I tell you? Have her come up, and we shall see if I can succeed in keeping both wife and Empress close to my side. Many women have come this far to present themselves, assuring me and reassuring me that they are she. The one who I, knowing I already possessed her . . . yes, of course, I even tried sometimes . . . nothing to be ashamed of: after all, it's my wife! But all of them, when they said they were Bertha and told me they were from Susa – I have no idea why – began laughing! [*As if confidentially:*] Do you understand? In bed – I without these clothes – she too . . . yes, my God, with no clothes . . . a man and a woman . . . it is only natural. When we're like that we no longer think about who we are and our dress, hanging there, hovers like a ghost! [*And in another tone of voice, in confidence to the* DOCTOR:] And I think, Monsignor, that ghosts, in general, are basically nothing more than small disarrangements of the spirit: images that one is unable to contain within the realm of sleep. They reveal themselves also in the waking hours, during the day, and they frighten us. I am always full of fear when at night I see them before me – so many discomposed images, that laugh, unseated from their horses. Sometimes I am even afraid of my own blood that is pulsing in my arteries like the gloomy thud of footsteps in distant rooms in the silence of the night . . . But that's enough of that, I have kept you standing here much too long. My respects, my Lady, my kind regards, Monsignor.

> [*At the threshold of the main door to where he has accompanied them he dismisses them, accepting their bows.* LADY MATILDA *and the* DOCTOR *leave. He closes the door and turns around suddenly, changed.*]

Clowns! Clowns! Clowns! A piano made of colours! All I had to do was touch it: white, red, yellow, green . . . And that other fellow there: Peter Damian. Ah, ha! Perfect! Figured him right out! He's afraid to appear before me again!

> [*He says this in a gay and gushing frenzy, moving around from one place to another, turning his eyes, until all of a sudden he no longer sees* BERTHOLD, *who is more than stunned and full of fear from the unexpected change. He stops in front of him and points him out to the other three companions, they, too, bewildered by amazement.*]

Just look at this imbecile standing here now watching me with his mouth hanging open. [*He takes him by the shoulders and shakes him.*] Don't you understand? Don't you see how I handle them, how I play them for what they're worth, how I make them appear before me as frightened clowns! And one thing only frightens them, oh: that I tear off their ridiculous masks and reveal the disguise, as if it were not my very self who forced them into masquerading to satisfy my own pleasure of playing the madman!

LANDOLPH, HAROLD, ORDULPH [*upset, amazed, looking at each other*]: What? What did he say? But then, this means . . .

HENRY IV [*at their exclamations he suddenly turns and shouts imperiously*]: That's enough! Enough of this! I'm fed up with all this! [*Then suddenly, as if having thought it over he cannot come to terms with it and is unable to believe it:*] By God! What impudence to appear here before me, at this time, with her lover at her side . . . And with the nerve to pretend they were doing it out of pity, so as not to infuriate a poor wretch already out of the world, out of time, out of life! Eh, otherwise that poor wretch, imagine if he would have put up with such tyranny! They, of course, every day, every moment expect others to be how they want them to be, but that's not an oppression, that — why it's their way of thinking, their way of seeing, of feeling: each to his own! You have your own way too, no? Certainly! Now what would yours be like? Like that of the flock, miserable, fleeting, uncertain . . . And those others take advantage of this, they put you down and make you accept their way, to make you feel and see as they do! Or at least they think they do. Because, then, what have they succeeded in imposing? Words! Words that anyone can interpret and repeat in his own way! Ah, but that is just how so-called public opinion is formed! And it means trouble for that man who one fine day finds himself stamped with one of these words that everyone repeats! For example, 'crazy'! For instance, who knows, 'imbecile'! Would you mind telling me how a person can keep quiet when he knows that out there somebody is going around doing his best to persuade others that you are just the way he pictures you to be, doing his best to fix you in the estimation of others according to his own personal judgement of you? 'Crazy', 'crazy'! I do not mean to say that now I do it as a joke! Before, before I hit my head falling from a horse . . . [*He stops short, noticing that the four men are getting nervous, more perplexed and amazed than ever before.*] You look one another in the eyes? [*He imitates grotesquely their look of amazement.*] Ah, eh! Such a revelation! Am I or am I not? Eh, why not? Yes, of course, I am crazy! [*He becomes terrifying.*] Well, by God, in that case, down on your knees! On your knees! [*He forces each of them to kneel down one by one.*] I order all of you to kneel down before me — yes, like that! Now touch the floor with your foreheads three times. Down!

Everybody must assume this position before crazy people! [*At the sight of the four of them kneeling he quickly feels his ferocious gaiety fade away, and he is annoyed.*] Up, off with you, sheep. On your feet! You obeyed me, did you not? You could have put me in a straitjacket. Crush a person with the weight of a single word? But it is nothing! What is it? A fly! All of life is crushed this way by the weight of the word – the weight of the dead. Here I am, right here. Can you seriously believe that Henry IV is still alive? Nevertheless, here I am, and I talk and order you around, you the living! I want you this way! Does this seem to be a joke to you as well: that the dead continue to lead their lives? Yes, here it is a joke, but once you leave here, into the living world . . . The day is breaking. All of time is before you. The dawn! This day we have ahead of us, you say, we'll make of it whatever we like! Yes? You will? Say goodbye to all traditions! Goodbye to old inventions. Go on and speak! Repeat all those words that have always been said! Do you think you are alive and living? Remasticate the life of the dead! [*He stops in front of* BERTHOLD, *who is by now stupefied.*] You don't understand a thing, do you? What is your name?

BERTHOLD: I? . . . Eh . . . Berthold . . .

HENRY IV: What do you mean, Berthold, you fool! Here, just between the two of us, what's your name?

BERTHOLD: My na . . . name is . . . my name is really Fino . . .

HENRY IV [*feeling the sense of admonition and looks of warning coming from the other three, he immediately turns to them in order to silence them*]: Fino?

BERTHOLD: Fino Pagliuca, yes sir.

HENRY IV [*turning again to the others*]: Of course, I've heard you use your names talking among yourselves – many times! (*To* LANDOLPH:) Your name is Lolo, no?

LANDOLPH: Yes, sir . . . [*Then, in a burst of joy:*] Oh my God! . . . But then!

HENRY IV [*at once, brusquely*]: What?

LANDOLPH [*suddenly, turning pale*]: No . . . I mean . . .

HENRY IV: Am I no longer crazy? Of course not! Can't you see me? We're playing a joke on those who think I am. [*To* HAROLD:] I

know your name is Franco . . . [*To* ORDULPH:] And you, wait
now . . .

ORDULPH: Momo!

HENRY IV [*as above*]: That's it: Momo! Nice, isn't it?

LANDOLPH [*as above*]: But then this means . . . Oh God . . .

HENRY IV: What? Nothing! Let's have a good, long laugh over it
. . . [*And he laughs.*] Ha, ha, ha, ha, ha, ha!

LANDOLPH, HAROLD, ORDULPH [*looking at one another, uncertain,
bewildered, between joy and dismay*]: He's cured! Is it true? How is
he?

HENRY IV: Quiet! Quiet! [*To* BERTHOLD:] You're not laughing?
Are you still offended? Of course not! My words weren't directed
at you, you know? It's convenient for everyone, you understand?
It's convenient for everybody to make others think that certain
people are crazy in order to have an excuse to keep them shut
away. Do you know why? Because you can't put up with
hearing them speak. What can I say about those people, the ones
who have just left? That one is a whore, the other a filthy
libertine, the other an imposter . . . It is not true! No one can
believe it! But everyone stands there listening to me, and they are
struck with fear. Well now, I would like to know why, if it is
not true. You cannot possibly believe what crazy people say! And
yet, they stand there listening like this: with their eyes wide open
from fright. Why? Tell me, you tell me, why? I'm calm now,
see?

BERTHOLD: But because . . . perhaps, they think that . . .

HENRY IV: No, dear friend . . . no, my dear . . . Look me straight in
the eyes. I am not saying it is true, rest assured! Nothing is true!
But now look me in the eyes!

BERTHOLD: Yes, there you are, so now what?

HENRY IV: You see it? Do you see it? You yourself. Now you have
it, too, that fear in your eyes! Because I appear to you to be
crazy. There's the proof! There's the proof for you! [*And he
laughs.*]

LANDOLPH [*gathering his courage, speaking for the others, exasperated*]:
What proof?

HENRY IV: This fright of yours, because now, once again, I appear to you to be crazy! And yet, by God, you know it! You believe me. Until now you believed that I was crazy! Is that true or isn't it? [*He looks at them a while, sees them terrified.*] But you see it. You feel that it can also turn into terror, this fear of yours – something that makes you feel the ground beneath your feet disappear and takes away the air you breathe. It must be that way, gentlemen. Do you know what it means to find yourself standing in front of a crazy person? To find yourself face to face with a person who shakes the foundations of everything you have built up in and around you: that logic, the logic of all your constructions! Eh! What do you expect! Crazy people, bless them, construct without logic. Or with their own logic that flies like a feather! Voluble! Voluble! This way today and what way tomorrow, who knows! You hold strong and they no longer hold. Voluble! Voluble! You say: 'This cannot be!' and for them everything can be. But you say that it is not true. And why not? Because it does not seem to be true to you, to you, to you [*points to the three of them*] and a hundred thousand others. Eh, my dear fellows! One would have to see, then, what it is, instead, that seems to be true to these other hundred thousand who are not considered to be crazy. And what a show they put on with their concordance, the flowers of logic. I know that for me, when I was a child, the moon in the well appeared to be real. So many things seemed real! And I believed all those other things that other people told me, and I was blissful. Because how terrible it is, terrible if you do not hold on very tight to what seems true to you today and to what will seem true to you tomorrow, even if it is the opposite of what seemed true to you yesterday! How awful it is to have to flounder, the way I have, in the thought of this terrible thing which drives one truly mad: that if you are next to someone and looking into his eyes – the way I looked one day into a certain person's eyes – then you can imagine what it is like to be a beggar in front of a door through which you shall never be able to enter. The one who does enter will never be you with your own interior world and the way you see it and touch it, but rather someone unknown to you, like that other one who in his own impenetrable world sees you and touches you . . .

[*A long sustained pause. The shadows in the room begin to grow darker, increasing that sense of being lost and the profound consternation which the four disguised men share. The Great Disguised One remains detached and absorbed in the thought of the horrible misery which is not only his but everybody's. Then he pulls himself together and starts looking for the four men, whom he feels are no longer around him, and says:*]

It has grown dark here.

ORDULPH [*quickly, moving forward*]: Shall I get the lamp?

HENRY IV [*ironically*]: The lamp, yes . . . You think I do not know that as soon as I turn my back with my oil lamp in hand to go to bed, you turn on the electric lights for yourselves in here as well as in the throne-room: I pretend not to see it . . .

ORDULPH: Ah! Well, then . . .?

HENRY IV: No, it would blind me. I want my lamp.

ORDULPH: Here you are, it's already prepared behind the door.

[*He goes to the main exit, opens the door, takes a few steps in and returns immediately with an antique lamp, the kind you hold by a ring at the top.*]

HENRY IV [*taking the lamp and then pointing to the table in the gallery*]: There we are: a little light. Sit down, there around the table. But not like that! In a nice, relaxed way . . . [*To* HAROLD:] There you are. You sit like that . . . [*He poses him; then to* BERTHOLD:] And you like that . . . [*Poses him.*] This way, that's it! . . . [*He, too, sits down.*] And me here . . . [*Turning his head towards one of the windows:*] One should be able to order a nice ray of decorative light from the moon . . . It is useful, it helps us, the moon. I feel a need for it inside me and often I lose myself in gazing at it from my window. Who would believe from looking at her that she would know that eight hundred years have gone by and that I, seated at my window, cannot be the real Henry IV looking at the moon like any poor, ordinary man might do? But look now, look at this magnificent nocturnal scene: the Emperor among his faithful counsellors . . . Don't you find it pleasant?

LANDOLPH [*softly to* HAROLD, *as if not to break the spell*]: Eh, do you understand? And to think it wasn't true.

HENRY IV: True, what's that?

LANDOLPH [*faltering, as if to excuse himself*]: No . . . it's . . . because as I was saying to him [*indicating* BERTHOLD] – he just took his new position in your service – I was saying just this morning: what a shame that dressed up this way, and then with so many lovely costumes there in the wardrobe . . . and with a room like that one . . . [*Points to the throne-room.*]

HENRY IV: So then? It's a shame, you say?

LANDOLPH: Well, that is . . . that we didn't know . . .

HENRY IV: That you were staging this comedy here for fun?

LANDOLPH: Because we thought that . . .

HAROLD [*to help him out*]: Yes, that it was to be taken seriously!

HENRY IV: What do you mean? Doesn't it seem serious to you?

LANDOLPH: Eh, but if you say . . .

HENRY IV: I say that you are fools! You should have known how to stage it for yourselves, this deception of yours; not to act it out in front of me or in front of those who come to visit me from time to time; but like this, this way, the way you are naturally, from day to day, in front of no one, [*to* BERTHOLD, *taking him by the arm*] only for yourself, do you see, in this fiction of yours you could have eaten, slept and even scratched a shoulder if you felt an itch, feeling yourself alive, truly alive, living in the history of the eleven-hundreds, here at the Court of your Emperor Henry IV! And to think that from here, from this remote age of ours, so colourful and sepulchral, to think that at a distance of eight centuries back, far back, the people of the nineteen-hundreds are squabbling in the meantime, struggling in endless anxiety merely to know what fortune has in store for them, to see how they will be treated by fate which holds them in such anguish, in so much agitation. While you, instead, are already a part of history! With me! No matter how sad my lot, how horrible the facts, how bitter the battles and sorrowful the events: it is already history and none of it can ever change, it can never change, do you understand? It's become all fixed for ever: from there you could have rested comfortably, admiring how every effect follows obediently from its cause, with perfect logic, and how every happening unfolds precisely and coherently in its every detail. The pleasure, the pleasure of history, oh yes, how grand it is!

LANDOLPH: Ah, beautiful, beautiful!

HENRY IV: Beautiful, but finished! Now that you know about it, I can no longer go on with it! [*Takes the lamp to go to bed.*] Furthermore, neither could any of you, if up until now you haven't understood the reason for it. No I am sick of it! [*More or less to himself, with violent but contained anger:*] By God! I am going to make her sorry she ever came here! As a mother-in-law, oh, she goes and dresses up herself for me . . . and he as an abbot . . . And with them they even bring a doctor to study me . . . And who knows, they may even be hoping to cure me . . . Clowns! I would like to have the satisfaction of slapping at least one of them in the face: yes, he's the one. Isn't he a famous swordsman? He'll run me through . . . But we'll see, we'll see . . .

[*A knock at the main door.*]

Who is it?

VOICE OF JOHN: *Deo gratias!*

HAROLD [*very happy, as if because of the possibility of playing another joke*]: Ah it's John, it's John, coming as he does every night to play the monk.

LANDOLPH: [*to* ORDULPH]: It's got to look like the truth, you understand?

HENRY IV: Precisely. Like the truth! Because only in that way can truth never be a joke! [*He goes to open the door and lets in* JOHN, *who is dressed as a humble friar with a rolled-up parchment under his arm.*] Come in, come in, Father! [*Then, assuming a grave and tragic tone of gloomy resentment:*] All of the documents concerning my life and my reign that have dealt favourably with me have been destroyed deliberately by my enemies. This only has escaped destruction, this, my life written by a humble monk who is devoted to me – and you would laugh at it? [*He turns lovingly to* JOHN *and invites him to sit in front of the table.*] Sit down, Father, sit here. And the lamp next to you. [*He takes the lamp which he is still holding and puts it next to him.*] Write, write.

JOHN [*unfolding the roll of parchment and preparing to take dictation*]: I am ready now, Your Majesty.

HENRY IV [*dictating*]: 'The decree of peace proclaimed at Mayence helped the poor and the good just as it harmed the bad and the powerful.'

[*The curtain begins to fall.*]

'It brought abundance to the former, hunger and misery to the latter . . .'

ACT THREE

The throne-room, dark. In the dark the back wall is hardly visible. The canvases of the two portraits have been removed and in their place, in the empty frames surrounding the hollow niches, having taken their positions in exactly the same pose as in those portraits, are FRIDA *dressed as the Marchesa of Tuscany, as in the Second Act, and* CARLO DI NOLLI *dressed as Henry IV.*

As the curtain rises for a moment the scene appears empty. The door to the left opens and HENRY IV *enters, holding the lamp by the ring at its top, turns round and speaks to the four young men and* JOHN, *who are supposedly in the adjoining room into which he speaks, as at the end of the Second Act.*

HENRY IV: No. Stay there. Do not get up. I shall manage on my own. Good night. [*He closes the door and moves, sad and tired, to cross the room, heading for the second exit to the right which leads to his quarters.*]

FRIDA [*As soon as she sees that he has moved slightly beyond the height of the throne, she whispers from her niche like one who is about to faint from fear*]: Henry . . .

HENRY IV [*stopping at the sound of the voice, as if sliced down the back by the razor of betrayal, turns his terrified face to the back wall and is instinctively about to raise his arm for protection*]: Who calls me? [*It is not a question, it is an exclamation quivering with a chill of terror, and it does not expect an answer from the darkness and the horrible silence of the room which all of a sudden fills him with the fear that perhaps he is, indeed, crazy.*]

FRIDA [*at that exclamation of terror, no less terrified by the part she has agreed to play, repeats in a voice a bit louder*]: Henry . . . [*But she stretches her neck out a little from her niche in the direction of the other niche, even though she has tried to play her part the way she had been told to.*]

[HENRY IV *cries out and lets the lamp fall from his hand in*

127

order to put his arms around his head and makes a move to run off.]

[*jumping from the niche onto the ledge and shouting like a crazy woman:*] Henry . . . Henry . . . I'm frightened . . . I'm frightened . . . [*And while* DI NOLLI *in turn jumps onto the ledge and from there down to the floor and runs to* FRIDA *who, continuing her fitful screaming, is on the verge of fainting, everyone rushes into the room from the exit to the left: the* DOCTOR, LADY MATILDA, *who is also dressed as the Marchesa of Tuscany,* TITO BELCREDI, LANDOLPH, HAROLD, ORDULPH, BERTHOLD, JOHN. *One of them quickly turns on the light: it is a strange glow coming from light bulbs hidden in the ceiling in such a way that only the area above the scene is illuminated. The others, paying no attention to* HENRY IV, *who stands there watching, stunned by that unexpected eruption of people following the terrifying moment which still causes his entire body to tremble, run with great concern to support and comfort* FRIDA, *who is still shaking as she raves and moans in the arms of her fiancé. Everyone is speaking in confused fashion.*]

DI NOLLI: No, no, Frida . . . Here I am . . . I'm here with you!

DOCTOR [*coming with the others*]: Enough! Enough! There is nothing more to be done . . .

LADY MATILDA: He's cured, Frida! He's cured! Look, you see?

DI NOLLI [*amazed*]: Cured?

BELCREDI: It was just for fun! Calm yourself!

FRIDA [*as above*]: No! I'm frightened! I'm frightened!

LADY MATILDA: But of what? Look at him; see for yourself if it isn't true! It's not true!

DI NOLLI [*as above*]: Not true? What are you saying? Cured?

DOCTOR: Seems so! As far as I'm concerned . . .

BELCREDI: Of course! They told us so! [*Points to the four young men.*]

LADY MATILDA: Yes, for quite some time! He confided in them!

DI NOLLI [*now more indignant than amazed*]: But how? If until a little while ago . . .?

BELCREDI: Hmm! He was acting and laughing behind your back, and also at us who in good faith . . .

DI NOLLI: Is it possible? Also at his sister, right up until her death?

HENRY IV [*who has kept apart from the others, peering at one and then at another under accusation and derision of what all believe to be a cruel joke of his which has now been revealed; the glimmer in his eyes shows that he is considering some kind of revenge which the contempt raging inside him will not allow him to express clearly as yet; at this point he jumps up, offended, with the clear idea of accepting as the truth the fiction which they have insidiously prepared, shouting at the nephew]:* Come on now! Come on, keep talking!

DI NOLLI [*stunned by the shout*]: What do you mean 'come on'?

HENRY IV: It is not only 'your' sister who is dead!

DI NOLLI [*as above*]: My sister! She was yours, I say, whom up to the last moment you forced to appear here as your mother, Agnes!

HENRY IV: And was she not 'your' mother?

DI NOLLI: My mother? My mother, precisely!

HENRY IV: But for me she is dead, 'old and far away', your mother! You have just descended, fresh, from there. [*Points to the niche from which he jumped down.*] And what do you know, how do you know that I have not wept for her a long time, a very long time, in secret, dressed even as I am?

LADY MATILDA [*puzzled, looking at the others*]: What is he saying?

DOCTOR [*extremely impressed, observing him*]: Not so loud, quiet, for Heaven's sake!

HENRY IV: What am I saying? Asking all of you if Agnes was not the mother of Henry IV! [*He turns to* FRIDA *as if she were really the Marchesa of Tuscany.*] It seems to me that you, Marchesa, ought to know!

FRIDA [*still frightened, getting closer to* DI NOLLI]: No, not I! I don't know!

DOCTOR: There, the delirium is returning. Quiet, now, all of you.

BELCREDI [*indignant*]: What delirium, Doctor? He's started acting his part again!

HENRY IV [*quickly*]: I? You have just emptied those two niches over there and he is standing here before me as Henry IV and . . .

BELCREDI: It's about time we stopped with this joke!

HENRY IV: Who said joke?

DOCTOR [*to* BELCREDI, *loudly*]: Do not provoke him, for the love of God!

BELCREDI [*not paying attention to him, louder*]: But they said so, they. [*Points again to the four young men.*] They did! They!

HENRY IV [*turning to look at them*]: You? You said joke?

LANDOLPH [*timid, embarrassed*]: No . . . what I really said was cured!

BELCREDI: And now that's enough of this! Don't you think, Marchesa, that the very sight of him [*indicates* DI NOLLI] as well as yourself dressed that way is becoming somewhat of an intolerable puerility?

LADY MATILDA: Oh, shut up, won't you! Who cares about the dress any more, if he is truly cured.

HENRY IV: Cured? Yes, I am cured! [*To* BELCREDI:] Ah, but not to end this all as quickly as you think! [*Attacks him.*] Do you realize that for twenty years no one has ever dared appear before me here like you and that gentleman? [*Pointing to the* DOCTOR.]

BELCREDI: Of course, I know it! In fact, this morning I, too, appeared before you dressed . . .

HENRY IV: As a monk, yes I know!

BELCREDI: And you took me for Peter Damian, and I certainly didn't laugh, believing, in fact . . .

HENRY IV: That I was crazy! Do you feel like laughing seeing her dressed like this, now that I am cured? And yet, you might have remembered that to my eyes, the way she looks, now – [*Interrupts himself with a show of contempt.*] Ah! [*And quickly turns to the* DOCTOR:] Are you a doctor?

DOCTOR: I, yes . . .

HENRY IV: And you also had a hand in dressing her up as the Marchesa of Tuscany? Do you realize, Doctor, that for a moment there you ran the risk of darkening my mind with madness again? By God, you had talking portraits, you had them jump out alive from their frames . . . [*Contemplates* FRIDA *and* DI NOLLI, *then looks at the* MARCHESA *and finally he looks at the costume he himself is wearing.*] Ah, the combination is very beautiful . . . Two couples . . . Very good, Doctor, very good: for a crazy man . . . [*A slight gesture of the hand towards* BELCREDI:] To him now it must seem like a carnival party out of season, hmm? [*He turns to look at him.*] And now, off with this masquerade costume of mine as well, so that I may leave here with you. Isn't that so?

BELCREDI: With me? With us?

HENRY IV: Where, to the club? In dress suit and white tie? Or home, the both of us together, with the Marchesa?

BELCREDI: Wherever you wish! You wouldn't prefer to continue on here, all alone, and perpetuate what was an unfortunate carnival-day joke, would you? It's really incredible, unbelievable, how you could have done it, once you were free of the misfortune that befell you!

HENRY IV: Indeed! But you see, the fact is that falling from my horse and hitting my head, I actually did go crazy, I did, but I do not know for how long . . .

DOCTOR: Ah, that's it, that's it! Did it last long?

HENRY IV [*very quickly, to the* DOCTOR]: Yes, Doctor, a long time: about twelve years. [*And at once, talking again to* BELCREDI:] And not to be able to see anything any more, my dear fellow, of all that happened after that carnival day, that happened for you and not for me: things, how they changed; friends, how they betrayed me, how my place was taken by others, for example . . . I don't know, let's say in the heart of the lady you loved; who had died and who had disappeared . . . and all this, you know, was really no joke to me, as it seems to you!

BELCREDI: No, but this is not what I am saying. I am talking about afterwards.

HENRY IV: Ah, yes? Afterwards? One day . . . [*He stops and turns to the* DOCTOR.] An extremely interesting case, Doctor. Study me, study me with care! [*Trembling as he speaks:*] All by itself, who knows how, one day, the damage here . . . [*touches his forehead*] I don't know, repaired itself. Little by little I open my eyes, and I am not sure at first whether or not I am still asleep or awake. Then, yes, I am awake; I start touching one thing and another; I see things clearly again . . . Ah! then – as he says [*indicating* BELCREDI] – well, off then, off with this masquerade costume, this nightmare! Let's open the windows; let's breathe in life! Let's run out. Away. [*All of a sudden calming his fervour:*] Where? To do what? To have everybody pointing me out in secret as Henry IV,

no longer like this, but arm in arm with you, among my dear
life-long friends!

BELCREDI: Of course not! What are you saying? Why?

LADY MATILDA: Who could any longer . . .? It is not even imagin-
able! It was an unfortunate incident!

HENRY IV: But if even before that everyone would call me crazy!
[To BELCREDI:] And you know it! You who more than anyone
else would become furious with those who tried to defend me!

BELCREDI: Oh, come now, it was only out of fun!

HENRY IV: Take a look at my hair; look here. [He shows him the hair
on his head.]

BELCREDI: But mine is grey, too!

HENRY IV: Yes, but with this difference: I had mine turn grey on
me here, as Henry IV, you see? And never was I even vaguely
aware of it! I realized it all of a sudden, one day, when I opened
my eyes again, and it was a shock, because at once I understood
that not only my hair but all the rest of me as well must have
turned grey, and everything collapsed, everything was over, and
I realized that I had arrived hungry as a bear to a banquet that
was already over.

BELCREDI: Forgive me, but what about the others?

HENRY IV [at once]: I know, they couldn't wait to see me cured, not
even those who, riding behind me, spurred my harnessed horse
until it bled . . .

DI NOLLI [shocked]: What? What?

HENRY IV: Yes, treacherously, to make the horse rear and me fall!

LADY MATILDA [at once, in horror]: But this is the first I've heard of
it!

HENRY IV: Was this also supposed to be done just for fun?

LADY MATILDA: But who did it? Who was riding behind the two of
us?

HENRY IV: Who it was does not matter. All of those who went on
feasting and who by this time would have given me their
leftovers, Marchesa, of lean or flabby pity on some thin slice of
remorse stuck to their filthy plate. Thank you! [Turning suddenly
to the DOCTOR:] Well then, Doctor, see if this case isn't something
truly new to the annals of insanity! I preferred to remain crazy,

having found everything here ready and willing for this new delight of sorts. Live it I would, with the most lucid consciousness, this insanity of mine, and in so doing take vengeance on the brutality of a rock that had bruised my head! The loneliness, this solitude which appeared so squalid and empty to me when I opened my eyes again, I decided to deck out at once and even better with all the colours and all the splendour of that far-off carnival day when you [*looks at* LADY MATILDA *and points out* FRIDA *to her*], Marchesa – there you were, right there – triumphed! I decided to oblige all those who would come into my presence to conform to it, by God, and now for my own amusement, to conform to that ancient and famous masquerade which had been for you but not for me the joke of the day! I would do it up so it would last for ever – no longer a joke, oh no, but the reality of true madness! Here everyone in disguise, with a throne-room, and these four counsellors of mine: secret and, you understand of course, traitors! [*Immediately he turns towards them.*] I would like to know what you think you gained by revealing that I was cured! If I am cured, there's no longer any need for you, and you will be let go! To confide in someone else – that, yes, that is truly crazy! Ah, but now it is my turn to accuse you! Did you know? They thought they, too, together with me would be able to play the same joke on you without your knowing it.

[*He bursts out laughing; the others laugh also but disconcertedly, except for* LADY MATILDA.]

BELCREDI [*to* DI NOLLI]: Ah, did you hear that . . . not bad at all . . .

DI NOLLI [*to the four young men*]: You?

HENRY IV: You must forgive them! This [*taking a hold of the clothes he is wearing*], this for me is the caricature, both evident and voluntary, of that other masquerade which is continuous, happening every minute and in which we are involuntary clowns [*indicates* BELCREDI] when, without knowing it, we masquerade ourselves with what we think we are – the clothes, what you see them wearing, you must forgive them, they still are unable to see it as part of their actual selves. [*Turning again to* BELCREDI:] You know, you get accustomed to it quite easily! It takes nothing to go around like this, as a tragic character [*imitates how a tragic character walks around*] in a room like this! Listen to this, Doctor. I remember a priest – Irish without a doubt – handsome, who was dozing in the sun one November day, his arm resting on the back of a bench in a public garden, drowned in the golden delight of that mild warmth which for him must have been summer-like. You may be sure that in that moment he was not aware of being a priest nor of where he was. He was dreaming. And who knows what he was dreaming. A rascal of a boy passed by. He had torn a flower from the ground, stem and all, and, passing by, he tickled the priest, here, at the neck. I saw him open his laughing eyes and he smiled blissfully from the forgetfulness of his dream. But let me tell you that all at once he regained his composure stiffly in his priest's robes, and there returned to his eyes the same seriousness that you have seen in mine, because the Irish priests defend the seriousness of their Catholic faith with the same zeal that I do the sacrosanct rights of hereditary monarchy. Ladies and gentlemen, I am cured because I know how to play the part of a madman to perfection, right here; and I do it quietly. The trouble with you is that you live in your own madness with such agitation that you do not even know or see it!

BELCREDI: We've reached the conclusion, you see: we, now, are the crazy ones!

HENRY IV [*managing to contain an outburst*]: But if the two of you, both you and she [*indicating the* MARCHESA], are not crazy, would you have come here to see me?

BELCREDI: I, in all truth, came here believing that you were the crazy one here.

HENRY IV [*suddenly, loudly, pointing to the* MARCHESA]: And she?

BELCREDI: Ah she, I do not know ... I can see that she is quite enchanted by all that you say ... fascinated by this 'conscious' insanity of yours! Let me tell you, Marchesa, dressed the way you are at present, you could even remain here and live it out right now.

LADY MATILDA: How insolent you are!

HENRY IV [*at once to calm her*]: Pay no attention to him; don't bother about him. He keeps trying to provoke me, in spite of the

Doctor's warning him not to do so. [*Turning to* BELCREDI:] But why should I get upset any more by what happened between us; the part you had with her in my misfortunes [*indicates the* MARCHESA *and now turns to her and points out* BELCREDI *to her*] and the part he now has, with you. This is what my life is! It is not your life! Yours, in which you have grown old, I did not live! [*To* LADY MATILDA:] Is this what you wanted to tell me, to show me this, by means of this sacrifice of yours, dressing yourself up this way under advisement of the Doctor? Oh, very well done, Doctor, as I told you: 'What we were like then, hmmm? and how we are now?' But I am not crazy according to your way of thinking, Doctor. I am very well aware that he [*indicates* DI NOLLI] cannot be me, because Henry IV is who I am. I, here, for twenty years, you understand, fixed in this eternal masquerade. She is the one who lived these years [*indicates the* MARCHESA], she is the one who enjoyed them, these twenty years, and has become – behold her there – someone I can no longer recognize, because I know her in this way [*indicates* FRIDA *and draws close to her*] – for me, this is she – for ever. You seem like so many children that I am able to frighten. [*To* FRIDA:] And you really got frightened, my child, by the game they persuaded you to take part in without knowing that for me it could not be the game they thought it would be. Oh, most formidable of miracles: the dream that has become alive in you – more than alive! You were there, an image; they've made your body come to life. You're mine! You are mine! All mine! Mine by right! [*He puts his arm around her laughing like a madman while everybody else, terrified, is shouting. When they run to tear* FRIDA *from his arms, he becomes terrifying and shouts to his four young men:*] Hold them back! Hold on to them! I order you to hold them back!

[*The four young men, amazed, as if fascinated, automatically try to hold back* DI NOLLI, *the* DOCTOR, BELCREDI.]

BELCREDI [*quickly freeing himself, rushes at* HENRY IV]: Let her go! Let go of her! You are not crazy!

HENRY IV [*in a flash, drawing the sword from the side of* LANDOLPH *who is next to him*]: Am I not crazy? Here, take that!

[*He pierces him in the stomach. A cry of horror. Everyone runs to help* BELCREDI, *who is crying out in turmoil.*]

DI NOLLI: Did he wound you?

BERTHOLD: He's wounded him! He's wounded him!

DOCTOR: I said this would happen!

FRIDA: Oh God!

DI NOLLI: Frida, come here!

LADY MATILDA: He's crazy! He is mad!

DI NOLLI: Hold him!

BELCREDI [*while they are taking him away through the left exit, protesting furiously*]: No! You're not crazy! He is not crazy! He is not crazy!

    [*They leave through the left exit shouting and they keep on shouting beyond the exit until above the other cries is heard one that is more acute than the rest coming from* LADY MATILDA, *followed by silence.*]

HENRY IV [*remaining on stage in the midst of* LANDOLPH, HAROLD *and* ORDULPH, *his eyes wide open and terrified by the life of his own fiction which in a single moment has forced him into committing this crime*]: And now, yes ... Now I have no choice ... [*He calls his men around him as if to protect himself.*] Here together, together here ... and for ever!

SO IT IS (IF YOU THINK SO)

A parable in three acts

LIST OF CHARACTERS

COUNCILLOR AGAZZI
DINA *his daughter*
AMALIA *his wife*
LAMBERTO LAUDISI *her brother*
MR PONZA *secretary to Agazzi*
MRS PONZA *his wife*
MRS FROLA *his mother-in-law*
THE GOVERNOR
CENTURI *the Police Commissioner*
MR SIRELLI ⎱
MRS SIRELLI ⎰ *friends of the Agazzi family*
MRS CINI *a friend of Mrs Sirelli*
MRS NENNI *a friend of Mrs Cini*
A BUTLER *in the Agazzi household*
A GENTLEMAN
A SECOND GENTLEMAN
OTHER LADIES AND GENTLEMEN

Place: in an Italian province.
Time: the present.

ACT ONE

Living-room in the home of COUNCILLOR AGAZZI. *Main entrance door at the back; side exits to right and left*

SCENE ONE

[AMALIA, DINA, LAUDISI]

When the curtain goes up LAMBERTO LAUDISI, *in an irritated mood, is walking around the living-room. He is around 40, energetic, elegant, dressed in good taste, wearing a violet-coloured smoking jacket with black lapels and braiding.*

LAUDISI: Ah, so, then, he did go to take the matter up with the Governor?

AMALIA [*around 45, grey hair, makes a show of her own sense of importance due to the position of her husband in society; however, she makes it understood that if it were left to her, she could play her role without him and would behave herself quite differently on many occasions*]: My God, Lamberto, just for one of his subordinates!

LAUDISI: A subordinate, at the office, but not at home!

DINA [*19 years old; gives the impression of understanding everything better than her mum and dad, but this attitude is softened by the graceful charm of youth*]: But he managed to get his mother-in-law a place right here next to us – on our same floor!

LAUDISI: Didn't he have the right to? There was a small place free, and he rented it for his mother-in-law. Are you telling me that a mother-in-law is obliged to come and pay her respects [*exaggerating, purposely drawing it out*] to the wife and daughter of her son-in-law's boss in their home?

AMALIA: Who said anything about being obliged? It seems to me that we were the ones, I and Dina, who first took steps to call on her, and *we were not received.*

LAUDISI: And for what reason has your husband gone to call on the Governor now? To make an act of courtesy the law?

AMALIA: If anything: a just act of reparation! Because you just do not allow two ladies to be left standing stock-still in front of a door.

LAUDISI: An outrage! It's outrageous! So then people shouldn't be allowed to do what they want in their own home?

AMALIA: Eh, you don't seem to want to take into account that it was *we* who wished to take the first polite steps towards a stranger!

DINA: Now, now, my dearest uncle, don't be angry now. We might as well be honest about it and admit, if you will, that we were so courteous out of curiosity. Forgive me, but don't you find that quite natural?

LAUDISI: Ah, natural, of course! Because you don't have anything better to do.

DINA: No, Uncle dear, wait now. Let's say: here you are, right here, minding your own business. OK. I come in. And here, right on top of this little table I, cool as cool can be, put down, no, better yet, with the look of some gentleman over there, with a hang-dog face – let's say I, what for example – I put down a pair of the cook's shoes.

LAUDISI [*excitedly*]: What do the cook's shoes have to do with anything?

DINA [*at once*]: There, you see? You're amazed! It seems a strange thing to you, and immediately I ask why.

LAUDISI [*taken aback, with a cold smile, but eventually recovering*]: Oh, aren't you a dear! You're smart, but remember that you're talking to me! You came and you put down on this little table here the cook's shoes with the express purpose of provoking my curiosity; and certainly, since you were doing it on purpose, you can't blame me if I ask: 'But why those cook's shoes right there on top of the little table?' What you must now do is prove to me that this Mr Ponza of ours – that peasant and scoundrel, as your father calls him – brought his mother-in-law to live in the apartment next to ours, nevertheless, on purpose!

DINA: All right! He may not have done it on purpose. But you cannot deny that this man lives in a way strange enough to arouse the curiosity of the entire town. It's very natural. Look here! He arrives. He rents a small apartment on the top floor of that gloomy tenement, there, on the outskirts of town facing the orchards. Have you seen the place? I mean, inside?

LAUDISI: I suppose you went and had a look at it?

DINA: Yes, Uncle dear! With Mamma. And we're not the only ones, you know? The whole town's been to see it. There's a courtyard, a very dark one! – seems like a deep well – there's a little iron railing up high, way up on the fifth floor, going around a balcony and baskets that hang from it with ropes.

LAUDISI: And so, what of it?

DINA [*with astonishment and indignation*]: He's put his wife up there!

AMALIA: And the mother-in-law, here, next to us!

LAUDISI: In a lovely apartment, for his mother-in-law, in the middle of the city!

AMALIA: Thank you very much. And he forces her to live apart from her daughter.

LAUDISI: Who says so? Why couldn't it be she, instead, the mother, in order to have more freedom?

DINA: No, no, my dear uncle, everyone knows that it's his fault!

AMALIA: Look here, we all understand that a daughter, once she is married, may leave her mother's home to go and live with her husband, even if it's in another city. But that a poor mother, unable to cope with living far away from her daughter, follows her, and in a city where she, too, is a stranger, is forced to live apart from her – come on, now, you will admit that this is not – not at all – easy to understand!

LAUDISI: Of course! The mind of a mud turtle. Does it take that much to imagine that through her fault or through his, or even through nobody's fault, there may be some sort of incompatibility of character, by which, even in such conditions as these . . .

DINA [*interrupting, amazed*]: What, Uncle dear? Between the mother and the daughter?

LAUDISI: Why between mother and daughter?

AMALIA: And why not between those two? They are always together, the two of them, he and she.

DINA: Mother-in-law and son-in-law. And it is precisely this that amazes everyone!

AMALIA: He comes here every evening to keep his mother-in-law company.

DINA: He even comes during the day: one or two times.

LAUDISI: Do you think they make love, mother-in-law and son-in-law?

DINA: Of course not! What are you saying? A poor old lady like that!

AMALIA: But he never brings her daughter to her! He never brings her with him, never, never does he bring his wife to see her mother!

LAUDISI: That poor little thing must be ill . . . She probably has to stay at home . . .

DINA: Not so! She goes to see her, the mother . . .

AMALIA: Sure she goes . . . yes! So that she can see her from a distance! It's a proven fact this poor mother has been prohibited from going up to her daughter's place!

DINA: She is allowed to speak to her only from the courtyard!

AMALIA: From the courtyard, do you understand!

DINA: To her daughter up there who leans over the balcony as if from the sky! This poor little thing enters the courtyard, pulls on the rope of the basket; the bell rings up there; the daughter looks down, and she talks to her from down there, from that well, twisting her neck, like this! Can you imagine! And it's not as though she sees her, blinded as she is by the light that pours down from up there!

[*There is heard a knocking at the door and the* BUTLER *appears.*]

BUTLER: With your permission?

AMELIA: Who is it?

BUTLER: Mr and Mrs Sirelli with another lady.

AMALIA: Ah, well, have them come in.

[*The* BUTLER *bows and is off.*]

SCENE TWO

[*The* SIRELLI COUPLE, MRS CINI *and those already there*]

AMALIA [*to* MRS SIRELLI]: My dear madam!

MRS SIRELLI [*on the plump side, hearty-looking, still young, over-dressed in elegant provincial style; with ardent, unsatisfied curiosity; bitter towards her husband*]: I took the liberty of bringing my good friend, Mrs Cini, along. She was so anxious to meet you.

AMALIA: It is a pleasure, madam. Won't you please make yourself comfortable. [*She makes the presentations.*] This is my daughter Dina, my brother Lamberto Laudisi.

SIRELLI [*bald, around 40, fat, somewhat dandified with pretensions of elegance, polished squeaky shoes; bowing*]: Madam. Miss. [*Shakes* LAUDISI's *hand.*]

MRS SIRELLI: Ah, my dear madam, we come here as to the very font itself. We are two poor pilgrims thirsting for news.

AMALIA: News of what, my dears?

MRS SIRELLI: Why, about this blessed new Secretary at the government office. The whole town talks of nothing else!

MRS CINI [*an unattractive-looking old lady full of greedy maliciousness, though affecting an air of innocence*]: We are all a bit curious . . . very curious in fact!

AMALIA: But we know about as much as everyone else does, believe me, madam.

SIRELLI [*to his wife, as if he has just won a battle*]: Just as much as I know, and perhaps less! [*Then, turning to the others:*] The reason why this poor mother is not allowed to go to her daughter's home to see her, I tell you, only they know! Only they know the true reason why!

AMALIA: I was just discussing it with my brother.

LAUDISI: I think you are all crazy!

DINA [*at once, to prevent everyone from listening to her uncle*]: Because the son-in-law, they say, will not allow her to.

MRS CINI [*in a complaining voice*]: That is not sufficient, miss.

MRS SIRELLI [*pursuing it*]: Not sufficient at all! There's more to it!

SIRELLI [*making a gesture with his hands to get their attention*]: A fresh piece of news just now verified. [*Syllabizing:*] He keeps her locked up!

AMALIA: The mother-in-law?

SIRELLI: No, madam, the wife!

MRS SIRELLI: The wife! The wife!

MRS CINI [*moaning voice*]: Locked up!

DINA: Do you see that, Uncle? And you wanted to defend . . .

SIRELLI [*amazed*]: What? You were ready to defend that monster?

LAUDISI: I have no intention at all of defending him! What I am saying is that your curiosity − if you will forgive me for saying so, ladies − is insufferable, if for no other reason than the fact that it is useless.

SIRELLI: Useless?

LAUDISI: Useless! Useless, my friends.

MRS CINI: But we're trying to get to the bottom of this and find out.

LAUDISI: Find out what, if you please? What can we really know about other people? Who they are . . . what they are . . . what they are doing . . . why they are doing it . . .

MRS SIRELLI: By asking for news, getting information . . .

LAUDISI: In that case, there is no person here more up to date on all goings on than yourself, madam − why, with a husband like yours always so well informed about everything!

SIRELLI [*trying to interrupt*]: I beg your pardon . . . excuse me but . . .

MRS SIRELLI: Ah no, dear, listen: he's right! [*Turning to* AMALIA:] It is the truth, my dear, with my husband who always professes to know it all, I never manage to find out anything!

SIRELLI: And I believe it! She is never satisfied with what I tell her! She always wonders about one thing or another that I tell her. Then she's convinced that it cannot possibly be quite the way I told her. And then finally she comes to the conclusion that it is precisely the opposite of what I've told her!

MRS SIRELLI: Hold on now. If some of the things you've told me . . .

LAUDISI [*laughs loudly*]: Hah, hah, ha. Allow me madam. Let me answer your husband. My dear man, how do you expect your wife to be satisfied with the things you tell her, if you, as is of course most natural, tell them as they appear to be to you?

MRS SIRELLI: Which means: as they cannot possibly be!

LAUDISI: Ah, madam, forgive me, but on this point you are wrong! I assure you that for your husband things are exactly the way he tells you they are.

146

SIRELLI: As they are in reality! As they really are!

MRS SIRELLI: Not at all! You are always wrong!

SIRELLI: You're the one who is always wrong, believe me! I'm not wrong!

LAUDISI: Not so, my friends! Neither one of you is wrong. Allow me? I will prove it to you. [*He gets up and stands in the middle of the room.*] Both of you are here looking at me. You do see me, don't you?

SIRELLI: But of course we do.

LAUDISI: No, no, don't be so quick to answer, my dear fellow. Come here, come here.

SIRELLI [*looks at him with a smile, perplexed, a bit disturbed, as if reluctant to lend himself to a game he does not understand*]: Why?

MRS SIRELLI [*urging him to go in an irritated voice*]: Come on, get over there.

LAUDISI [*to SIRELLI who goes hesitantly*]: You see me? Take a better look at me. Now touch me.

MRS SIRELLI [*to her husband, who hesitates to touch him*]: Come on, touch him!

LAUDISI [*to SIRELLI, who raised a hand to touch just his shoulder*]: Like that. Very good. You are sure that you touched me just the way you see me, true?

SIRELLI: I should think so.

LAUDISI: You have no doubts about it. Of course not! Now return to your place.

MRS SIRELLI [*to her husband, who remains dumbfounded in front of LAUDISI*]: No use standing there batting your eyes. Go back there now and sit down!

LAUDISI [*to MRS SIRELLI once her husband has returned to his place*]: Now, if you will, madam, come here. [*At once, anticipating:*] No, no – rather, I shall come to you. [*He goes before her and gets down on one knee.*] You see me, true? Raise one of those lovely little hands of yours and touch me. [*And as MRS SIRELLI, who is seated, places a hand on his shoulder, he bends to kiss it.*] Pretty little hand!

SIRELLI: Hey there, just a minute.

LAUDISI: Pay no attention to him! Are you also sure of touching

me as you see me? You have no doubts about it. But whatever
you do, do not tell your husband, nor my sister, nor my niece,
nor Mrs . . .

MRS CINI [*prompting*]: Cini.

LAUDISI: Cini – do not tell them how you see me, because, were
you to do this, all four of them would tell you that you are
wrong while, in fact, you are not at all wrong, because I am
really the way you yourself see me. But this does not prevent
me, my dear madam, from also being really what I am for
your husband, my sister, my niece, and the lady here, Mrs . . .

MRS CINI [*prompting him*]: Cini –

LAUDISI: Cini, because they, too, are in no way wrong.

MRS SIRELLI: Then, you change for each one of us?

LAUDISI: Of course I change, madam! And you do not, perhaps?
You do not change?

MRS SIRELLI [*precipitously*]: Ah no, no, no, no. I can assure you that
I am never changing!

LAUDISI: And neither am I from my point of view, believe me!
And I say that all of you are wrong if you do not see me as I see
myself! That is not to say that it is not quite some presumption as
much on my part as on yours, dear madam.

SIRELLI: Do you mind telling me what if anything can be concluded
from all this quibbling?

LAUDISI: Do you really think I'm not coming to a conclusion? Oh,
that's a good one! I find you all exhausted from your search to
find out who and what other people are, and how things are, as if
other people or things were simply this or that particular way in
their own right.

MRS SIRELLI: So according to you, then, one can never know the
truth?

MRS CINI: My, if we cannot believe even in what we see and touch!

LAUDISI: Yes, believe me, madam! And that is why I say: respect
that which others see and touch, even if it is the opposite of what
you yourself see and touch.

MRS SIRELLI: Now listen here! I'm turning my back and refusing to
speak to you. I have no intention of going crazy!

LAUDISI: No, no! All over! Please continue your discussion about

Mrs Frola and Mr Ponza, her son-in-law. I shall not interrupt you again.

AMALIA: Thank God for that! And you might be better off, dear Lamberto, if you moved over there into the next room!

DINA: Into the other room with you, Uncle dear. That's right. Go on!

LAUDISI: No, why should I? I enjoy hearing all of you talk. But I promise not to say another word. At the very most, I'll have a laugh or two to myself, and if once in a while a loud laugh slips out, you will just have to forgive me!

MRS SIRELLI: And to think that we came here in order to learn . . . I beg your pardon, madam, but doesn't this Ponza fellow work for your husband?

AMALIA: The office is one thing, the home another, madam!

MRS SIRELLI: I understand, of course! But haven't you even attempted to see the mother-in-law next door?

DINA: And how we have! Madam, twice we tried!

MRS CINI [startled, and then anxious and intent]: Ah, so then! So you have spoken to her?

AMALIA: We were not invited in, my dear.

MRS SIRELLI, SIRELLI, MRS CINI: Oh my! Oh! Why? Why in Heaven's name?

DINA: This very morning, too . . .

AMALIA: The first time we waited there in front of the door for over a quarter of an hour. No one came to open the door, and we weren't even able to leave a calling-card – and then we tried again today . . .

DINA [expressing horror with a hand gesture]: And *he* came to the door.

MRS SIRELLI: What a face! Really! It looks so evil! That face of his has upset the entire town! And then the way he dresses, always in black. The three of them dress in black, even the old lady. Isn't that true? The daughter?

SIRELLI [with disgust]: But no one has ever seen the daughter. I've told you that a thousand times. She's probably dressed in black too. They come from a little town in Marsica.

AMALIA: Yes, destroyed it seems, totally –

SIRELLI: – completely, razed to the ground by the last earthquake.

DINA: I've heard that they lost every one of their relatives.

MRS CINI [*anxious to get back to the subject that was interrupted*]: All well and good. But go on, then . . . he opened the door?

AMALIA: As soon as I saw him in front of me with that face of his, I found that I didn't have enough voice left in my throat to tell him we had come to pay his mother-in-law a visit. And he, nothing, you realize? Not even a thank you.

DINA: Not exactly. He did bow.

AMALIA: But hardly . . . like this, merely, with his head.

DINA: More important, though, are those eyes. Tell about those eyes! They're the eyes of a beast, not a man.

MRS CINI [*as above*]: And then? What did he say after that?

DINA: Totally embarrassed –

AMALIA: – all dishevelled, he told us his mother-in-law was indisposed . . . that he was grateful for our concern . . . and he just stood there, on the threshold, just waiting for us to leave.

DINA: How mortifying!

SIRELLI: What a rude boor! You can be sure it's his fault, you know? He probably keeps his mother-in-law under lock and key too!

MRS SIRELLI: What nerve, I tell you! To behave like that to a lady who is the wife of a superior!

AMALIA: Ah, but this time my husband really got indignant: he took it as a grave lack of respect on the man's part and he went straight to the Governor insisting on an apology.

DINA: Oh, good, here's Daddy now!

SCENE THREE

[COUNCILLOR AGAZZI *and the above*]

AGAZZI [*50 years old, red hair, rather unkempt, a beard, gold-rimmed glasses, authoritarian manner, scornful*]: Oh, my dear Sirelli. [*He approaches the sofa, bows and shakes* MRS SIRELLI'*s hand.*] Madam.

AMALIA [*introducing* MRS CINI]: My husband – Mrs Cini.

AGAZZI [*bows, shakes her hand*]: Delighted, indeed. [*Then turning in a rather solemn way to his wife and daughter:*] I warn you that Mrs Frola will be here shortly.

MRS SIRELLI [*clapping her hands with delight*]: Ah, is she coming? Really coming here?

AGAZZI: Why, I had no choice. How could I allow a clear piece of rudeness like that occur in my own home and to my own women?

SIRELLI: Why, I should say not. We were just now discussing that very issue!

MRS SIRELLI: And it would have been most proper to take this occasion –

AGAZZI [*anticipating*]: – to inform the Governor of the talk going around town concerning this gentleman? Eh, believe you me: I did just that!

SIRELLI: Ah, good, very good!

MRS CINI: It's inexplicable, such goings on. Truly inconceivable!

AMALIA: Downright brutal! Do you know that he keeps both of them under lock and key!

DINA: No, Mamma, we don't know about the mother-in-law.

MRS SIRELLI: But we are certain about his wife!

SIRELLI: And what about the Governor?

AGAZZI: Yes . . . Eh . . . he was very . . . yes, profoundly impressed.

SIRELLI: Well, I should hope so!

AGAZZI: Some of the talk had already reached him, and . . . and he, too, now sees the advisability of clearing up this mystery, to come to the truth of the matter.

LAUDISI [*laughs out loud*]: Ha! ha! ha! ha!

AMALIA: The only thing missing now was a nice laugh from you!

AGAZZI: And why is he laughing?

MRS SIRELLI: Why, because he claims it is impossible to discover the truth!

SCENE FOUR

[BUTLER, *the above characters, then* MRS FROLA]

BUTLER [*appearing at the threshold of the door and announcing*]: With your permission, Mrs Frola.

SIRRELI: Oh, here she is now.

AGAZZI: Now we'll see if it is not possible, my dear Lamberto!

MRS SIRELLI: Splendid! Ah, I am really delighted!

AMALIA [*rising*]: Shall we have her come in?

AGAZZI: No, please wait and keep your seat. Wait for her to come in. Seated, everyone seated. We must remain seated. [*To the* BUTLER:] Show her in.

> [*The* BUTLER *leaves. Shortly after,* MRS FROLA *enters and everyone gets up.* MRS FROLA *is a lovely old lady, modest, very friendly, with much sadness in her eyes, tempered, however, by a constant, sweet smile on her lips.* AMALIA *steps forward and holds out her hand to greet her.*]

AMALIA: Please do come in, madam. [*Taking her by the hand, she makes the presentations.*] My very good friend Mrs Sirelli – Mrs Cini – my husband – Mr Sirelli – my daughter Dina – my brother Lamberto Laudisi. Please make yourself comfortable, madam.

MRS FROLA: I am so very sorry and I beg your forgiveness for having neglected my social duties until now. You, madam, were so kind as to honour me with a visit when it was I that should have come to you first.

AMALIA: Among neighbours there is no need to ask whose turn it was first. All the more so, since you were new in town and here all alone, I thought, who knows, you might need . . .

MRS FROLA: Thank you, thank you . . . too kind you are . . .

MRS SIRELLI: Madam, you are alone in town, are you not?

MRS FROLA: No, I have a married daughter who has also come to town recently.

SIRELLI: And your son-in-law is the new Secretary at the Government Building: Mr Ponza, isn't it?

MRS FROLA: Precisely so. And I do hope that the good Councillor Agazzi will forgive both myself and my son-in-law.

AGAZZI: To tell the truth, madam, I was somewhat put out –

MRS FROLA [*interrupting*]: And you are right, quite right! But you really must forgive him. Believe me, we were so upset by the unfortunate thing that happened to us . . .

AMALIA: Of course! You went through that terrible disaster.

MRS SIRELLI: You lost all your relatives?

MRS FROLA: Oh yes, all . . . All of them, madam. There is hardly a trace left of our town: it's there just in a pile of ruins with open fields around it. Deserted.

SIRELLI: I know! We heard about it!

MRS FROLA: I had only a sister who also had a daughter, but unmarried. But for my son-in-law the disaster was far more serious. His mother, two brothers, a sister, brother-in-law, sister-in-law and two little nephews.

SIRELLI: A slaughter!

MRS FROLA: They are disasters that last a lifetime: they leave you stunned!

AMALIA: Of course they do!

MRS SIRELLI: Just like that it happened. From one moment to the next. It's enough to drive one mad!

MRS FROLA: You think of nothing else but that. And we do things without intending to, Councillor.

AGAZZI: Oh, please madam, no need to . . .

AMALIA: It was also on account of this unfortunate event that my daughter and I came to pay you a visit first.

MRS SIRELLI [*burning with curiosity*]: Of course! Knowing that you were all alone, poor dear! And yet, please excuse me, madam, but dare I ask you how is it that when you have a daughter here in town . . . and after a disaster like that . . . well it seems to me that it would create a need for the survivors to be united, to be all together –

MRS FROLA [*continuing to save her from embarrassment*]: While I am left alone here this way, true?

SIRELLI: Yes, of course, and it does seem strange, to be honest about it.

MRS FROLA [*sorrowfully*]: Ah, I understand what you are saying. [*Then, as if attempting to get out of it:*] But, you know, I am of the opinion that when a son or daughter get married, they should be left to themselves to lead their own life – I do feel this.

LAUDISI: Very good! A most suitable response! Their life must be another kind now with this new relationship between husband and wife.

MRS SIRELLI: But not to the point – excuse me for saying so Laudisi – of excluding one's own mother from one's life!

LAUDISI: Who said exclude? We are talking now – if I have understood correctly – about a mother who understands that her daughter cannot and shall not remain bound to her as she once was, since now she has another life of her own.

MRS FROLA [*with keen gratitude*]: That is it; precisely so, sir! Thank you! You have said exactly what I wanted to say!

MRS CINI: But I imagine your daughter comes; she must come here often to keep you company.

MRS FROLA [*ill at ease*]: Yes . . . of course . . . we see one another, certainly . . .

SIRELLI [*quickly*]: However, your daughter never leaves the house. At least no one has ever seen her.

MRS CINI: She probably has her little ones to look after.

MRS FROLA [*speaking up at once*]: No, no children yet. And perhaps, now, they will never have any. She's been married for seven years now. She has a lot to do in the house, of course. But this is not really the reason. [*She smiles sorrowfully, and she adds in another attempt to avoid the issue:*] We women, you know, who come from the little country towns are used to staying at home most of the time.

AGAZZI: Even when one has a mother one could visit? – a mother who no longer lives with us?

AMALIA: But the lady certainly visits her daughter!

MRS FROLA [*quickly*]: Ah, certainly! Of course I do! I go once or twice a day!

SIRELLI: And once or twice a day you climb all those stairs up to the last floor of that tenement?

MRS FROLA [*turning pale, and still trying to convert the torture of this interrogation into a smile*]: Er, no. Actually I do not climb the stairs. You are right, sir: it would be too much for me. I do not go upstairs. My daughter leans over the balcony facing the courtyard and . . . we see each other, and we talk.

MRS SIRELLI: Just that and nothing more? Don't you ever see her up close?

DINA [*putting her arm around her mother's neck*]: I, as a daughter, would not expect my mother to climb ninety or a hundred steps for me. But I could never be satisfied with merely seeing her and speaking to her from a distance, without being able to hug her and feel her close to me.

MRS FROLA [*clearly upset and embarrassed*]: You are right! Er, yes, clearly so, but I must explain. I would not want any of you to think that my daughter is what she is not: that she has little affection, little consideration for me; or believe that I, her mother . . . Ninety or a hundred little steps could never stand in the way of a real mother, though she be old and weary, when she knows that up there is the gift of being able to hold tight to her heart her very own daughter.

MRS SIRELLI [*triumphantly*]: Ah, there you have it! That's what we have all been saying, madam. There must be a reason!

AMALIA [*deliberately*]: You see, Lamberto, there is one. There is a reason!

SIRELLI [*quickly*]: Your son-in-law, no?

MRS FROLA: Oh, for the love of God, please do not think badly of him! He is such a fine young man. You can't imagine how good he is! The delicate and tender affection, the endless kindness and concern he has for me – not to mention the love and solicitude he has for my daughter. Ah, believe me when I tell you, never could I have wished for a better husband for my daughter!

MRS SIRELLI: But . . . what then?

MRS CINI: So he is not the reason, then!

AGAZZI: Of course! It doesn't seem to me in the least possible for a man to prohibit his wife from going to see her mother or preventing a mother from going to visit a while with her daughter in her home!

MRS FROLA: No, it has nothing to do with prohibiting! I did not say that it was he who prohibited it! We are the ones, we, Councillor, my daughter and I, who refrain from visiting one another, of our own accord; out of consideration for him.

AGAZZI: But how, if I may ask, could he be offended by such a thing? I do not see it!

MRS FROLA: Do not be angry, Councillor – it's a feeling . . . a feeling, my friends, difficult, perhaps, to understand. However, when understood, believe me, it is no longer difficult to sympathize with, although it involves without a doubt no slight sacrifice both on my part and that of my daughter.

AGAZZI: You must admit, madam, that all the things you are telling us are at best quite strange?

SIRELLI: Strange it certainly is; enough so to arouse as well as justify one's curiosity.

AGAZZI: As well as, we also add, some suspicion.

MRS FROLA: Concerning him? For the love of God please don't say that! What suspicion, Councillor?

AGAZZI: None at all! Please do not upset yourself. I am simply saying that one *might* suspect.

MRS FROLA: Oh no, no! Suspicions of what? Ours is a perfect agreement. We are happy, very happy, my daughter as much as myself.

MRS SIRELLI: Could it, perhaps, be a case of jealousy?

MRS FROLA: Jealous of her mother, of me? I don't think you can call it that. Although, to tell the truth, I wouldn't know. It's this way: he wants his wife's heart all for himself, so much so that even the love my daughter must have for her mother (and he recognizes that love, of course, and why shouldn't he) he wants that love to reach me through him – that's it – it must pass through him!

AGAZZI: Well, I must say! That sounds like downright cruelty to me – that does!

MRS FROLA: No, no, not cruelty! Please don't say cruelty, Councillor! It's something quite different, believe me. I find it difficult to explain . . . Nature, that's it. No, that's not it . . . Perhaps – oh God what to call it – it's more like a sort of illness, if you will. It's like a fullness of love – shut in – that's it: yes, something exclusive within which his wife must live, shut in, never leaving it and into which other persons may never enter.

DINA: Not even her mother?

SIRELLI: That's a real case of egoism, it is!

MRS FROLA: Perhaps. But an egoism that sacrifices all of its *self* – an egoism that gives the lady it loves all of its world to live in. In fact, perhaps the egoism would be all mine were I to want to force my way into this world all closed round by love and within which my daughter lives so happily, and so adored! This much, my friends, should suffice for a mother, isn't that true? In any case, since I do see my daughter and do speak to her . . . [*With a gracious gesture of confidentiality:*] The basket that I pull up and down there in the courtyard always carries in it a few words in a letter with the day's news. For me, this is all I need. And, anyway, by now I have grown accustomed to it. I am resigned to it, there, to the situation, if you will. It no longer makes me suffer.

AMALIA: Well, after all, if they're happy with it . . .!

MRS FROLA [*rising*]: Oh, yes! As I told you. Because he is such a good man, believe me he is. He couldn't be better, really! We all have our weaknesses and we must have indulgence for one another. [*Says her goodbyes to* AMALIA:] Madam. [*She says goodbye to* MRS SIRELLI *and* MRS CINI, *then* DINA; *then, turning to* COUNCILLOR AGAZZI:] I do hope you have forgiven me . . .

AGAZZI: Oh, madam, think nothing of it. We are most grateful for your visit.

MRS FROLA [*says goodbye with a nod of her head to* SIRELLI *and* LAUDISI, *then turning to* AMALIA]: No, please, do not get up, madam . . . please don't trouble yourself . . .

AMALIA: No, but of course. I must see you to the door, madam.

[MRS FROLA *leaves accompanied by* AMALIA *who returns shortly after.*]

SIRELLI: Well now! Are you all happy with the explanation?

AGAZZI: You call it an explanation? There's something mysterious about the whole thing!

MRS SIRELLI: Who knows what pain that poor woman must be suffering!

DINA: And the daughter as well – my God!

MRS CINI [*from the corner of the room, where she has hidden herself in order not to show her tears, with a piercing outburst*]: Her trembling voice could hardly hold her tears back!

AMALIA: Ah, yes! And when she said that a hundred stairs to climb would be like nothing if only she could hold her daughter close to her heart.

LAUDISI: What I noticed above all else was a concern – no, more than that — a determination to protect her son-in-law from any suspicion.

MRS SIRELLI: How could she excuse him? Excuse violence? cruelty?

SCENE FIVE

[BUTLER, *the same as above, and then* PONZA]

BUTLER [*appearing on the threshold*]: Commendatore, there is a Mr Ponza who wishes to be received.

MRS SIRELLI: Oh my! It's the man himself!

[*General surprise and a flow of anger, curiosity, close to bewilderment.*]

AGAZZI: Received by me?

BUTLER: Yes, sir, that is what he said.

MRS SIRELLI: For Heaven's sake, please have him come in, Commendatore. I am a bit afraid of the man, but I must admit I am enormously curious to see this monster up close!

AMALIA: What is it he wants?

AGAZZI: We'll see. Sit down. Down all of you. We must sit down. [*to the* BUTLER:] Show him in.

[*The* BUTLER *bows and leaves. Shortly after,* PONZA *enters. He is short, with a dark complexion, grim-looking, dressed all in black, black thick hair, low forehead, big black moustache. He constantly clenches his fists and speaks forcefully, with a kind of violent tone which he finds difficult to control. From time to time with a black-bordered handkerchief he wipes the perspiration from his face. While he speaks his eyes remain unchangeably hard, fixed and dismal.*]

AGAZZI: Come, come in please, Mr Ponza! [*Making the presentations:*] The new Secretary, Mr Ponza — my wife — Mrs Sirelli — Mrs Cini — my daughter — Mr Sirelli — my brother-in-law Laudisi. Please make yourself comfortable.

PONZA: Thank you. This will only take a moment of your time.

AGAZZI: You wish to talk to me in private?

PONZA: No, I can . . . I can discuss the subject in front of all of you. In fact . . . It is . . . It's a declaration which I feel obliged to make on my part.

AGAZZI: Does it concern the matter of your mother-in-law's calling on my wife? Just forget all about it, because . . .

PONZA: No, it's not about that, Commendatore. I feel I must tell you that Mrs Frola, my mother-in-law, would most certainly have called on you first, long before your wife and your daughter were so very kind as to honour her with their first visit, if I had not done everything possible to prevent her from coming. I cannot allow her to pay a visit nor to receive them.

AGAZZI [*with proud resentment*]: But why, if you don't mind explaining?

PONZA [*growing more and more angry in spite of his efforts to control himself*]: My mother-in-law has probably spoken to you about her daughter and that I have forbidden her from going into my house to see her?

AMALIA: Oh, not at all! The lady showed the greatest respect for you and she spoke so kindly about you!

DINA: She had nothing but good things to say about you.

AGAZZI: And that she refrains from entering your daughter's home out of respect for certain feelings of yours which we frankly must say we do not understand.

MRS SIRELLI: In fact, if we were to say exactly what we think . . .

AGAZZI: Well, yes, let's bring it out in the open: to us it seems cruel – the essence of cruelty!

PONZA: I am here precisely in order to clear up this matter, Commendatore. The condition of this woman is a most pitiful one indeed. But no less pitiful than my own, for the fact that I am compelled to come here and make apologies to explain to you my misfortune which only . . . only a kind of violence like this could compel me to reveal. [*He stops for a moment and looks at everybody, then he says slowly, emphasizing each syllable:*] Mrs Frola is insane, mad.

EVERYONE [*with a start*]: Mad?

PONZA: For four years now.

MRS SIRELLI [*with a shout*]: My God! But she doesn't seem mad in the least!

AGAZZI [*amazed*]: What? Mad?

PONZA: She doesn't seem to be, but she *is* mad! And her madness consists precisely in believing that I do not want to let her see her daughter. [*With a terrible look and a sort of ferocious excitement:*] And what daughter, for God's sake? Why, her daughter has been dead for four years!

EVERYONE [*at once*]: Dead? – Oh! . . . But how? Dead?

PONZA: It's been four years. This is why she went mad.

SIRELLI: But what about the woman you are living with now?

PONZA: I married her two years ago. She is my second wife.

AMALIA: And Mrs Frola believes that your wife is still her daughter?

PONZA: In a way she was fortunate, if one can call it that. One day from the window of her room where she was under doctor's care she saw me walking down the street with my second wife and she believed that she had seen in my wife her own daughter alive, and she started laughing and trembling all over. All of a sudden she was lifted from the dismal despondency into which she had fallen to find herself now in the midst of this other madness, at first exultant, extremely happy, then gradually becoming more and more calm, but distressed as she is within the resignation she herself gave in to. And nevertheless, she is happy, as you were able to see for yourselves. She insists on believing that it is not true her daughter is dead, but instead that I want to keep her daughter all to myself and never allow her to see her again. It is as though she were cured, so much so that to hear her speak, she does not seem in the least to be mad.

AMALIA: Never! Not at all!

MRS SIRELLI: Ah yes, and she actually says she is happy this way.

PONZA: She tells this story to everyone. For me she has a great deal of true affection and gratitude, because I do everything I can to favour her condition, and at the cost of great sacrifice. I must maintain two households. I oblige my wife, who fortunately lends herself compassionately to foster constantly this illusion of hers, the illusion that she is her real daughter. She comes to the window, speaks to her, writes to her. But charity – yes – and duty – yes, but up to a certain point, ladies and gentlemen! I cannot force my wife to live with her. As it is she lives in a prison, poor woman, under lock and key with the fear that she might enter the house at any moment. Yes, true, she is a tranquil person and has a gentle disposition, but you must understand, my wife would feel absolutely terrified at having to accept the caresses of this woman.

AMALIA [*reacting with a mixture of horror and pity*]: Ah, but of course, the poor thing. Can you imagine?

MRS SIRELLI [*to her husband and* MRS CINI]: Ah, so then, she agrees to being locked up that way – do you understand?

PONZA [*to cut short*]: Commendatore, you understand now why I could not allow her to call on you here unless I were absolutely forced to do so.

AGAZZI: Ah yes, now I see. I understand, now I understand everything.

PONZA: A person with a misfortune like mine should keep to himself. I was really forced to have my mother-in-law come here – it was my duty to make this declaration to you all; I mean, I did it out of respect for the office which I occupy and with regard for the responsibility of a public official. I could not have everyone in town believing in such an absurdity: that out of jealousy or for some other reason I am preventing a poor old mother from seeing her daughter. [*He gets up.*] My apologies, ladies and gentlemen, for having, though unwillingly, disturbed you. [*He bows.*] Commendatore! [*He bows, then, in front of* LAUDISI *and* SIRELLI, *bowing his head:*] Gentlemen. [*And he exits through the main door.*]

AMALIA [*astonished*]: Ah . . . so then, she is mad!

MRS SIRELLI: The poor thing! Mad.

DINA: And that's the reason why! She believes that she's her mother, and the other one is not her daughter! [*In horror she hides her face with her hands.*] Oh God!

MRS CINI: But who in the world would ever have guessed!

AGAZZI: Eh . . . I don't know! From the way she was talking –

LAUDISI: – you already get the picture?

AGAZZI: No . . . but it's true that . . . well she never seemed to find the right words!

MRS SIRELLI: Well, how could you expect her to, being out of her mind that way!

SIRELLI: Yes, but, forgive me for a moment: it's rather strange for a crazy person, isn't it! I agree, of course, she wasn't talking rationally. But that way of hers to search for an explanation why her son-in-law would not allow her to see her daughter; her effort to justify it and then adapt herself to excuses which she herself has invented . . .

AGAZZI: Oh, that's beautiful! That's the very proof of her madness! In this search of hers to find excuses for her son-in-law, without ever finding one that is acceptable.

AMALIA: Why, yes! She would say something, and then retract what she said.

AGAZZI [to SIRELLI]: Does it seem to you that, if she were not insane, she would accept such conditions as these: never to see her daughter except through a window with the alleged excuse of that morbid love of a husband who wants his wife all for himself?

SIRELLI: I see. And crazy as she is, she accepts it? And she is resigned to it? It seems strange to me somehow. Something strange about it. [To LAUDISI:] And what do you have to say about it?

LAUDISI: Me? Not a thing!

SCENE SIX

[BUTLER, the same as above, then MRS FROLA]

BUTLER [knocking at the door and appearing in a disturbed way on the threshold]: I beg your pardon. Mrs Frola is here again!

AMALIA [with alarm]: Oh God, and now what? Won't we ever be able to get rid of her any more?

MRS SIRELLI: Eh, I understand, you mean now that we know that she's crazy!

MRS CINI: My God, who knows what she's going to say now? Oh, I can't wait to hear it!

SIRELLI: I'm curious too. You know, I'm not really convinced she's mad.

DINA: Look now, Mamma. There's nothing to be afraid of. She is so calm!

AGAZZI: We have to have her in. Of course we must. Let's hear what she wants. And in case we'll take measures. But everybody seated, sit down. We have to be sitting down. [*To the* BUTLER:] Have her come in.

  [*The* BUTLER *withdraws.*]

AMALIA: Help me now, for Heaven's sake. I have no idea of how to talk to her now!

  [MRS FROLA *comes in again.* AMALIA, *a bit frightened, gets up and goes towards her; the others look on bewildered.*]

MRS FROLA: May I?

AMALIA: Please do, please come in, madam. As you can see, my friends are still here with me –

MRS FROLA [*in an extremely sad but friendly manner, smiling*]: – and they are looking at me . . . as you are, too, my good friend. You are all looking at me as if I were crazy. Isn't that true?

AMALIA: Why no, madam, what do you mean?

MRS FROLA [*with deep regret*]: Ah, better to have been rude, madam, and left you behind my door the way I did the first time. But I never thought that you would come back again and force me into this visit, the consequences of which, unfortunately, I could already foresee.

AMALIA: But no, please believe me. We are delighted to see you again.

SIRELLI: The lady seems quite worried . . . we don't know why. Let her speak.

MRS FROLA: Didn't my son-in-law leave here just a little while ago?

AGAZZI: Ah, yes he did! But he came . . . he came, madam, in order to discuss office matters with me, you see.

MRS FROLA [*wounded and dismayed*]: Eh! You tell that merciful little lie in order to put my mind at rest . . .

AGAZZI: No, no, madam. Rest assured, I'm telling you the truth.

MRS FROLA [*as above*]: Tell me, was he calm at least? Did he speak calmly?

AGAZZI: But of course, calm, very calm. Isn't that the truth?

  [*Everyone joins in confirming his words.*]

MRS FROLA: Oh my God, I know you are trying to reassure me, but it is I, on the other hand, who wish to reassure you concerning my son-in-law.

MRS SIRELLI: In what way, madam? We've told you before that —

AGAZZI: — that he spoke to me about office business . . .

MRS FROLA: But you see I can tell from the way you are looking at me! Please try to understand. It is not a question of me at all! From the way you look at me I can tell that he came here to prove something which I — not for all the money in the world — would ever have revealed! You are all witnesses to the fact that a little while ago the questions you asked me — and believe me, they were very harsh ones for me — I did not really know how to answer, and I gave you an explanation of the way we live that could not possibly satisfy anyone. And I realize this. But how could I give you the true reason? Oh, how could I tell you all, what he tells you: that my daughter has been dead for four years and that I am a poor old madwoman who believes her daughter is still living and that her husband will not let me see her?

AGAZZI [*stunned by the profound tone of sincerity in* MRS FROLA's *way of speaking*]: Ah, but what do you mean, your daughter?

MRS FROLA [*quickly, anxiously*]: You know it is the truth. Why do you want to hide it from me? He told you, didn't he . . .

SIRELLI [*hesitating as he studies her*]: Yes . . . in fact . . . he said . . .

MRS FROLA: I know he did! And I also know how much it must have upset him to be forced to say this about me! How unfortunate, Commendatore, that it took so much suffering, so much sorrow to live, and we could only endure by living the way we live. I understand, yes I do, that it must look weird to people and provoke scandal and arouse all sorts of suspicions. But on the other hand, if he is an excellent employee, zealous and scrupulously honest . . . Certainly, you've seen this for yourself in the office, haven't you?

AGAZZI: To tell the truth, no, I haven't had a chance to do so yet.

MRS FROLA: For the love of God, please do not judge him on appearances! He is the best. Everyone he worked for has said so. And I ask you why then must people torment him with their prying into his family life, into this misfortune of his which, I repeat, he has already managed to master and which, if revealed, might well compromise his career?

AGAZZI: Oh no, madam, do not distress yourself like this. No one wants to torment him.

MRS FROLA: Oh my God, how do you expect me not to suffer when I see him forced to give everyone such an absurd explanation – more than absurd, it's awful. Are they really expected to believe that my daughter is dead? That I am crazy? That the woman he lives with is his second wife? But it is all necessary, believe me, he needs to have it this way! It is the only thing that restores his tranquillity, his faith – it is the only way for him. He himself, however, is aware of the absurdity of what he is saying, and forced as he is to talk about it, he gets all wrought up and excited. You must have seen this for yourselves!

AGAZZI: Yes, in fact, he was . . . he was a bit excited.

MRS SIRELLI: Oh God, what's happening? But, then, this means he's the one.

SIRELLI: Of course, it's got to be him! [*Triumphantly:*] Ladies and gentlemen, I always said it was!

AGAZZI: Come on now! Is that really possible?

[*Everyone becomes very agitated.*]

MRS FROLA [*quickly, joining her hands*]: No, for Heaven's sake no, my friends! What are you thinking? This is the only matter that he cannot stand to have mentioned. I ask you now, would I leave a daughter of mine alone with him, if he were truly crazy? And then again you have the proof of all this in your own office, Councillor, where he fulfils all his duties and does so better than anyone else could.

AGGAZI: Ah, but, madam, you will have to explain yourself more clearly. Is it possible that your son-in-law came to us with a story he entirely invented?

MRS FROLA: Yes sir, yes. That's right. I will explain the whole thing to you! You must try to understand him, Councillor.

AGAZZI: What are you saying? There is no truth at all to the story that your daughter is dead?

MRS FROLA [*horrified*]: Oh no! God forbid!

AGAZZI [*extremely irritated, shouting*]: Well then, he is the crazy one!

MRS FROLA [*beseeching*]: No, no . . . look . . .

SIRELLI [*triumphant*]: But yes, of course, by God it must be him!

MRS FROLA: No, look here; please look! He is not mad; he is not crazy. Please let me have my say now! All of you have seen him: he has a very strong temperament; violent . . . When he married he was taken with a veritable frenzy of love. My daughter was very delicate and at risk of almost having her life destroyed by him. Under doctor's advice and with the consent of all the relatives including his own (who now, poor things, no longer exist) his wife had to be taken away from him secretly and placed in a sanatorium. And then, he, who was already a bit angry, naturally, due to that . . . that excessive love of his, not finding her at home any more . . . Ah, I tell you, my friends, he fell into a state of furious despair. He believed that his wife was truly dead. He wouldn't hear another word about it. He decided to dress in black. He did a lot of crazy things. And there was no possible way of getting this idea out of his mind – so much so that when (just after a year had passed) my daughter had regained her health, a pretty little thing again, and was brought back to him, he said no, that this was not the woman, not any more. Ah, my friends, how terrible it was! He would go up to her, and it would seem he was about to recognize her, and then, again: no, no . . . And to get him to accept her again, with the help of friends we had to pretend to have a second wedding.

MRS SIRELLI: Ah, this, then, is why he says that . . .

MRS FROLA: Yes, but I'm certain that not even he believes it any more, and hasn't for quite some time now. But he still feels the need to have others believe it. He can't do without it! And that way, you see, he feels more sure of himself. Perhaps because, from time to time, there still flashes through his mind the fear that this pretty little wife of his may be taken away from him again. [*In a low voice, smiling confidentially:*] This is why he keeps her locked up – to have her all to himself. But he does adore her! I'm certain of this. And my daughter is happy. [*She rises.*] I'll be going now, because I wouldn't want him to rush back to my place and not find me there, especially in the nervous state he is in. [*She sighs sweetly, shaking her joined hands.*] It takes a great deal of patience! That poor little thing has to pretend not to be herself, but rather someone else. And I . . . well, oh my, I . . . have to be crazy, my friends. But I don't mind, so long as it gives him some tranquillity. Oh please don't bother, I know the way out. My respects, friends, and good afternoon.

[*Saying goodbye and bowing she hurries out the main door. All remain standing, amazed, dumbfounded, staring at each other. Silence.*]

LAUDISI [*moving into their midst*]: So, there you are taking a good look at each other. Ah, ha! And the truth? [*Bursts out laughing.*] Ha, ha, ha, ha!

ACT TWO

The study in COUNCILLOR AGAZZI's *home. Antique furnishings; old paintings on the walls; entrance in the rear with portière; entrance on the left, also with portière, that leads into living-room; to the right a big fireplace with large mirror resting on the mantel; on the desk a telephone; a small sofa, armchairs, other chairs, etc.*

SCENE ONE

[AGAZZI, LAUDISI, SIRELLI]

AGAZZI *is standing by the desk with the telephone receiver to his ear.* LAUDISI *and* SIRELLI *are seated, looking at him expectantly.*

AGAZZI: Hello! – Yes. – Is this Centuri? – Well then? – Yes, fine. [*Listens for a long time, then:*] What's that you said? Really? [*Again he listens for a long time, then:*] I understand, but it wouldn't hurt to give the matter a bit more of your attention . . . [*Another long pause, then:*] How very strange. It's hard to believe that you can't . . . [*Pause.*] I understand, yes . . . oh, I see. [*Pause.*] OK, then, see what you can do . . . Goodbye. [*He puts down the receiver and steps forward.*]

SIRELLI [*anxiously*]: Well, then?

AGAZZI: Nothing.

SIRELLI: They can find nothing?

AGAZZI: Everything's either missing or destroyed: town hall, archives, all vital statistics.

SIRELLI: But at least, how about the testimony of some survivor there?

AGAZZI: There's no record of survivors; and even if there were some, by this time it would be very difficult to find them!

SIRELLI: So you're saying that there's nothing left to do but believe one or believe the other, just like that, without any proof?

AGAZZI: Unfortunately!

LAUDISI [*rising*]: You want my advice? Believe the both of them!

AGAZZI: Sure, and what if –

SIRELLI: – if one says white and the other black?

LAUDISI: Well, then, don't believe either one of them!

SIRELLI: You must be joking. We lack verification, dates and documents, but the truth, by God, has got to be on one side or the other!

LAUDISI: Documented facts, really. And what would you hope to learn from them?

AGAZZI: Now listen here! The daughter's death certificate, for example, if the lady is the crazy one (unfortunately it can't be found, because nothing at all can be found) but there had to be such documents there; they could be found tomorrow; and if so – once the document is found – it would be clear that he was right, the son-in-law.

SIRELLI: You would deny such evidence if tomorrow such documentation were handed to you?

LAUDISI: Me? I don't deny anything; not me! I wouldn't dare to! You people, not I, are the ones who have to have records and documentation in order to affirm or negate! I would have no use for them, because for me the truth is not to be found in them but rather in the mind of these two individuals into which I cannot even imagine gaining entrance except in as much as I learn from those things they tell me.

SIRELLI: That's perfect! And isn't it true that each of them is saying the other one is crazy? Either he's crazy or she's crazy! There's no getting out of that! Which one is it?

LAUDISI: First of all, it is not true that they are saying this about each other. He is saying it, Mr Ponza, about his mother-in-law. Mrs Frola denies it not only of herself but also of him. What she says, at most, is that he was at one time a bit out of his mind from being too much in love. But now he is fine and healthy as can be.

SIRELLI: Ah, so then, you are leaning, as I am, in the direction of what the mother-in-law is saying?

AGAZZI: The fact is, if you go by what she is saying, everything can be explained perfectly.

LAUDISI: But everything can be explained just as well if you go according to what he, the son-in-law, has to say!

SIRELLI: Well, then, neither one is crazy! But one of them has to be, for God's sake!

LAUDISI: And which one of them is it? You can't tell, can you – just as no one else can either. And it's not just because those documents you go searching for have been wiped out, lost or destroyed through some kind of accident – a fire, an earthquake, or what have you – but because those people have invalidated those documents inside themselves, within each of their souls. Why can't you understand that? She has created for him, or he for her, a fantasy that has the same consistency of reality itself and in which both of them live in perfect accord and at peace with one another. And this reality of theirs can never be destroyed by any document, because they breathe this world of theirs. They see it and feel it and touch things within it! Granted, this document you talk about might serve your purpose – that is, to relieve you of this stupid curiosity of yours. But you don't have it, and so here you are, damned to the marvellous torment of finding here before your eyes on the one hand a world of fantasy and on the other a world of reality, and you are unable to distinguish one from the other.

AGAZZI: Philosophy, my dear fellow, philosophy! We'll see, we're going to see right now if it isn't possible!

SIRELLI: First we listened to one of them and then to the other one; now, if we bring them together, face to face, do you mean to say that we will not discover which of the stories is fantasy and which is reality?

LAUDISI: All I ask is your permission to keep on laughing when it's over.

AGAZZI: OK, that's fine! We'll see who laughs the loudest at the end. Let's not lose any time! [*He goes to the exit at the left, and calls out:*] Amalia, madam, come in, come in now!

SCENE TWO

[AMALIA, MRS SIRELLI, DINA *and the above*]

MRS SIRELLI [*to* LAUDISI, *with a threatening finger*]: Again, not you again!

SIRELLI: He's incorrigible!

MRS SIRELLI: How do you manage to keep from getting caught up, like the rest of us are now, in this frenzy to get to the bottom of this mystery which is about to drive everyone here crazy? I couldn't get to sleep last night because of it!

AGAZZI: For Heaven's sake, madam, don't bother with him!

LAUDISI: Better that you listen to my brother-in-law; he'll make it possible for you to sleep tonight.

AGAZZI: So then. Let's get things straight. I have it. You all go over to Mrs Frola's . . .

AMALIA: Will she receive us?

AGAZZI: Oh God, I would certainly think so!

DINA: It's our duty to return her call.

AMALIA: But hasn't he forbidden her from receiving or paying calls?

SIRELLI: At first, yes! Because then no one knew a thing. But now that Mrs Frola, forced by the circumstances, has spoken up and in her own way explained the reasons for her actions –

MRS SIRELLI [*continuing*]: – she would probably be more than happy to talk to us about her daughter.

DINA: And she's such a friendly person! Ah, as far as I'm concerned, I want you to know he's the crazy one!

AGAZZI: Let's not rush; we don't want to make a hasty judgement. I want you to listen to me now. [*He looks at his watch.*] Just stay a little while; fifteen minutes, not more.

SIRELLI [*to his wife*]: And for God's sake, be careful!

MRS SIRELLI [*becoming angry*]: And why are you telling me this?

SIRELLI: Well, because once you get going, talking . . .

DINA [*in order to prevent the two of them from arguing*]: A quarter of an hour, fifteen minutes; I'll be sure to be careful.

AGAZZI: I'll just go to my office and be back here by eleven. In approximately twenty minutes.

SIRELLI [*eagerly*]: And what do I do?

AGAZZI: Wait. [*To the ladies:*] A little before then, with some excuse or another, you must convince Mrs Frola to come here.

AMALIA: What . . . what excuse?

AGAZZI: Whatsoever excuse! You'll think of something in the course of your conversation. You certainly ought to know how to do that! You're not women for nothing! And then you have Dina and then there's madam . . . You understand that you must go into the living-room. [*He goes to the door on the left and opens it wide, and moves the portière to one side.*] This door must stay this way – wide open – just like this so that we can hear you talking from in here. I leave these papers that I am supposed to take with me here on the desk. They are documents that specifically require Ponza's attention. I pretend to forget them, and with this pretext I bring him back here. Then . . .

SIRELLI [*as above*]: I'm sorry, but what about me . . . when must I come in?

AGAZZI: A few minutes past eleven, you – when the ladies are already in the living-room and I am right here with him, you come by to pick up your wife. I'll have you brought to me. Then I'll invite everyone to join us in here.

LAUDISI [*quickly adding*]: And the truth will be revealed!

DINA: But certainly, Uncle, when we have the two of them here face to face . . .

AGAZZI: God in Heaven! Don't listen to him! Go on, let's get on with it. We have no time to lose!

MRS SIRELLI: Come, let's go, yes, we must. As for you, I'm not even going to say goodbye to you!

LAUDISI: Well then, I'll just have to say goodbye to myself on your behalf, madam! [*With one hand he shakes the other.*] Good luck!

[*Exit* AMALIA, DINA *and* MRS SIRELLI.]

AGAZZI [*to* SIRELLI]: And we should go, too, no? Right away.

SIRELLI: Yes, let's go. Goodbye, Lamberto.

LAUDISI: Goodbye, goodbye.

[*Exeunt* AGAZZI *and* SIRELLI.]

SCENE THREE

[LAUDISI *alone, then the* BUTLER]

LAUDISI [*walking around the study for a while, smiling derisively to himself and shaking his head; then he stops in front of the large mirror over the mantelpiece; he looks at his image and starts speaking to it*]: Oh, so there you are! [*He greets his image by raising two fingers, giving a cunning wink of the eye, and laughs sarcastically:*] Tell me, old friend, which one of the two of us is crazy? [*He raises a hand and points his index finger at his image that, in turn, points a finger at him. Another sarcastic laugh, then:*] Ah yes, I know: I say 'You' and you with your finger point at me. Come on now, let's admit it, just between the two of us, the two of us know each other quite well, don't we? The trouble is that other people just do not see you the way I do! And so then, dear friend, what becomes of you? As for me, I can say that here in front of you I can see myself and I can touch myself – but you, what do you become, how do other people see you? A ghost, my friend, a ghostly image! And yet, you see all these crazy people? Paying no attention to that image they carry around with them, inside themselves, they run around full of curiosity, chasing after the ghostly image of others. And they believe that it is something different.

BUTLER [*having entered, is amazed at hearing* LAUDISI's *final words at the mirror; then he calls*]: Mr Lamberto.

LAUDISI: Ah, oh yes.

BUTLER: Two ladies are here. Mrs Cini and another lady.

LAUDISI: They want to see me?

BUTLER: They asked for madam. I told them she was visiting Mrs Frola next door, and then . . .

LAUDISI: And then?

BUTLER: They looked at each other, then they fiddled with their gloves, and said, 'Oh really, is that so?' and they asked me, in an anxious way, if there were no one at all in the house.

LAUDISI: You, of course, you told them that there was no one at home?

BUTLER: I answered that you were here.

LAUDISI: Me? No, I'm not. If at all, it's only the person they take me for who is at home!

BUTLER [*annoyed more than ever*]: What did you say?

LAUDISI: Excuse me, but do they both seem to you to be the same fellow?

BUTLER [*as above, attempting miserably a smile with mouth open wide*]: I do not understand.

LAUDISI: With whom are you speaking?

BUTLER [*struck dumb*]: What do you mean ... with whom am I speaking? ... With you ...

LAUDISI: And are you absolutely certain that I am the same person that those ladies out there are asking to see?

BUTLER: But ... I really wouldn't know. They said the brother of madam ...

LAUDISI: My dear fellow! Ah ... yes, in that case it is I. I am the one ... Have them come in, show them right in.

[*The* BUTLER, *while making his exit, turns around several times to look back at* LAUDISI *as if he no longer believes his eyes.*]

SCENE FOUR

[*The same as above,* MRS CINI, MRS NENNI]

MRS CINI: May I come in?

LAUDISI: Come right in, come in, please, madam.

MRS CINI: They told me that madam is not here. I have brought with me my friend, Mrs Nenni.

[*She introduces her: she is an old lady even more unattractive and affected than herself and like her friend full of greedy curiosity, but wary, and a bit confused.*] She was so looking forward to meeting Mrs –

LAUDISI [*at once*]: – Frola? –

MRS CINI: – no, no: your sister!

LAUDISI: Oh she's coming, she'll be here in a while. Mrs Frola, too. Please make yourselves at home, won't you? [*He invites them to sit on the small sofa, then graciously squeezes in to sit between them.*] May I? This sits three quite comfortably. Mrs Sirelli is also over there, you know?

MRS CINI: Yes, that's right, the butler told us.

LAUDISI: The whole thing has been orchestrated, you know. It's going to be some scene! A scene to end all scenes! In a little while, at eleven o'clock. Right here.

MRS CINI [*bewildered*]: Orchestrated? What has been? Pray tell.

LAUDISI [*mysteriously, first with a gesture pointing the index fingers of both hands at each other, then, with his voice*]: The meeting. [*A gesture of admiration then:*] A great idea!

MRS CINI: What . . . what meeting?

LAUDISI: The two of them. First he comes in here.

MRS CINI: Mr Ponza?

LAUDISI: Yes, and she'll be over there. [*Points to the living-room.*]

MRS CINI: Mrs Frola, that is?

LAUDISI: Yes, madam. [*Once more, first with an expressive gesture of the hand, then with the voice:*] But then, both of them here, one in front of the other, and the rest of us around them watching and listening. A great idea!

MRS CINI: In order to what, to know what?

LAUDISI: The truth. But we already know that. Now the only thing left to do is the unmasking.

MRS CINI [*with surprise and most anxiously*]: Ah, they know it? Who is it? Which of the two is it? Who, who is it?

LAUDISI: Let's see. Why don't you guess who? Who do you say it is?

MRS CINI [*chuckling, hesitant*]: Well . . . I . . . It's . . .

LAUDISI: He or she? Let's see . . . Guess . . . Go on and give us a guess!

MRS CINI: I . . . I say it is him. It's him!

LAUDISI [*looks at her a bit then*]: It's him.

MRS CINI [*chuckling with joy*]: Yes. It is? Ah! That's it. Of course! Certainly! It must have been, it had to be him!

MRS NENNI [*chuckling with joy*]: Him! We all said it was. All of us women said so!

MRS CINI: But how, how did you find out? Some kind of proof turned up, isn't that true? Documents?

MRS NENNI: Through police headquarters, no? We all said that's what would happen! Once the Governor's authority is behind it there's no chance of not discovering the answer!

LAUDISI [*With his hand he motions to them to come closer to him; then he says to them softly and mysteriously, weighing each syllable*]: The licence for the second marriage.

MRS CINI [*as if she had just been punched in the nose*]: For the second?

MRS NENNI [*all upset*]: What, what? For the second marriage?

MRS CINI [*recovering, disappointed*]: But then . . . then he was right?

LAUDISI: Ah, documents, ladies. A licence for a second marriage, so it seems, speaks clearly.

MRS NENNI [*almost in tears*]: Then she's the crazy one!

LAUDISI: That's right. She's the one it seems.

MRS CINI: But how? First you said him and now you say her?

LAUDISI: Yes, but because the document, madam, this second marriage certificate, could very well be – just as Mrs Frola assured us – a fake one prepared with the help of friends to foster that fixation of his that his wife was no longer his first one but another woman.

MRS CINI: Ah, you mean a public document like that one can be worthless?

LAUDISI: That is, I mean . . . It has the value, ladies, the value each of you wishes to give it. After all, aren't there also those little letters that Mrs Frola says she receives every day from her daughter by means of that basket hanging out there in the courtyard. There are such little letters, true?

MRS CINI: Yes, and so?

LAUDISI: And so: documents, madam! Aren't these little letters also documents? It's just a matter of how much value you wish to give them. Mr Ponza steps in and claims they are false documents prepared to foster Mrs Frola's fixation –

MRS CINI: Oh my, my, my, then we really know nothing for certain.

LAUDISI: What do you mean we know nothing? Let's not exaggerate! There are the days of the week, for example. How many are they?

MRS CINI: Why, er – seven.

LAUDISI: Monday, Tuesday, Wednesday . . .

MRS CINI [*invited to continue*]: Thursday, Friday, Saturday . . .

LAUDISI: And Sunday. [*Turning to the other lady:*] And the months of the year?

MRS NENNI: Twelve!

LAUDISI: January, February, March . . .

MRS CINI: We understand! You're trying to make fun of us, aren't you?

SCENE FIVE

[*The same as above and* DINA]

DINA [*having raced to the doorway at the rear*]: Uncle, please . . . [*She stops, having seen* MRS CINI.] Oh, Mrs Cini, you're here?

MRS CINI: Yes, I came with Mrs Nenni –

LAUDISI: – who is so anxious to meet Mrs Frola.

MRS NENNI: Why no, I beg your pardon . . .

MRS CINI: He keeps making fun of us! Ah, my dear young lady! He's got us all mixed up, you know. It's like a train entering the station: pa poum, pa poum, pa poum – constantly switching from one track to another. We're all dizzy!

DINA: Oh! He's so naughty these days, and with all of us as well. Pay no attention. I don't think I'll be needing anything else. I'll just go back and tell Mamma that you people are here; and that should do it. Ah yes, Uncle, you should hear her, what a darling little old lady she is. Oh, the way she talks. The goodness in that lady! And that little place of hers, so nice and tidy, everything just right, all those little white embroidered doilies on the furniture. And she showed us all those little letters her daughter wrote her.

MRS CINI: Yes . . . but . . . if, as Mr Laudisi was just saying . . .

DINA: And what does he know? He hasn't read them!

MRS NENNI: Couldn't they be fake?

DINA: Fake? No chance of it! Don't listen to a word he says! Do you think a mother could ever be fooled by the way her own

daughter expresses herself? The last letter, the one from yesterday
– [*She is interrupted when she hears the sound of voices coming through
the open door to the adjoining living-room.*] Ah, here they are!
They're already here, I'm sure! [*She goes to the living-room door to
look.*]

MRS CINI [*running after her*]: Is *she* with her, with Mrs Frola, is she?

DINA: Yes. Come on now, come with me. We must all be in the
living-room. Is it already eleven o'clock, Uncle?

SCENE SIX

[*The same as above,* AMALIA]

AMALIA: [*rushing in, from the living-room door, she, too, in an agitated
state*]: I think we can very well do without it now! There's no
more need for proof!

DINA: Of course! I think so too! It would be ridiculous to proceed.

AMALIA [*sorry and anxious, hastily greeting* MRS CINI]: My dear lady.

MRS CINI [*introducing* MRS NENNI]: Mrs Nenni who has come here
with me to . . .

AMALIA [*hastily greeting* MRS NENNI *as well*]: A pleasure, madam.
[*Then:*] No doubt about it! He's the one!

MRS CINI: He's the one? Is it true? He *is* the one!

DINA: If we could only forestall Daddy and put an end to deceiving
the poor old lady.

AMALIA: Oh yes! But we've brought her here now! I really feel
like I am betraying her at this point!

LAUDISI: Of course! Indecent, outrageous. You are right! All the
more so now that I am beginning to think that it is quite evident
that she has got to be the one! It is she, I'm certain!

AMALIA: She? How! What are you saying?

LAUDISI: She, she, she.

AMALIA: Oh stop it!

DINA: We are absolutely certain of the opposite now. That we are!

MRS CINI *and* MRS NENNI [*overjoyed*]: Yes, yes, it's yes, isn't it?

LAUDISI: Precisely! Since all of you are so sure it is he!

DINA: Let's go, let's move to the other room. Can't you see he's doing it on purpose?

AMALIA: Yes, we must go, let's go now, ladies. [*In front of the door to the left:*] Step this way, if you please.

[MRS CINI, MRS NENNI, AMALIA *leave.* DINA *is also just about to leave.*]

LAUDISI [*calling her over*]: Dina!

DINA: I just won't listen to you! No! and no!

LAUDISI: Why don't you shut that door over there, if you still think it is ridiculous to proceed.

DINA: And what about Daddy? He left it open like that. He's about to arrive with the other one now, and if he were to find it closed . . . You know how Daddy can be at times!

LAUDISI: But you can persuade him – especially you – that there is no longer any need to keep it open. Aren't you convinced, hmm?

DINA: I couldn't be more convinced!

LAUDISI [*with a challenging smile*]: So close it then!

DINA: You would like to see me start doubting again, wouldn't you? I'm not closing it. But only because of Daddy.

LAUDISI [*as above*]: Would you like me to close it?

DINA: If you are willing to take the responsibility!

LAUDISI: But I am not as certain as you are that he is the crazy one.

DINA: Now you just come into the living-room with me and listen to the lady the way we have, and you'll soon see that you, too, will no longer have any doubts. Are you coming?

LAUDISI: Yes, I'm coming. And I'm closing the door, you know. And on my own responsibility.

DINA: Ah, you see? And even before you hear her talk!

LAUDISI: No, my dear. Because I am sure that by this time your father thinks the same as the rest of you do: that this test is useless.

DINA: Are you sure about that?

LAUDISI: But of course. Right now he is talking to him. By this time he will have been convinced that *she* is the crazy one. [*He walks resolutely to the door.*] I am shutting it.

DINA [*quickly stopping him*]: No. [*Then correcting herself:*] I'm sorry . . . if you really think so . . . well then, let's leave it open . . .

LAUDISI [*with his usual laugh*]: Ha, ha, ha . . .

DINA: But just for Daddy's sake!

LAUDISI: And Daddy will say so just for your sake! Let's leave it open.

[*In the adjoining room a piano starts playing an old aria full of gracefulness, sweet and sad, from 'Nina mad with love' by Paisiello.*]

DINA: Ah, there she is . . . do you hear? She's playing. She's actually playing!

LAUDISI: The little old lady?

DINA: Yes, and she told us that at one time her daughter would always play this very same old tune. Listen how sweetly she plays. Come, let's go.

[*Both of them leave by the door on the left.*]

SCENE SEVEN

[AGAZZI, PONZA, *then* SIRELLI]

The stage, as soon as LAUDISI *and* DINA *have made their exits, remains empty for a while. The sound of the piano continues from the other room.* MR PONZA, *entering the rear door with* COUNCILLOR AGAZZI, *hears that music and becomes deeply disturbed; and his emotion will gradually increase as the scene unfolds.*

AGAZZI [*at the rear doorway*]: After you, please. Go in. [*He sees* MR PONZA *into the room, then he enters and heads for the desk to get the papers he pretends to have forgotten there.*] Well now, I'm sure I must have left them here! Please sit down, won't you?

[MR PONZA *remains standing, looking with agitation towards the living-room door from where the sound of the piano is coming.*]

Ah, here they are, just as I thought! [*He picks up the papers and moves towards* MR PONZA *as he leafs through them.*] It's a case of litigation, as I was telling you – a big mess that has been dragging on for years. [*He, too, turns towards the living-room, irritated by the sound of the piano.*] This music . . . ! What a time to be playing! [*He makes a scornful gesture while turning around, as if he were saying to himself 'Those stupid women!'*] Who's playing? [*He goes through the doorway to the living-room; he sees* MRS FROLA *at the piano and is astounded.*] Ah! Just look at that!

PONZA [*approaching* AGAZZI, *agitated*]: In the name of God, is she here? Is she playing?

AGAZZI: Yes, your mother-in-law. And how well she plays!

PONZA: What's going on? You've brought her here again? And you're making her play the piano?

AGAZZI: I don't see that it can do any harm.

PONZA: Oh no, for the love of God, no! Not this music! It's what her daughter used to play!

AGAZZI: Is it painful for you to listen to it, perhaps?

PONZA: Not for me! It's painful for her! Incalculable pain! And yet I've warned you, Councillor, as I did those ladies, about the condition of that poor, unfortunate woman!

AGAZZI [*trying to calm* PONZA *as he becomes more and more emotional*]: Yes, yes . . . but you see –

PONZA [*continuing*]: – she must be left in peace! She must not receive calls nor make any! I am the only person, I alone, who knows how to handle her! You're destroying her! Destroying her!

AGAZZI: I'm surely not. Why? My wife and daughter are also well aware . . . [*He is interrupted suddenly by the music stopping in the living-room and the burst of applause coming from there.*] There you are, you see . . . you can hear it for yourself . . .

[*From the next room the following exchange of words is clearly heard.*]

DINA: But you still play so well, madam!

MRS FROLA: I? Ah, but my Lina! If you hear my Lina, how she plays!

PONZA [*trembling, wringing his hands*]: Her Lina! Did you hear? She said her Lina!

AGAZZI: Of course, her daughter.

PONZA: But she is saying *plays*! She says *plays*!

[*Again, from inside the living-room, the distinct words:*]

MRS FROLA: Ah, no, she cannot play any more – not since that time! And this, perhaps, is what gives her the most pain, poor thing!

AGAZZI: Seems quite natural ... She thinks her daughter is still alive ...

PONZA: But they shouldn't let her say such things! She shouldn't ... She must not say this. Did you hear? Not *since that time* ... She said not *since that time* – referring to *that* piano, I'm sure. But you couldn't know this: the piano belonged to my poor dead wife!

[*Arriving at this moment is* SIRELLI *who, hearing the last few words of* PONZA *and noting his extreme exasperation, is struck dumb.* AGAZZI, *who also appears bewildered, signals him to come closer to him.*]

AGAZZI: Please, have the ladies come in here!

[SIRELLI, *keeping his distance, goes to the door at the left and calls to the ladies.*]

PONZA: Ladies? In here? No, no! I would rather ...

SCENE EIGHT

[MRS FROLA, AMALIA, MRS SIRELLI, DINA, MRS CINI, MRS
NENNI, LAUDISI, *the same as above*]

The ladies, at a signal from SIRELLI *(full of amazement), enter a bit frightened.* MRS FROLA, *who notices her son-in-law in that emotional state of his, all quivering and animal-like, becomes frightened. Assailed by him with extreme violence in the following scene, she exchanges expressive glances of understanding with the other ladies. The scene unfolds rapidly and in a very excited manner.*

PONZA: You, here? Here again? What are you here for?

MRS FROLA: I came ... don't be upset ...

PONZA: You came here to speak again ... What did you say? What did you tell these ladies right here?

MRS FROLA: Nothing, I swear! Nothing!

PONZA: Nothing? What do you mean nothing? I heard it myself! And this man heard it when I did! [*Indicates* AGAZZI.] You said 'she plays'! Who plays? Lina plays? You are well aware of the fact that your daughter died four years ago!

MRS FROLA: But of course, my dear. Calm yourself. Oh yes, yes, I know.

PONZA: 'And she cannot play any more – not since that time,' you said. Of course she can't play any more – not since that time! How could she play if she's dead?

MRS FROLA: You're right. Certainly! Isn't that what I said, ladies? I said she could not play any more – not since that time. If she is dead!

PONZA: Then why do you still think about that piano?

MRS FROLA: I? No. I don't think about it any more! I never think about it!

PONZA: I destroyed that piano! And you know I did! When your daughter died! So that this other woman wouldn't play it – in any case she doesn't even know how to play! You know she docsn't play.

MRS FROLA: She doesn't even know how to play! Why of course!

PONZA: And what was her name, her name was Lina, isn't that true? Your daughter was Lina. Right here and now I want you to tell everyone what my second wife's name is! Tell everybody right here and now, because you know very well what her name is! – What is her name?

MRS FROLA: Julia! Julia is her name! Quite right. Yes, it's absolutely true, my friends, her name is Julia!

PONZA: Her name then is Julia, not Lina! And don't try winking at anybody in the meantime suggesting that her name may not be Julia!

MRS FROLA: Why I . . . no! I didn't wink!

PONZA: I saw you! You did wink! I clearly saw you do it! You want to ruin me! You are trying to make these people think that I still want to keep her all for myself, your daughter all for me, as if she were not dead. [*He breaks into horrible sobbing.*] As if she were not dead!

MRS FROLA [*quickly hurrying towards him, with infinite tenderness and humility*]: Of course not, no, my dear boy. Come now, try to calm yourself. I never said anything of the kind . . . Isn't that true? I didn't, did I, ladies?

AMALIA, MRS SIRELLI, DINA: But of course, of course not! She never said that! She always said the girl was dead! She did.

MRS FROLA: It's true, isn't it? I said she was dead! Why of course I did. And that you are so very good to me! [*To the ladies:*] Isn't that true? It's true, isn't it? I try to ruin you? I cause you trouble? I?

PONZA [*bustling, terrible*]: But you in the meantime go around to other people's houses looking for pianos so that you can play your daughter's tunes on them and say that Lina played them like that, and even better than that!

MRS FROLA: No, it was . . . I did it . . . just to . . . just to try . . .

PONZA: You can't! You must not! How could you possibly have thought of playing the same thing again that your dead daughter used to play?

MRS FROLA: You're right, yes you are, ah, you poor thing . . . you poor thing! [*Moved to compassion, she starts to cry.*] I won't do it again! I won't ever do it again!

PONZA [*attacking her terribly from close up*]: Go! Get out of here! Out! Go on!

MRS FROLA: Yes . . . yes . . . I'll go, I'm going . . . Oh God!

[*As she withdraws, she is making beseeching gestures to all present to be considerate towards her son-in-law, and weeping she withdraws.*]

SCENE NINE

[*The same as above except for* MRS FROLA]

They are all full of pity and fear as they remain in their places watching PONZA. *But as soon as his mother-in-law has left, he, at once, regaining his normal composure, now changed and calm, says simply:*

PONZA: I must beg your pardon for this sad spectacle which I was forced to present to you in order to mend the damage which, without your wanting to, and without your knowing it, you are doing to this unfortunate soul with your compassion.

AGAZZI [*amazed as all the others*]: What do you mean? You were just pretending?

PONZA: I had to, my friends. Don't you see that this is the only way to do it in order to keep up the illusion for her. You see I have to shout out the truth that way, as if it were part of my madness? Please forgive me and please allow me to take my leave. I really must rush off to see her now.

LAUDISI [*making his way into the midst of them*]: And there you have it, ladies and gentlemen, the truth revealed! [*Bursts out laughing.*] Ha! ha! ha! ha!

ACT THREE

Same scene as in Second Act.

SCENE ONE

[LAUDISI, BUTLER, COMMISSIONER CENTURI]

LAUDISI *is stretched out in an easy chair and is reading. Through the door at the left leading to the living-room the confused noise of many voices can be heard. The* BUTLER *from the door at the rear ushers in* COMMISSIONER CENTURI.

BUTLER: Please wait here, if you will, while I go to call the Commendatore.

LAUDISI [*turning and catching a glimpse of* CENTURI]: Oh, it's you, Commissioner! [*He rises quickly and calls back the* BUTLER *who is about to leave.*] Pst! Wait. [*To* CENTURI:] Any news?

CENTURI [*tall, stiff, frowning, around 40 years old*]: Yes, a bit.

LAUDISI: Ah, good! [*To the* BUTLER:] Never mind. I'll call my brother-in-law myself later on.

  [*He indicates with a movement of his head the door at the left. The* BUTLER *bows and leaves.*]

  You have performed a miracle! You saved a town! Do you hear? Listen to them shouting! Well then, you've got solid news and facts?

CENTURI: From a few people we were finally able to track down.

LAUDISI: From Mr Ponza's town? Fellow citizens who know the facts?

CENTURI: Yes sir. Somes dates, not many, but reliable.

LAUDISI: Ah, good! good! Now what have we got, for example?

CENTURI: Ah, here we are. I have here the communications that were sent me. [*He takes from the inside pocket of his jacket a yellow envelope that is open, containing a sheet of paper, and hands it to* LAUDISI.]

LAUDISI: Let's see! Let's see now. [*He takes the sheet of paper from the envelope and begins to read it carefully, interpolating from time to time with different tones of voice: now with an 'ah', now with an 'eh', expressing satisfaction, then doubt, then a kind of commiserating tone, and finally one of complete disillusionment.*] No, there's nothing here! Nothing definite in this report, Commissioner.

CENTURI: It's all we were able to find out.

LAUDISI: But all those same doubts that were there before are still there now! [*He looks at him, then with sudden decision:*] Would you like to do some real good, Commissioner, to render an outstanding service to the citizens of this town and for which service the good Lord above will certainly reward you?

CENTURI [*looking at him perplexed*]: What service is that? I wouldn't know.

LAUDISI: Now let me explain. Sit here. [*Points to the desk.*] Tear this sheet of useless information that proves nothing in two, and here on the other half write down something that is precise and clear.

CENTURI [*stunned*]: So? How? What information?

LAUDISI: Oh, any information. Say anything! Your choice! Write it down in the name of those two fellow countrymen that you succeeded in tracking down. Do it for the good of everyone: to bring this whole town back to its old tranquil self! They all want the truth and it doesn't matter which truth so long as it is something specific, categorical. And you are the one to give it to them! Give them the truth!

CENTURI [*forcefully, getting heated up, nearly offended*]: But how can I give it to them, if I do not have it? Would you have me make a forgery? I am surprised that you dare to propose such a thing to me. And I use the word 'surprised' not for lack of something stronger! Enough of this! Do me a favour, tell the Councillor at once that I am here, will you?

LAUDISI [*spreads out his arms in defeat*]: At your service and at once!

[*He moves towards the door at the left; he opens it. Immediately the shouting from the people in the living-room becomes louder. But as soon as LAUDISI steps through the door, the shouting comes to a quick stop. And from inside the living-room the voice of LAUDISI is*] *heard announcing: 'Ladies and gentlemen, Commissioner Centuri is here, and he bears with him specific information from people who know!' Applause, cheering and congratulations welcome this news!* COMMISSIONER CENTURI *expresses worry, since he is well aware of the fact that the information he brings will not be nearly enough to satisfy such expectations.*]

SCENE TWO

[*The same as above,* AGAZZI, SIRELLI, LAUDISI, AMALIA, DINA, MRS SIRELLI, MRS CINI, MRS NENNI *and many other ladies and gentlemen*]

They all rush in through the door at the left with AGAZZI *heading the group. They are still stirred up, exultant, clapping their hands and shouting: 'Good job, hurray, for Centuri!'*

AGAZZI [*with hands held out*]: My dear Centuri: I knew you could do it! I knew all along you would come out on top!

EVERYONE: Good work! Excellent! Let's see! Let's see! We can't wait to see the proof! Who's the one? Who is it?

CENTURI [*stunned, bewildered, lost*]: Why no . . . well you see . . . I, Councillor . . .

AGAZZI: Ladies and gentlemen, for Heaven's sake! Quiet, please.

CENTURI: I have done my best, yes I have. But if Mr Laudisi told you from over there –

AGAZZI: – that you bring us specific information! –

SIRELLI: – exact dates! –

LAUDISI [*loud, resolute, anticipating*]: – not many, it's true, but precise! From people he was able to track down. From Mr Ponza's home town! People who know!

EVERYONE: Finally! Ah, at last, at last!

CENTURI [*shrugging his shoulders and handing the paper to* AGAZZI]: There you have it – for you, Councillor.

AGAZZI [*unfolding the sheet in the midst of the crowd that has rushed to surround him*]: Ah, let's see now! Let's take a look.

CENTURI [*resentful, drawing close to* LAUDISI]: But you, Mr Laudisi . . .

LAUDISI [*at once, strong*]: For God's sake let him read, won't you? Let him read!

AGAZZI: Ladies and gentlemen, please give me a chance. A little room, please. There, that's better. Now I can read.

[*There is a moment of silence. Then the silence is interrupted by the voice of* LAUDISI, *ringing out loud and clear.*]

LAUDISI: But I've already read it!

EVERYONE [*leaving* COUNCILLOR AGAZZI *and noisily rushing around* LAUDISI]: Oh really? So then? What does it say? What do we know, then?

LAUDISI [*choosing his words with care*]: There is irrefutable proof as testified to by a fellow townsman of Mr Ponza that Mrs Frola has been in a sanatorium.

EVERYONE [*with regret and disappointment*]: Oh!

MRS SIRELLI: You say Mrs Frola?

DINA: Is she really the one, then?

AGAZZI [*having now read the paper, he shakes it about and shouts*]: No, no! Not at all! It doesn't say anything like that here!

EVERYONE [*again, leaving* LAUDISI *and rushing around* AGAZZI *shouting*]: Ah, what then? What does it say? What's in there?

LAUDISI [*loudly to* AGAZZI]: But of course. It says 'Mrs'! It specifically says 'Mrs'!

AGAZZI [*louder*]: Nothing of the kind! The witness says: 'It seems to him.' He's not at all certain! And in any case he doesn't know if it was the mother or the daughter in the sanatorium.

EVERYONE [*with satisfaction*]: Ah!

LAUDISI [*insisting*]: But it must be the mother, no doubt about it.

SIRELLI: What in the world! No, it's the daughter, friends, the daughter!

MRS SIRELLI: In fact, it's just what the lady herself told us!

AMALIA: There you have it! Very good, indeed! It was when they secretly took her away from her husband –

DINA: – precisely, and put her away in a nursing home!

AGAZZI: And you see now, the witness does not even come from the same town! He says he often went there . . . that he doesn't remember all that well . . . that he seems to remember hearing people mention something or other . . .

SIRELLI: Ah, so then, it's all just hearsay!

LAUDISI: I beg your pardon, but if you are all so convinced that Mrs Frola is right, what are you still looking for? For God's sake put an end to it once and for all! He's the crazy one, and that's the end of it!

SIRELLI: That would be fine, if it were not for the fact that the Governor, my dear fellow, believes the opposite and has quite openly sided with Mr Ponza, giving him his complete support.

CENTURI: Yes, sir, that's true. The Governor believes in Mr Ponza. He also told me that!

AGAZZI: But that's because the Governor has not yet spoken to the lady next door.

MRS SIRELLI: He surely hasn't! He spoke only with him!

SIRELLI: As far as that goes, there are others here who feel the same way as the Governor does.

A GENTLEMAN: I, I, for one, certainly do! Because I know of a similar case, I do: a mother who went crazy over the death of the daughter, and she believes that the son-in-law does not want to let her see this daughter of hers. Exactly the same situation!

SECOND GENTLEMAN: No, no. There's something extra in your story. That son-in-law of yours has remained a widower and has no woman living with him. While, here, this Mr Ponza has a woman living with him at home . . .

LAUDISI [suddenly struck by a new idea]: Oh God, did you hear that, ladies and gentlemen? There you have it: the clue that solves the mystery! My God! You've found it! Eureka! [Slapping the SECOND GENTLEMAN on the back:] Very good! Excellent, dear sir! Did you hear that?

EVERYONE [perplexed, not understanding]: What does he mean? What?

SECOND GENTLEMAN [stunned]: What did I say? I don't know . . .

LAUDISI: What do you mean what did you say? You solved the problem! Eh, just take it easy now, ladies and gentlemen! [To AGAZZI:] Will the Governor be coming here by any chance?

AGAZZI: Yes, we're expecting him . . . But why do you ask? Explain!

LAUDISI: It makes no sense for him to come here to speak with Mrs Frola. At present he believes the son-in-law. Once he speaks with the mother-in-law not even he will know which of the two to believe any more! No, no! This requires something quite different to be done by the Governor – something only he can do!

EVERYONE: What? What?

LAUDISI [*glowing*]: You don't see? Didn't you hear what this gentleman said? Mr Ponza has 'a woman' at home with him! The wife.

SIRELLI: Get the wife to talk? Why of course! Eh, of course!

DINA: But if she is kept like a prisoner, that poor thing!

SIRELLI: The Governor will have to authorize it and make her talk!

AMALIA: Of course, she's the only one who can tell the truth!

MRS SIRELLI: Not necessarily so! She'll say what her husband wants her to say!

LAUDISI: Sure! But only if she has to talk in front of him! Of course!

SIRELLI: She should speak to him privately, just the two of them!

AGAZZI: And the Governor could certainly insist with the power of his authority that she confess to him, in a strictly private way, how things really stand. Of course! Definitely! What do you think of that, Centuri?

CENTURI: Eh, no question about it, if that's what the Governor wishes.

AGAZZI: It's true. It's the only thing to do. We ought to call him and spare him the inconvenience of having to come here. You'll see to it, won't you, Centuri?

CENTURI: Yes sir! My compliments. Ladies. Gentlemen. [*He bows and leaves.*]

MRS SIRELLI [*clapping her hands*]: Of course! Bravo, Laudisi!

DINA: Bravo! Bravo, my little Uncle! What a great idea!

EVERYONE: Bravo! Bravo! It's the only way! The only way to do it!

AGAZZI: But of course! Wonder why we didn't think of it before?

SIRELLI: No wonder at all! No one has ever seen her! It's as though that poor thing never existed!

LAUDISI [*as if struck by a new idea*]: Oh! But, forgive me for asking, are you really sure that she does exist?

AMALIA: What are you saying? My God, Lamberto!

SIRELLI [*with a fake laugh*]: Are you really questioning her existence as well?

LAUDISI: Hold it, let's slow down a bit. You yourselves said that no one has ever seen her!

DINA: Come on now! There is always madam who sees her and talks to her every day.

MRS SIRELLI: And then the son-in-law would support that fact as well.

LAUDISI: That's all well and good! But reflect now for a moment. To be strictly logical there can be nothing but a ghost living in that house.

EVERYONE: A ghost?

AGAZZI: That's enough of that! Stop with that business, once and for all!

LAUDISI: Let me go on. The ghost of a second wife, if Mrs Frola is correct. Or the ghost of the daughter if Mr Ponza is right. Now it remains to be seen, my friends, if for either of them this ghost is really a person in her own right. Having reached this point, it seems to me there may even be some room for doubt!

AMALIA: Oh, come now! You would like to drive us all as crazy as you are!

MRS NENNI: Oh God, I can feel a chill running up and down my spine!

MRS CINI: I don't see what enjoyment you get from frightening us like that.

EVERYONE: No! Of course not! He's joking! He's only joking!

SIRELLI: She's a woman of flesh and bones – you can be sure of it! And we'll make her talk. We will get her to talk!

AGAZZI: And you're the very one who proposed that she talk to the Governor!

LAUDISI: I did, yes – if there truly is a woman up there; I mean, an ordinary woman. But listen carefully, my friends, when I tell you that there cannot possibly be any ordinary woman living up

there. No there is not! At least I have doubts right now that there
is.

MRS SIRELLI: My God, he really does want to drive us crazy!

LAUDISI: Eh! You'll see. We will see!

EVERYONE [*in confusion*]: But there are other people who have
seen her. She looks out into the courtyard! She writes those little
letters! He's just doing it on purpose to make fun of us!

SCENE THREE

[*The same as above,* CENTURI *now returned*]

CENTURI [*amid the agitation of all he enters excitedly announcing*]: The
Governor. The Governor is here!

AGAZZI: What? Here? Well then what did you do?

CENTURI: I met him on the street with Mr Ponza heading this
way . . .

SIRELLI: Ah, he's with him.

AGAZZI: Oh God, no! If he is coming with Ponza he'll go
to madam next door. Please, Centuri, stand in front of the
door and ask him on my behalf if he would be so kind as to
stop for a moment by my place first, as he promised me he
would.

CENTURI: Yes sir, leave it to me. I'm going right now. [*He hurries
out the door in the rear.*]

AGAZZI: Would you people be kind enough to move over there
into the living-room for a while.

MRS SIRELLI: But be sure you make him see the point. It's the only
way. It's the only way!

AMALIA [*in front of the door to the left*]: This way, ladies, if you
please.

AGAZZI: You stay, Sirelli. And you, too, Lamberto.

[*All the other ladies and gentlemen leave through the door at the left.*]
[*To* LAUDISI:] I want you to let me do the talking, if you will.

LAUDISI: As for me, no problem at all! In fact, if you want me to
leave too . . .

AGAZZI: No, no. Better if you stay – ah, here he is now.

SCENE FOUR

[*The same as above, the* GOVERNOR, CENTURI]

GOVERNOR: [*around 60 years of age, tall, fat, good-natured, easy-going*]: Good old Agazzi! Oh, you here too, Sirelli? My dear Laudisi! [*Shakes everyone's hand.*]

AGAZZI [*with a gesture inviting him to sit*]: Forgive me for having asked you to come here first.

GOVERNOR: It was my intention to come, just as I had promised you I would. But in any case I certainly would have dropped by afterwards.

AGAZZI [*noticing* CENTURI *standing behind him*]: Please, Centuri, come on in. Sit right here.

GOVERNOR: Ah, Sirelli, I've heard all about you! I've heard you're quite worked up about the goings on with our new Secretary.

SIRELLI: Oh no, believe me, Governor, everyone in town is no less worked up than I am.

AGAZZI: It's the truth, yes, everyone is extremely concerned.

GOVERNOR: And I can't seem to see the reason why!

AGAZZI: Because you didn't happen to be in on certain scenes that we happened to witness, having, as we do, the mother-in-law living right here next to us.

SIRELLI: I beg your pardon, Governor, but you haven't heard what the poor lady has to say yet.

GOVERNOR: I was just on my way to do so. [*To* AGAZZI:] I had promised you to talk to her here at your place, as you wanted me to do, but then the son-in-law himself came and begged me, implored me, in fact, to go to her place and put an end to all this gossip. I'm sorry, but do you think he would have done this if he were not more than certain that I had the proof of what he is affirming from my visit here with the lady?

AGAZZI: Oh certainly! Because in front of him, that poor little thing –

SIRELLI [*suddenly cutting in*]: – would have said just what he wanted her to say, Governor! And this is the proof that she is not the crazy one!

AGAZZI: We had the same thing happen to us here yesterday.

GOVERNOR: But of course, my dear boy, because he's purposely trying to make her believe that he is the crazy one. He warned me about that. And, in fact, how else could he keep this poor unfortunate creature in her illusion? It's torture, believe me, a real torture for that poor man!

SIRELLI: All well and good! Unless, of course, she is the one who is trying to keep him in his illusion that her daughter is dead so that he can feel sure his wife will not be taken from him again. In this case, you can easily see, Governor, the torture would be the lady's and not his.

AGAZZI: And that's the doubtful part. And when such doubt as this has entered the mind –

SIRELLI: – as it has entered everybody's! –

GOVERNOR: – doubt? Eh, no, on the contrary, it seems to me that not even the shadow of a doubt remains in you people. Just as I must confess there remains none for me from the opposite point of view. What about you Laudisi?

LAUDISI: I'm sorry, Governor, I promised my brother-in-law to keep my mouth shut.

AGAZZI [*reacting quickly*]: Come off it now! What are you saying? If you're asked, you answer! Yes, I told him not to talk, but do you know why? Because for two days now he's been having fun confusing the issue! Making the waters more muddy!

LAUDISI: Don't believe him, Governor. It's exactly the opposite. I've done everything I could to clear them up – these waters.

SIRELLI: Sure! You know how he cleared things up? By insisting that it is impossible to discover the truth and then by raising the doubt that Ponza is living in his house not with a woman but with a ghost!

GOVERNOR [*enjoying himself*]: Isn't that something? Oh, I like that!

AGAZZI: For the love of God! You know how he is: no sense listening to him!

LAUDISI: Nevertheless, Governor, you were invited to come here because of me!

GOVERNOR: Why, do you also think I would do well to talk with the lady next door?

LAUDISI: For Heaven's sake, no! You would do very well to stick with what Ponza tells you!

GOVERNOR: Ah, good! Then you, too, believe that Mr Ponza . . .?

LAUDISI [*at once*]: No. Just as much as I wish everyone here would stick to what Mrs Frola tells them – and put an end to it!

AGAZZI: Did you get that? Can you call that reasoning, what he just said?

GOVERNOR: Allow me, won't you? [*To* LAUDISI:] According to you, then, we can believe what madam says as well?

LAUDISI: And how you can! Every last word of it – just as much as you can whatever he says!

GOVERNOR: Forgive me, but then what?

SIRELLI: If they are saying the opposite?

AGAZZI: [*irritated, resolutely*]: Do me a favour and listen to me! I am not leaning, nor do I have any intentions of leaning as yet in the direction of one or the other. He may be right. She may be right. But we have got to settle this! And there is only one way to do it.

SIRELLI: And he's the one who suggested it! [*Indicates* LAUDISI.]

GOVERNOR: Ah, really? Well then, let's hear it!

AGAZZI: Given the fact that we haven't found any positive proof, the only thing left to do is the following: that you, given your authority, obtain a confession from the wife.

GOVERNOR: From Mrs Ponza?

SIRELLI: But not in the presence of her husband, of course!

AGAZZI: That way she will be able to tell the truth!

SIRELLI: That she is the lady's daughter, as we find fit to believe –

AGAZZI: – or a second wife who is willing to play the part of the daughter, as Mr Ponza would have us believe –

GOVERNOR: – and just as I myself believe without reservation! And why not! I agree, it seems to be the only way. Believe me, that poor man wants nothing better than to convince everybody that he is right. He proved to be so very agreeable to everything I suggested. He would be the happiest of all. And your minds, my friends, would at once be put at ease. Do me a favour, Centuri.

[CENTURI *rises*.]

Go and call Mr Ponza for me; he's right here next door. Ask

196

him on my behalf if he wouldn't mind coming here for a moment.

CENTURI: At once, sir! [*He bows and leaves by the door at the rear.*]

AGAZZI: Eh, if only he consents!

GOVERNOR: You'll see, he'll agree to it immediately! And it'll all be over within a quarter of an hour. Here, right here, in front of your very selves.

AGAZZI: What? Here in my house?

SIRELLI: Do you think he'll want to bring his wife here?

GOVERNOR: Leave it to me! Yes, right here – because, otherwise – I'm sure of it – you people would always suppose that I –

AGAZZI: – never, for God's sake no! We would never!

SIRELLI: Perish the thought!

GOVERNOR: Come on now! Since you know for sure that I feel he is in the right, you'd always be thinking that in order to hush up the matter, dealing as it does with a public servant, I . . . No, no, I want you to be present also. [*Then to* AGAZZI:] Your wife?

AGAZZI: She is in the other room with some other ladies.

GOVERNOR: So, you've established a real conspiracy headquarters on the premises!

SCENE FIVE

[*The same as above,* CENTURI, PONZA]

CENTURI: May I come in? Mr Ponza is here.

GOVERNOR: Thank you, Centuri.

[PONZA *appears on the threshold.*]

Come in, please step inside, my dear Ponza.

[PONZA *bows.*]

AGAZZI: Please make yourself comfortable.

[PONZA *bows again and sits down.*]

GOVERNOR: You know these gentlemen – Sirelli . . .

[PONZA *rises and bows.*]

AGAZZI: Yes, I've already introduced them. My brother-in-law Laudisi.

[PONZA *bows.*]

GOVERNOR: I've asked you to come here, dear Ponza, to tell you that here, with these friends of mine ... [*He interrupts himself, noticing that from the moment he started talking* PONZA *gave signs of great uneasiness and nervousness.*] Is there something you want to say by any chance?

PONZA: Yes. That it is my intention, Governor, to request an immediate transfer.

GOVERNOR: But why? I'm sorry, but just a while ago, you were speaking to me with such understanding.

PONZA: I have become the target here, Governor, of outrageous persecution.

GOVERNOR: Come now! Let's not exaggerate now!

AGAZZI [*to* PONZA]: Excuse me but when you said 'persecution', did you mean on my part?

PONZA: On everyone's part! And for this reason I am leaving. I am leaving, Governor, because I can no longer tolerate this relentless inquisition, this ferocious prying into my private life which ends up by doing irreparable damage to a work of charity which cost me so much pain and so much sacrifice. I love that poor old lady more than if she were my mother, and yesterday, right here, I had to see myself forced to treat her in the most cruel and horrible way. And just now I found her over there in such a state of dejection and so nervous –

AGAZZI [*interrupting, calm*]: That's strange. Because madam always spoke to us in a very calm way. On the contrary, all that nervousness we have found to be in you, Mr Ponza – and it is there right now as well!

PONZA: Because all of you have no idea of what you are making me go through.

GOVERNOR: Come now, my dear Ponza, calm yourself. What's the matter? Remember, I am here and you know with what faith and sympathy I listened to all you had to say. Isn't that the case?

PONZA: Forgive me. Yes, you did, and I am grateful to you, Governor.

GOVERNOR: So then. Look at it this way: you worship your poor mother-in-law as if she were your mother? Well now, I want you to know that all these friends of mine here are so curious to know the truth because they, too, are fond of the lady.

PONZA: But they are killing her, Governor, and I've warned them about it more than once!

GOVERNOR: Bear with me now. It will be over for good, you'll see, as soon as it's all cleared up. Right now, if you like. It's very simple. You possess the simplest and the surest means of removing any doubts these people may have. I, of course, do not need to have any removed, since I have none!

PONZA: But they won't believe me, no matter what I say!

AGAZZI: That is not true. When you came here after your mother-in-law's first visit to us and told us she was insane, all of us, though we were surprised, we all believed you. [*To the* GOVERNOR:] But immediately after that, you understand, madam returned –

GOVERNOR: Yes, yes, I know, you told me [*turning to* PONZA, *he continues*] – came back and used the same reasoning that you yourself are using in the case of your mother-in-law. You must try to understand, then, if some tormenting doubt arises in the mind of one who hears the story of the poor lady after they have heard yours. In light of what your mother-in-law has to say these people here – well it's this way – they can no longer believe with certainty what you have to say, my dear Ponza. So, you see, it's clear: you and your mother-in-law – out of the picture. You simply step to one side for the moment! You are sure that you are telling the truth, as sure as I am that you are; so I don't see how you could have any objection to hearing that truth repeated here and now by the only person, other than the two of you, who can possibly confirm it.

PONZA: And who is that?

GOVERNOR: Why, your wife!

PONZA: My wife? [*With decisiveness, with scorn:*] Ah, no, never, Governor.

GOVERNOR: And why not, may I ask?

PONZA: I should bring my wife here for the satisfaction of these people who do not want to believe what I say!?

GOVERNOR [*quickly*]: And for my satisfaction, may I add! Why would this be a problem?

PONZA: But Governor . . . no, not my wife. Let us please leave my wife out of this. You'll have to believe in me!

GOVERNOR: Wait now, even to me it's beginning to look as if you're trying to do everything possible not to be believed!

AGAZZI: All the more so since he also tried in every way to prevent – and even at the cost of committing a double discourtesy towards my wife and my daughter – his mother-in-law from coming here to speak.

PONZA [*bursting out, exasperated*]: But what is it that all of you want from me? In the name of God, tell me! Isn't that poor, unfortunate woman enough to satisfy you? You want my wife, too! You want her to come here? Governor, I refuse to put up with such an outrage! My wife will not leave my house! I am not going to drag her out in front of anyone! It is enough for me to know that you believe me. And furthermore I am going right this moment to submit my request to be transferred from here! [*He gets up.*]

GOVERNOR [*banging his fist down on the desk*]: Now look here a moment! First of all, Mr Ponza, I will not tolerate your using that tone of voice in front of one of your supervisors as well as myself – after all, I have always treated you with great courtesy and much deference. In the second place, I must repeat that now you are beginning to make even me question this stubbornness of yours in refusing to furnish me with the proof which I – not anyone else – have requested in your own interest, and I see no harm in this! My colleague here and I are well acquainted with the manner in which one receives a lady in one's home . . . or even, if you like, we could come to your home . . .

PONZA: So, you really insist, then?

GOVERNOR: I tell you again: I ask you to do this for your own good. You know I could also insist on it as your superior.

PONZA: All right. All right, then! Since you put it in these terms, I will bring my wife here – anything to put an end to this matter! But what guarantee do I have that the poor little woman next door will not see her?

GOVERNOR: Ah, of course . . . because she *does* live next door . . .

AGAZZI [*at once*]: We could go to the lady's house.

PONZA: No, no, better not! I say it on your account. I wouldn't want any more surprises from you. They could produce horrible consequences.

AGAZZI: As for us, do not worry.

GOVERNOR: Or if not, you might consider bringing the lady to my office at your convenience.

PONZA: No, no – immediately, right here . . . at once . . . I'll stay over there and keep an eye on my mother-in-law. I'll go right now, Governor, so we can get it over with. Finished once and for all! [*He rushes out the rear exit.*]

SCENE SIX

[*The same as above, except for* PONZA]

GOVERNOR: I must confess I was not expecting such opposition on his part.

AGAZZI: And you'll see that he will probably convince his wife to say what he wants her to!

GOVERNOR: Ah no! Rest assured on that score. I'll question the lady myself!

SIRELLI: His state of exasperation continues, you see!

GOVERNOR: It is the first time that . . . ah . . . that . . . ah . . . I see him like this. Perhaps the idea of bringing his wife here –

SIRELLI: – of letting her out of prison! –

GOVERNOR: – oh, as for that – that he keeps her as if she were a prisoner – that can also be explained without recourse to the supposition that she is crazy.

SIRELLI: I'm sorry, Governor, but you haven't heard this poor woman's story yet.

AGAZZI: Of course, he says he keeps her like that for fear of the mother-in-law.

GOVERNOR: But even if this were not the case, it could be he is jealous of her – and that would be enough!

SIRELLI: To the extent, I'm sorry to have to say, of not providing her with at least one servant? He makes his wife do all the housework all by herself.

AGAZZI: And he goes to do the shopping every morning!

CENTURI: Yes sir, it is true. I saw him. He carries it into the house with the help of a sturdy little boy –

SIRELLI: – whom he never allows to pass through the door!

GOVERNOR: Oh God, my friends: even he deplored having to do this when he spoke to me about the matter.

LAUDISI: And his is an irreproachable information service!

GOVERNOR: He does it to save money, Laudisi! He has to support two households . . .

SIRELLI: Oh no, we're not saying it for that reason. I beg your pardon, Governor, but do you really think a second wife would put up with such –

AGAZZI [getting angry]: – the most menial house chores! –

SIRELLI [following up]: – for someone who was once the mother-in-law of her husband and who would, in fact, for her be a stranger?

AGAZZI: Come on now! I ask you: isn't that a bit too much?

GOVERNOR: Too much, yes –

LAUDISI [interrupting]: – for any ordinary second wife!

GOVERNOR [at once]: Let's admit it. Too much, yes. Nevertheless, even this, I must say, can be explained if not by generosity, then certainly by jealousy. And that he is a jealous man – crazy or not crazy – is not even questionable!

[At this point a clamour of confused voices is heard coming from the living-room.]

AGAZZI: Oh! What's going on over there?

SCENE SEVEN

[The same as above, AMALIA]

AMALIA [enters in great haste and in a state of consternation from the door to the left, announcing]: Mrs Frola! Mrs Frola is here!

AGAZZI: Oh, for God's sake no! How? Who sent for her?

AMALIA: No one! She just came, on her own!

GOVERNOR: No! For the love of God! Not now! Please make her leave, madam.

AGAZZI: Get her out quick! Don't let her come in! We must keep her out of here at any cost! If he were to find her here, it's going to look like a real ambush to him!

SCENE EIGHT

[*The same as above,* MRS FROLA, *all the others*]

MRS FROLA *comes in trembling, weeping, beseeching, handkerchief in hand, with an excited crowd of others around her.*

MRS FROLA: Oh please! For pity's sake, please! Please, Councillor, tell them! Tell everyone!

AGAZZI [*coming forward, very irritated*]: I must insist that you go away immediately! We cannot allow you to be here, not now!

MRS FROLA [*bewildered*]: But why? Why? [*To* AMALIA:] I am appealing to you, my good lady . . .

AMALIA: But look . . . you see, the Governor is there . . .

MRS FROLA: Oh! It is you, Governor! Please! I intended to come and see you!

GOVERNOR: No, madam, please try to understand! For the time being I am unable to talk to you. You really must leave here now! Please leave as quickly as possible.

MRS FROLA: Yes, I'll go away! I'm leaving this very day! I'm leaving, Governor, and I'm never coming back!

AGAZZI: Now, now, madam. Would you be so kind as to leave for a moment and wait in your apartment next door? Please do me this favour. And then you will be able to speak to the Governor.

MRS FROLA: But why? What's wrong? What's going on?

AGAZZI [*losing his patience*]: Your son-in-law is about to arrive! Is that clear enough for you?

MRS FROLA: Oh, he is? Oh, well, then, yes . . . yes, I'll leave . . . I'm leaving right away! There is just one thing I wanted to tell you all: you must stop all this! Out of pity for us, I beg you to stop! You think you are being good to me, but instead you are doing me great harm! I shall be forced to leave town if you continue to do what you're doing! I'll have to leave this very day. That way he may find some peace! But what is it you want? Why do you want him here right now? What is he coming here for? Oh, Governor!

GOVERNOR: Nothing, madam, please do not worry, don't worry, and now please just step out, won't you?

AMALIA: Come along now, madam. That's right. Try to understand.

MRS FROLA: Oh my God, my dear Mrs Agazzi, they are going to take away from me the only good thing I have left in life, the only comfort I have: the chance to see my daughter if only from a distance! [*She begins weeping.*]

GOVERNOR: Who told you such a thing? There is no need to leave town! We are merely asking you to withdraw from here now, for the moment. Not to worry!

MRS FROLA: But I am worried about him! It's for him I'm worried, Governor! I came here to beg everyone to help him. I came for him, not myself!

GOVERNOR: Yes, all right. And I don't want you to worry about him either. I promise you. You'll see, we'll have everything fixed in no time at all!

MRS FROLA: And how? I can see that everyone here is out to get him!

GOVERNOR: Not at all, madam! It's not true! And then I am here, in case, to help him. Please don't worry!

MRS FROLA: Oh, thank you! At least *you* understand . . .

GOVERNOR: Yes, yes, madam, I do understand.

MRS FROLA: I've told all these people so many times that it was an unfortunate thing that happened in the past and is now over with and must be left in the past.

GOVERNOR: Yes, you are right, madam . . . You have my word, I understand!

MRS FROLA: We are happy living the way we do. My daughter is happy. And so . . . You see to it, you must see to it, because if you don't, I have no choice but to leave the town! I really must. And I shall never see her again, not even from a distance, the way I do now . . . For the love of God, please leave him alone!

[*At this point the crowd begins to stir; some begin to make gestures, others are looking at the door; a repressed voice here and there makes itself heard.*]

VOICES: Oh God, there she is! There she is!

MRS FROLA [*noticing the alarm and uneasiness in the group of people, she groans, perplexed and trembling*]: What is it? What's happening?

SCENE NINE

[*The same as above,* MRS PONZA, *then* PONZA]

Everyone moves to one side and the other to make way for MRS PONZA, *who comes forward in a rigid manner, dressed in mourning, with her face covered by a thick, black, impenetrable veil.*

MRS FROLA [*letting out a piercing cry of unrestrained joy*]: Oh, Lina! Lina! Lina! Lina!

[*She rushes up and throws her arms around the veiled woman with the passion of a mother who has not been able to embrace her daughter for years and years. But at the same time from outside the room there comes a cry from* PONZA *who immediately afterwards rushes onto the scene.*]

PONZA: Julia! Julia! Julia!

[*At the sound of his cry* MRS PONZA, *though still in the embrace of* MRS FROLA, *draws her body up stiffly.* PONZA, *rushing in, suddenly notices his mother-in-law so totally lost in the embrace of his wife and cries out in rage:*]

Ah, just as I thought! Cowards, so this is how you use me, by taking advantage of my good faith!

MRS PONZA [*turning her veiled head, with austere solemnity*]: Do not be afraid! Do not fear! Go now.

PONZA [*softly, lovingly, to* MRS FROLA]: Yes, let's go. Let's go . . .

MRS FROLA [*releases herself from the embrace, and, trembling all over, and humble, at once echoes his words in her concern for him*]: Yes, yes . . . let us go, my dear, come, let's go . . .

[*The two of them, with an arm around each other, exchanging affections, each weeping in his own way, withdraw as they whisper tender words to one another. Silence. Everyone on stage, having kept their eyes on the both of them until the moment they vanished, now turn their eyes in bewilderment and emotion to the veiled woman.*]

MRS PONZA [*having watched them through her veil, speaking with dark solemnity*]: What else could you want from me, after this, ladies and gentlemen? Here, as you have seen, we have an unfortunate incident that must remain hidden, because only in that way can the remedy which compassion provides be of any use.

GOVERNOR [*moved*]: And we do want to respect compassion, madam. We would, however, like you to tell us –

MRS PONZA [*speaking slowly and articulating*]: – what? The truth? The truth is simply this. Yes, I am the daughter of Mrs Frola –

EVERYONE [*with a sigh of satisfaction*]: – Ah! –

MRS PONZA [*at once, as above*]: – and Mr Ponza's second wife –

EVERYONE [*stunned and deluded, submissively*] – Oh! But how?

MRS PONZA [*at once, as above*]: Yes. And for myself no one! I am no one!

GOVERNOR: Ah, no, for yourself, madam, you are either one or the other!

MRS PONZA: No, ladies and gentlemen, I am the one you believe me to be. [*She looks through her veil at everyone for a moment; then she withdraws. Silence.*]

LAUDISI: There you have it, my friends, that's the voice of truth! [*He gives them all a look of derogatory defiance.*] Are you happy now? [*Bursts out laughing.*] Ha! ha! ha! ha!

[*Curtain.*]